Ultimate Quick Bread Cookbook

S. L. Watson

DEDICATION

To everyone who loves easy baking!

CONTENTS

Introduction

Over 350 recipes for savory and sweet quick breads, muffins, biscuits, scones, cornbreads, hushpuppies, fritters and more. All of your favorite easy to make breads in one cookbook.

Also included are my favorite flavored butters to enhance the breads. Easy recipes for savory and sweet butters. Don't just save the butters for breads, they are also great on meats and vegetables.

I love to make biscotti from quick breads. Cut day old quick bread slices into strips. For sweet quick breads, lightly brush melted butter over the breads. For savory quick breads, lightly brush vegetable or olive oil over the strips. Bake at 300° until dry.

1 SAVORY BREADS

It is crucial to any quick bread recipe that you do not over mix the batter. You only want to mix the batter until the batter is moistened and combined. Properly mixed batter will produce the rounded top on quick breads and muffins.

Always preheat the oven before making any breads. I mainly use dried herbs in breads but you can substitute your favorite fresh herb if desired. You can also make pancakes and waffles from muffin batters. Use 1/4 cup batter for each pancake and use the amount of batter recommended in your waffle maker's instructions. Watch the batters closely as sweet batters will burn easily.

Blue Cheese Shallot Bread

Makes one loaf

1/2 cup chopped shallots
1/4 cup plus 3 tbs. cold unsalted butter
2 cups all purpose flour
1 tbs. granulated sugar
2 1/2 tsp. baking powder
1 tsp. salt
1 tsp. ground mustard
1 egg
1 cup whole milk
3/4 cup crumbled blue cheese
2 tbs. grated Parmesan cheese

In a skillet over medium heat, add the shallots and 3 tablespoons butter. Saute the shallots for 4 minutes or until the shallots are tender. Remove the skillet from the heat.

In a mixing bowl, add the all purpose flour, granulated sugar, baking powder, salt and ground mustard. Stir until combined. Add 1/4 cup butter to the bowl. Using a pastry blender, cut the butter into the dry ingredients until you have coarse crumbs.

In a small bowl, add the egg and milk. Whisk until combined and add to the dry ingredients. Stir only until the batter is moistened and combined. Add the shallots, blue cheese and Parmesan cheese. Stir only until combined.

Preheat the oven to 325°. Spray an 8 x 4 loaf pan with non stick cooking spray. Bake for 50 minutes or until a toothpick inserted in the center of the bread comes out clean. Remove the bread from the oven and cool the bread in the pan for 10 minutes. Remove the bread from the pan and cool completely before slicing.

Pepper Cheese Bread

Makes one loaf

2 1/2 cups all purpose flour
1 tbs. granulated sugar
1 1/2 tsp. coarse ground black pepper
1 tsp. baking powder
3/4 tsp. salt
1/2 tsp. baking soda
2 eggs
1 cup plain yogurt
1/2 cup vegetable oil
1/4 cup whole milk
1 tbs. spicy brown mustard
1 cup shredded cheddar cheese
1/4 cup thinly sliced green onion

Preheat the oven to 350°. Spray a 9 x 5 loaf pan with non stick cooking spray. In a mixing bowl, add the all purpose flour, granulated sugar, black pepper, baking powder, salt and baking soda. Stir until combined.

In a separate bowl, add the eggs, yogurt, vegetable oil, milk and mustard. Whisk until combined and add to the dry ingredients. Stir only until the batter is moistened and combined. Add the cheddar cheese and green onion. Stir only until combined.

Spoon the batter into the prepared pan. Bake for 45 minutes or until a toothpick inserted in the center of the loaf comes out clean. Remove the bread from the oven and cool the bread for 10 minutes in the pan. Remove the bread from the pan and serve warm or at room temperature.

Mozzarella Parmesan Loaf

Makes one loaf

1 1/2 cups Bisquick
1 cup shredded mozzarella cheese
1/4 cup plus 2 tbs. grated Parmesan cheese
1/2 tsp. dried oregano
1/2 cup whole milk
1 beaten egg
2 tbs. melted unsalted butter

Preheat the oven to 400°. Spray an 8" round cake pan with non stick cooking spray. In a mixing bowl, add the Bisquick, mozzarella cheese, 1/4 cup Parmesan cheese, oregano, milk and egg. Whisk until the batter is moistened and combined. Spread the batter into the prepared pan.

Brush the melted butter over the top of the dough. Sprinkle 2 tablespoons Parmesan cheese over the dough. Bake for 20 minutes or until a toothpick inserted in the center of the loaf comes out clean. Remove the bread from the oven and cool the bread in the pan for 10 minutes. Remove the bread from the pan. Cut the bread into wedges and serve.

Cheesy Pecan Bread

Makes one loaf

2 cups all purpose flour
1 tbs. baking powder
3/4 tsp. salt
1/2 tsp. granulated sugar
1 cup shredded American cheese
1/2 cup chopped pecans
1 beaten egg
3/4 cup whole milk
2 tbs. melted unsalted butter

Preheat the oven to 350°. Spray a 9 x 5 loaf pan with non stick cooking spray. In a mixing bowl, add the all purpose flour, baking powder, salt, granulated sugar, American cheese and pecans. Whisk until combined.

In a small bowl, add the egg, milk and butter. Whisk until combined and add to the dry ingredients. Mix only until the batter is moistened and combined.

Spoon the batter into the prepared pan. Bake for 1 hour or until a toothpick inserted in the center of the loaf comes out clean. Remove the bread from the oven and cool the bread for 10 minutes in the pan. Remove the bread from the pan and cool completely before slicing.

Parmesan Walnut Bread

Makes one loaf

3 cups all purpose flour
2/3 cup granulated sugar
2/3 cup grated Parmesan cheese
4 tsp. baking powder
1/2 tsp. salt
1 egg
1 3/4 cups whole milk
1/3 cup vegetable oil
1 cup finely chopped walnuts

Preheat the oven to 350°. Spray a 9 x 5 loaf pan with non stick cooking spray. In a mixing bowl, add the all purpose flour, granulated sugar, Parmesan cheese, baking powder and salt. Whisk until combined.

In a small bowl, add the egg, milk and vegetable oil. Whisk until combined and add to the dry ingredients. Mix only until the batter is moistened. Add the walnuts and mix until the batter is combined.

Spoon the batter into the prepared pan. Bake for 50 minutes or until a toothpick inserted in the center of the loaf comes out clean. Remove the bread from the oven and cool the bread for 10 minutes in the pan. Remove the bread from the pan and serve.

Cheddar Zucchini Bread

Makes a 9" round pan

1 cup chopped onion
1/4 cup unsalted butter
2 1/2 cups Bisquick
1 tbs. minced fresh parsley
1/2 tsp. dried basil
1/2 tsp. dried thyme
3 beaten eggs
1/4 cup whole milk
1 1/2 cups shredded zucchini
1 cup shredded cheddar cheese
3/4 cup toasted chopped almonds

Preheat the oven to 400°. Spray a 9" round baking pan with non stick cooking spray. In a small skillet over medium heat, add the onion and butter. Saute the onion for 4 minutes. Remove the skillet from the heat.

In a mixing bowl, add the Bisquick, parsley, basil and thyme. Whisk until combined. In a small bowl, add the onion, eggs and milk. Whisk until combined and add to the dry ingredients. Mix only until combined. Fold in the zucchini, cheddar cheese and almonds.

Spread the batter into the prepared pan. Bake for 20 minutes or until a toothpick inserted in the center of the bread comes out clean. Remove the bread from the oven and serve.

Cheddar Bran Bread

Makes one loaf

1 1/2 cups all purpose flour
1 1/2 tsp. baking powder
1/4 tsp. baking soda
1/2 tsp. salt
3 tbs. unsalted butter, softened
1/3 cup granulated sugar
1 beaten egg
1 cup buttermilk
1 cup shredded cheddar cheese
1 cup bran cereal flakes

Preheat the oven to 350°. Spray an 8 x 4 loaf pan with non stick cooking spray. In a mixing bowl, add the all purpose flour, baking powder, baking soda and salt. Whisk until combined.

In a separate mixing bowl, add the butter and granulated sugar. Using a mixer on medium speed, beat until smooth and creamy. Add the egg and buttermilk to the bowl. Mix until combined. Add the dry ingredients and mix only until the batter is moistened and combined. Turn the mixer off and stir in the cheddar cheese and bran cereal flakes.

Spoon the batter into the prepared pan. Bake for 1 hour or until a toothpick inserted in the center of the loaf comes out clean. Remove the bread from the oven and cool the bread for 10 minutes in the pan. Remove the bread from the pan and cool completely before slicing.

Whole Wheat Cheddar Walnut Bread

Makes one loaf

2 cups whole wheat flour
1/4 cup granulated sugar
2 tsp. baking powder
1/4 tsp. salt
1/3 cup unsalted butter
1 cup whole milk
2 beaten eggs
1 cup chopped walnuts
1 cup shredded cheddar cheese

Preheat the oven to 350°. Spray a 9 x 5 loaf pan with non stick cooking spray. In a mixing bowl, add the whole wheat flour, granulated sugar, baking powder and salt. Whisk until combined. Add the butter to the bowl. Using a pastry blender, cut the butter into the dry ingredients until you have coarse crumbs.

In a small bowl, add the milk and eggs. Whisk until combined and add to the dry ingredients. Mix only until the batter is moistened and combined. Stir in the walnuts and cheddar cheese.

Spoon the batter into the prepared pan. Bake for 45 minutes or until a toothpick inserted in the center of the loaf comes out clean. Remove the bread from the oven and cool the bread for 15 minutes in the pan. Remove the bread from the pan and cool completely before slicing.

Avocado Pecan Bread

Makes one loaf

2 cups all purpose flour
1/2 tsp. baking soda
3/4 cup granulated sugar
1/2 tsp. baking powder
1/4 tsp. salt
1 beaten egg
1/2 cup whole milk
1/2 cup mashed ripe avocado
1 cup chopped pecans

Preheat the oven to 350°. Spray a 9 x 5 loaf pan with non stick cooking spray. In a mixing bowl, add the all purpose flour, baking soda, granulated sugar, baking powder and salt. Whisk until combined.

In a small bowl, add the egg, milk, avocado and pecans. Whisk until combined and add to the dry ingredients. Mix only until the batter is moistened and combined.

Spoon the batter into the prepared pan. Bake for 1 hour or until a toothpick inserted in the center of the loaf comes out clean. Remove the bread from the oven and cool the bread for 10 minutes in the pan. Remove the bread from the pan and cool completely before serving.

Parmesan Herb Bread

Makes one loaf

1 1/4 cups all purpose flour
3 tbs. plus 1 tsp. grated Parmesan cheese
1 1/2 tsp. granulated sugar
1 1/2 tsp. dried minced onion
1 1/4 tsp. dried Italian seasoning
1/2 tsp. baking soda
1/4 tsp. salt
1/2 cup sour cream
2 tbs. plus 2 tsp. whole milk
4 1/2 tsp. melted unsalted butter
1 egg white, beaten until foamy

In a mixing bowl, add the all purpose flour, 3 tablespoons Parmesan cheese, granulated sugar, onion, 1 teaspoon Italian seasoning, baking soda and salt. Whisk until combined.

In a separate bowl, add the sour cream, milk and butter. Whisk until combined and add to the dry ingredients. Mix only until the batter is moistened and combined.

Lightly flour your work surface. Place the dough on your surface and knead for 1 minute. Shape the dough into a round loaf. Spray a baking sheet with non stick cooking spray. Place the loaf on the baking sheet. Using kitchen scissors, cut a 1/4" deep cross in the loaf. Brush the loaf with the egg white. Sprinkle 1/2 teaspoon Italian seasoning and 1 teaspoon Parmesan cheese over the top of the bread.

Preheat the oven to 350°. Bake for 30 minutes or until the bread is golden brown. Remove the bread from the oven and cool for 5 minutes. Serve the bread warm.

Olive Bread

Makes one loaf

2 1/4 cups all purpose flour
4 tsp. baking powder
3/4 cup sliced pimento stuffed olives
1/4 cup granulated sugar
1 beaten egg
1 1/4 cups whole milk
2 tbs. melted unsalted butter

Preheat the oven to 375°. Spray a 9 x 5 loaf pan with non stick cooking spray. In a mixing bowl, add the all purpose flour, baking powder, olives and granulated sugar. Whisk until combined. Add the egg, milk and butter to a small bowl. Whisk until combined and add to the dry ingredients. Mix only until the batter is moistened and combined.

Spoon the batter into the prepared pan. Bake for 45 minutes or until a toothpick inserted in the center of the bread comes out clean. Remove the bread from the oven and cool the bread for 10 minutes in the pan. Remove the bread from the pan and cool completely before slicing.

Onion Barbecue Bread

This bread is great with any meal and is a huge hit at barbecues.

Makes one loaf

1 beaten egg
1/2 cup whole milk
3 tbs. dry onion soup mix
1/2 cup shredded cheddar cheese
1 1/2 cups Bisquick
2 tbs. grated Parmesan cheese
1 tbs. sesame seeds
2 tbs. melted unsalted butter

Spray a 9 x 5 loaf pan with non stick cooking spray. Preheat the oven to 400°. In a mixing bowl, add the egg and milk. Whisk until combined. Add the onion soup mix and cheddar cheese. Whisk until combined. Add the Bisquick and mix only until the batter is moistened and combined.

Spoon the batter into the prepared pan. Sprinkle the Parmesan cheese and sesame seeds over the top of the dough. Drizzle the melted butter over the top of the dough.

Bake for 25 minutes or until a toothpick inserted in the bread comes out clean and the bread is lightly browned. Remove the bread from the oven and cool for 10 minutes in the pan. Remove the bread from the pan and serve.

Onion Cheese Dinner Bread

Makes an 8" round cake pan

1 tsp. vegetable oil
1/2 cup chopped onion
1 beaten egg
1/2 cup whole milk
1 1/2 cups Bisquick
1 cup shredded American cheese
2 tbs. dried parsley flakes
2 tbs. melted unsalted butter

Preheat the oven to 400°. Spray an 8" round cake pan with non stick cooking spray. In a small skillet over medium heat, add the vegetable oil and onion. Saute the onion for 5 minutes. Remove the skillet from the heat.

In a mixing bowl, add the egg and milk. Whisk until combined. Add the Bisquick, onion, 1/2 cup American cheese and parsley flakes. Whisk until the batter is moistened and combined. Spread the batter into the prepared pan.

Sprinkle 1/2 cup American cheese over the top of the batter. Drizzle the butter over the top of the batter. Bake for 20 minutes or until a toothpick inserted in the center of the bread comes out clean. Remove the bread from the oven and serve.

Piccalilli Hot Bread

Makes 8 servings

2 cups Bisquick
2/3 cup whole milk
1 beaten egg
2 tbs. dried minced onion
1 tbs. vegetable oil
1/3 cup drained sweet pickle relish
1/4 cup grated American cheese

Spray an 8" square baking pan with non stick cooking spray. Preheat the oven to 400°. In a mixing bowl, add the Bisquick. In a small bowl, add the milk, egg, onion, vegetable oil and sweet pickle relish. Whisk until combined and add to the Bisquick. Mix only until the batter is moistened and combined.

Spread the batter into the prepared pan. Sprinkle the American cheese over the top. Bake for 20 minutes or until a toothpick inserted in the bread comes out clean and the bread is lightly browned. Remove the bread from the oven and serve.

Apple Cheddar Bread

This bread is great for ham, chicken or turkey sandwiches. Wonderful with salads and makes great croutons.

Makes one loaf

1 3/4 cups all purpose flour
1 tbs. baking powder
1/2 tsp. salt
1/8 tsp. cayenne pepper
4 bacon slices, cooked and crumbled
1 cup peeled and diced Granny Smith apple
3/4 cup shredded sharp cheddar cheese
1/2 cup toasted pecans, chopped
1 tsp. minced fresh rosemary
3 eggs
1/3 cup whole milk
1/3 cup vegetable oil
1 tbs. vegetable shortening

In a mixing bowl, add the all purpose flour, baking powder, salt and cayenne pepper. Whisk until combined. Add the bacon, apple, cheddar cheese, pecans and rosemary to a small bowl. Toss until combined.

Add the eggs, milk and vegetable oil to a small bowl. Whisk until combined and add to the dry ingredients. Mix only until the batter is moistened and combined. Add the bacon mixture and stir only until combined.

Grease an 8 x 4 loaf pan with the vegetable shortening. Make sure you get the shortening into the corners or the bread will stick. Spoon the batter into the pan. Preheat the oven to 350°. Bake for 50 minutes or until a toothpick inserted in the center of the bread comes out clean. The bread tends to brown fast so lightly cover the top of the bread with aluminum foil if needed .

Remove the bread from the oven and cool the bread in the pan for 10 minutes. Remove the bread from the pan and cool for 30 minutes before slicing.

Sally Lunn Quick Bread

Makes one loaf

1/2 cup vegetable shortening
1/2 cup granulated sugar
3 eggs
2 cups all purpose flour
3 tsp. baking powder
3/4 tsp. salt
1 cup whole milk

In a mixing bowl, add the vegetable shortening and granulated sugar. Using a mixer on medium speed, beat until smooth and creamy. Add the eggs and beat until smooth and combined. Add the all purpose flour, baking powder, salt and milk. Mix only until the batter is moistened and combined.

Preheat the oven to 425°. Spray a 9 x 13 baking pan with non stick cooking spray. Spoon the batter into the pan. Bake for 30 minutes or until a toothpick inserted in the bread comes out clean and the bread is golden brown. Remove the bread from the oven and serve.

Bacon Chipotle Cornbread

Makes an 8" cast iron skillet

3 tbs. unsalted butter
2/3 cup all purpose flour
2/3 cup plain white cornmeal
1 tbs. granulated sugar
1/2 tsp. baking powder
1/2 tsp. salt
1/4 tsp. baking soda
1 egg
1 cup buttermilk
3 chipotle peppers in adobo sauce, chopped
6 bacon slices, cooked and crumbled

Preheat the oven to 425°. Add the butter to an 8" cast iron skillet. Place the skillet in the oven until the butter melts and the skillet is sizzling hot.

In a mixing bowl, add the all purpose flour, cornmeal, granulated sugar, baking powder, salt and baking soda. Stir until combined. Add the egg and buttermilk to the bowl. Stir until the batter is smooth and combined. Add the chipotle peppers and bacon to the batter. Stir until combined.

Swirl the melted butter around the skillet sides to make sure the skillet is coated in the butter. Spoon the batter into the skillet. Bake for 20 minutes or until the cornbread is done and golden brown. Remove the cornbread from the oven and serve.

Black Bean & Sausage Cornbread

Makes 8 servings

1 lb. hot ground pork sausage
1 cup chopped green bell pepper
1 cup chopped red bell pepper
1 cup chopped onion
2 tbs. vegetable shortening
2 beaten eggs
1 1/3 cups whole milk
2 pkgs. yellow cornbread mix, 6 oz. size
1 cup shredded cheddar cheese
15 oz. can black beans, rinsed & drained

In a skillet over medium heat, add the sausage. Stir frequently to break the sausage into crumbles as it cooks. Cook for 5 minutes or until the sausage is well browned and no longer pink. Add the green bell pepper, red bell pepper and onion to the skillet. Cook for 5 minutes or until the vegetables are tender. Remove the skillet from the heat. Do not drain off the grease unless the sausage was very greasy.

Preheat the oven to 425°. Add the vegetable shortening to a 9 x 13 baking pan. Place the pan in the oven until the shortening melts. In a mixing bowl, add the sausage from the skillet, eggs, milk, cornbread mixes, cheddar cheese and black beans. Whisk until combined. Spoon the batter into the baking pan.

Bake for 25 minutes or until the cornbread is done and golden brown. Remove the pan from the oven and serve.

Kentucky Hot Brown Cornbread

Makes 4 servings

2 tbs. vegetable shortening
6 oz. pkg. cornbread mix
1/2 cup canned French fried onions
1/2 cup whole milk
1 beaten egg
1/4 cup unsalted butter
3 tbs. all purpose flour
2 cups whole milk
1 tsp. Worcestershire sauce
1/2 tsp. salt
1/4 tsp. cayenne pepper
1/4 tsp. black pepper
1 1/2 cups freshly grated Parmesan cheese
2 cups chopped cooked turkey
1 cup cooked bacon, crumbled
1 large tomato, sliced

Preheat the oven to 425°. Add the vegetable shortening to a 10" cast iron skillet. Place the skillet in the oven until the shortening melts and the skillet is hot. In a mixing bowl, add the cornbread mix, fried onions, milk and egg. Whisk until combined and pour the batter into the hot skillet.

Bake for 10 minutes or until the cornbread is set and light golden brown. Remove the skillet from the oven but leave the oven on. In a sauce pan over medium heat, add the butter. When the butter melts, add the all purpose flour. Stir constantly and cook for 1 minute. Add the milk to the pan. Stir constantly and cook for 5 minutes or until the sauce thickens and bubbles.

Add the Worcestershire sauce, salt, cayenne pepper, black pepper and 1/2 cup Parmesan cheese. Whisk until combined and remove the pan from the heat. Sprinkle the turkey over the cornbread. Spoon the sauce over the top of the cornbread. Sprinkle 1 cup Parmesan cheese and 1/2 cup bacon over the top.

Bake for 10 minutes or until the cornbread is done, hot and bubbly. Remove the skillet from the oven. Place the tomato slices over the top and sprinkle 1/2 cup bacon over the tomatoes. Serve hot.

Hot Water Cornbread With Variations

Makes 8 patties

2 cups plain white cornmeal
1/4 tsp. baking powder
1 1/4 tsp. salt
1 tsp. granulated sugar
1/4 cup half and half
1 tbs. vegetable oil
1 1/4 cups boiling water
Vegetable oil for frying

In a mixing bowl, add the cornmeal, baking powder, salt and granulated sugar. Whisk until combined. Add the half and half and vegetable oil. Whisk until well combined. Add 3/4 cup boiling water to the bowl. Whisk until combined.

Every cornmeal uses liquids differently. You need a batter similar to pancake batter. Add the remaining boiling water if needed. In a skillet over medium high heat, add vegetable oil to a depth of 1/2" in a skillet. You will need to cook the cornbread patties in batches.

Use 1/4 cup batter for each cornmeal patty. When the oil is hot, add the batter. Cook for 3 minutes on each side or until the cornbread is done and golden brown. Remove the patties from the skillet and drain on paper towels. Add vegetable oil as needed to fry all the patties.

Bacon Cheddar Hot Water Cornbread: Add 8 slices cooked and crumbled bacon, 1 cup shredded sharp cheddar cheese and 4 green onions to the batter after adding the boiling water. Cook as directed above.

Southwestern Hot Water Cornbread: Add 1 seeded and minced jalapeno pepper, 1 cup Mexican cheese blend, 1 cup thawed frozen whole kernel corn and 1/4 cup fresh chopped cilantro after adding the boiling water. Cook as directed above.

Country Ham Hot Water Cornbread: Add 1 to 2 cups, depending on taste, finely diced cooked country ham to the batter after adding the boiling water. Cook as directed above.

Baked Hot Water Cornbread: Omit the skillet directions. Preheat the oven to 475°. Pour 1/3 cup vegetable oil in the bottom of a 15 x 10 x 1 baking pan. Spread the oil all the way to the pan edges. Place the pan in the oven until the pan and oil are hot. Drop the batter, by 1/4 cupfuls, onto the hot pan. Bake for 12 minutes. Turn the patties over and bake for 5 minutes or until the patties are golden brown.

Sausage Tomato Gravy Over Bacon Cornbread

Makes 8 servings

1 lb. hot ground pork sausage
3 cans diced whole tomatoes, 28 oz. size
1/4 cup granulated sugar
1 tsp. salt
1/2 tsp. black pepper
1 tsp. chopped garlic
1 1/4 cups all purpose flour
1/4 cup water
1 lb. bacon, chopped
1 cup plain yellow cornmeal
1 tbs. baking powder
1 beaten egg
1 1/2 cups buttermilk
1/4 cup vegetable shortening

In a dutch oven over medium heat, add the sausage. Stir frequently to break the sausage into crumbles as it cooks. Cook for 8 minutes or until the sausage is well browned and no longer pink. Drain off any excess grease.

Add the tomatoes with juice, granulated sugar, salt, black pepper and garlic to the pan. Stir until well combined and bring the tomatoes to a boil. In a small bowl, whisk together 1/4 cup all purpose flour and water. Add to the pan. Stir constantly and cook for 2 minutes or until the gravy thickens and bubbles.

While the gravy is cooking, make the cornbread. In a large skillet over medium heat, add the bacon. Cook for 10 minutes or until the bacon is done and crispy. Remove the skillet from the heat. Pour the bacon and drippings into a mixing bowl.

Add the cornmeal, 1 cup all purpose flour, baking powder, egg and buttermilk to the bowl. Whisk until combined. Preheat the oven to 425°. Add the vegetable shortening to a 10" cast iron skillet. Place the skillet in the oven until the shortening melts and the skillet is piping hot. Add the cornbread batter to the skillet. Bake for 25 minutes or until the cornbread is done and golden brown.

Remove the cornbread from the oven and cut the cornbread into wedges. Spoon the sausage gravy over the cornbread and serve.

Onion Cornbread

Makes 8 servings

2 tbs. vegetable oil
1/4 cup unsalted butter
1 1/2 cups chopped onion
8 oz. pkg. cornbread mix
1 cup shredded sharp cheddar cheese
1 cup sour cream
1/2 cup whole milk
1 beaten egg
1/4 tsp. salt

Preheat the oven to 450°. Add the vegetable oil to an 8" square baking pan. Place the pan in the oven until the pan and the oil are sizzling hot. In a sauce pan over medium heat, add the butter and onions. Saute the onions for 5 minutes. Remove the pan from the heat.

Add the cornbread mix, cheddar cheese, sour cream, milk, egg and salt to the pan. Stir until the batter is moistened and combined. Pour the batter into the hot baking pan.

Bake for 25 minutes or until a toothpick inserted in the center of the cornbread comes out clean and the cornbread is golden brown. Remove the pan from the oven and invert onto a serving platter. Cut into squares and serve.

Sausage Cheddar Cornbread

Makes a 9" cast iron skillet

1 tbs. vegetable oil
8 oz. ground pork sausage
1 cup diced onion
1 jalapeno pepper, diced
8 oz. pkg. corn muffin mix
1 cup shredded cheddar cheese
1/3 cup whole milk
1 egg

Preheat the oven to 350°. Add the vegetable oil to a 9" cast iron skillet over medium heat. When the oil is hot, add the sausage, onion and jalapeno pepper. Stir frequently to break the sausage into crumbles as it cooks. Cook for 5 minutes or until the sausage is well browned and no longer pink. Remove the skillet from the heat. Spoon the sausage into a mixing bowl. Leave the sausage drippings in the skillet.

Add the corn muffin mix, 1/2 cup cheddar cheese, milk and egg to a separate mixing bowl. Mix until the batter is moistened and combined. Spoon the batter into the skillet used to cook the sausage. Spoon the sausage over the batter. Sprinkle 1/2 cup cheddar cheese over the top of the batter.

Bake for 20 minutes or until the cornbread is done and lightly browned. Remove the cornbread from the oven and serve. Store leftovers in the refrigerator.

Garlic Cornbread

Makes a 15 x 10 x 1 jelly roll pan

2 tbs. vegetable shortening
8 oz. pkg. cornbread muffin mix
3/4 cup cooked whole kernel corn
1/2 cup grated Parmesan cheese
1 tsp. garlic salt
3 tbs. melted unsalted butter

Preheat the oven to 375°. Grease a 15 x 10 x 1 jelly roll pan with the vegetable shortening. Prepare the cornbread mix according to the package directions for cornbread. Add the whole kernel corn to the batter and stir until combined. Spread the batter into the prepared pan.

Sprinkle the Parmesan cheese and garlic salt over the top of the batter. Drizzle the butter over the batter. Bake for 25 minutes or until the cornbread is done and lightly browned. Remove the pan from the oven and serve.

Mississippi Bacon Cornbread

Makes a 9 x 13 baking pan

1/4 lb. bacon
3 cups self rising cornmeal
3 eggs
2 1/2 cups whole milk
1/2 cup shredded cheddar cheese
2 tbs. granulated sugar
1 cup finely chopped onion
1 cup cream style corn
1/4 cup chopped red pimento
1/4 cup minced and seeded jalapeno pepper

Preheat the oven to 425°. In a large skillet over medium heat, add the bacon. Cook about 8 minutes or until the bacon is crisp. Remove the skillet from the heat and place the bacon on paper towels. Crumble the bacon. Place 2 tablespoons of the bacon drippings in a 9 x 13 baking pan. Place the pan in the oven until the bacon drippings are sizzling hot.

In a mixing bowl, add the cornmeal, eggs, milk, cheddar, cheese, granulated sugar, onion, corn, red pimento and jalapeno pepper. Whisk until the batter is moistened and combined. Add the bacon and stir until combined.

Spread the batter into the baking pan. Bake for 25 minutes or until the cornbread is golden brown. Remove the cornbread from the oven and serve.

Velveeta Cheese Onion Cornbread

Makes an 8 x 8 baking pan

1 tbs. vegetable shortening
1/2 cup chopped onion
2 tbs. unsalted butter
8 oz. pkg. cornbread muffin mix
1/2 cup sour cream
1/2 cup shredded Velveeta cheese

Preheat the oven to 400°. Add the vegetable shortening to an 8 x 8 baking pan. Place the pan in the oven until the shortening melts and the pan is sizzling hot.

In a small skillet over medium heat, add the onion and butter. Saute the onion for 3 minutes. Remove the skillet from the heat. Prepare the cornbread muffin mix according to package directions for cornbread. Add the onion and butter to the batter. Add the sour cream and Velveeta cheese to the batter. Whisk until combined.

Spread the batter into the prepared pan. Bake for 25 minutes or until the cornbread is done and golden brown. Remove the pan from the oven and serve.

Crackling Cornbread

Makes a 9" cast iron skillet

2 tbs. vegetable shortening
2 cups plain white or yellow cornmeal
1/2 tsp. baking soda
2 tsp. baking powder
2 tsp. salt
2 cups buttermilk
2 beaten eggs
1 cup chopped cracklings

Preheat the oven to 400°. Add the vegetable shortening to a 9" cast iron skillet. Place the skillet in the oven until the shortening melts and the skillet is sizzling hot.

Add the cornmeal, baking soda, baking powder and salt to a mixing bowl. Mix until combined. Add the buttermilk, eggs and cracklings to the dry ingredients. Mix until the batter is moistened and combined. Spoon the batter into the skillet.

Bake for 30 minutes or until the cornbread is done and golden brown. Remove the cornbread from the oven and serve. Store leftovers in the refrigerator.

Cheesy Cornbread With Variations

Makes a 10" cast iron skillet

2 tbs. vegetable shortening
1 cup self rising yellow or white cornmeal
1/2 tsp. baking soda
1/4 tsp. salt
1 1/2 cups shredded cheddar cheese
1/2 cup chopped onion
1 cup whole milk
3 tbs. bacon drippings
1 tsp. garlic powder
3 beaten eggs
1 cup cooked whole kernel corn
2 oz. jar diced red pimento, drained

Preheat the oven to 350°. Add the vegetable shortening to a 10" cast iron skillet. Place the skillet in the oven until the shortening melts and the skillet is sizzling hot.

In a mixing bowl, add the corn meal, baking soda and salt. Stir until combined. Add the cheddar cheese, onion, milk, bacon drippings, garlic powder, eggs, corn and red pimento. Stir until the batter is moistened and combined.

Spoon the batter into the hot skillet. Bake for 45 minutes or until the cornbread is golden brown. Remove the cornbread from the oven and serve.

Bacon Cheesy Cornbread: Add 6 slices cooked and crumbled bacon to the batter. Mix and bake as directed above.

Cheesy Green Chile Cornbread: Add a 4 oz. can drained diced green chiles to the batter. Mix and bake as directed above.

Cheesy Jalapeno Cornbread: Add 3 seeded and chopped jalapeno peppers to the batter. Mix and bake as directed above.

Sour Cream Jalapeno Cornbread

Makes a 9" square baking pan

1 tbs. vegetable shortening
1 1/2 cups plain white or yellow cornmeal
3 tsp. baking powder
1/2 tsp. salt
2 eggs
14 oz. can cream style corn
1 cup sour cream
1/2 cup vegetable oil
1 1/2 cups shredded cheddar cheese
3 jalapeno peppers, seeded and finely chopped

Preheat the oven to 350°. Add the vegetable shortening to a 9" square baking pan. Place the pan in the oven until the shortening melts and the pan is sizzling hot.

In a mixing bowl, add the cornmeal, baking powder and salt. Stir until combined. Add the eggs, corn, sour cream and vegetable oil. Whisk until the batter is smooth and combined. Add 1 cup cheddar cheese and jalapenos. Stir until combined.

Spoon the batter into the hot pan. Sprinkle 1/2 cup cheddar cheese over the top of the batter. Bake for 35 minutes or until a toothpick inserted in the center of the cornbread comes out clean. Remove the cornbread from the oven and serve.

Broccoli Cheese Cornbread

Makes 12 servings

4 eggs
1/2 cup melted unsalted butter
3/4 tsp. salt
8 oz. pkg. cornbread mix
10 oz. pkg. frozen chopped broccoli, thawed and drained
1 cup shredded cheddar cheese
1 cup chopped onion

Preheat the oven to 350°. Spray a 11 x 7 baking pan with non stick cooking spray. In a mixing bowl, add the eggs, butter and salt. Whisk until combined. Add the cornbread mix and mix until the batter is moistened. Add the broccoli, cheddar cheese and onion. Mix until combined.

Spread the batter into the baking pan. Bake for 30 minutes or until a toothpick inserted in the center of the cornbread comes out clean. Remove the cornbread from the oven and serve.

Pecan Cornbread

Makes 8 servings

1/3 cup plus 1 tbs. vegetable shortening
2 cups yellow self rising cornmeal
1 tbs. granulated sugar
1/2 tsp. cayenne pepper
2 cups buttermilk
1 egg
1 cup toasted pecans, finely chopped

Preheat the oven to 425°. Add the vegetable shortening to a 10" skillet. Place the skillet in the oven until the shortening melts and the skillet is sizzling hot.

In a mixing bowl, add the cornmeal, granulated sugar, cayenne pepper, buttermilk and egg. Whisk until combined. Remove the skillet from the oven and pour about 1/3 cup shortening into the batter. Add the pecans and stir until combined.

Spoon the batter into the hot skillet. Bake for 25 minutes or until the cornbread is done and golden brown. Remove the skillet from the oven and serve.

Blue Cheese Pecan Popovers

Makes 1 dozen

6 eggs
2 cups all purpose flour
2 cups whole milk
1/4 cup melted unsalted butter
1/2 tsp. salt
1/4 cup toasted pecans, chopped
2 tbs. chopped fresh chives
2 oz. crumbled blue cheese

Preheat the oven to 375°. Add the eggs, all purpose flour, milk, 2 tablespoons butter and salt to a blender. Process until smooth and combined. Grease your popover pans with 2 tablespoons melted butter.

Pour the batter into the pans filling them about 3/4 full. Sprinkle the pecans, chives and blue cheese over the top. Bake for 40 minutes or until the popovers are puffed and browned. Pierce each popover 3 times with a thin wooden skewer. Bake for 5 minutes or until the popovers are crisp. Remove the popovers from the oven and serve immediately.

Caramelized Onion & Swiss Popovers

Makes 8 servings

12 cups sliced onions
1 3/4 tsp. salt
1 cup all purpose flour
1 cup whole milk, at room temperature
3 eggs, at room temperature
2 tbs. melted unsalted butter
1/4 cup shredded Swiss cheese
1 tbs. chopped fresh chives
4 tsp. vegetable oil

In a non stick skillet over medium heat, add the onions and 1 teaspoon salt. Stir frequently and cook for 25 minutes. The onions should be golden brown and caramel colored when ready. Remove the skillet from the heat.

Preheat the oven to 425°. Place a 12 cup muffin tin in the oven to heat while you prepare the batter. In a blender, add the all purpose flour, milk, eggs, butter and 3/4 teaspoon salt. Process until smooth and combined.

Turn the blender off and stir in the Swiss cheese, chives and onions. Remove the muffin tin from the oven and spoon 1/2 teaspoon vegetable oil into 8 muffin cups. It is very important the placement of the popovers in the muffin pan. Fill the center 6 muffin cups and the center muffin cup on each side.

Spoon the batter into the muffin cups. Bake for 15 minutes or until the popovers are puffed and lightly browned. Reduce the oven temperature to 350°. Bake for 10 minutes or until the popovers are golden brown. Remove the popovers from the oven and immediately remove from the pan. Cool for 3 minutes before serving.

2 SAVORY MUFFINS

I make savory muffins every week. They are simple to make and most recipes freeze well. Be sure your oven is preheated and the muffin tin greased before adding the batter.

You can substitute cheeses and spices in most of the recipes for your favorite cheese and spice combination. You can also make pancakes and waffles from muffin batters. Use 1/4 cup batter for each pancake and use the amount of batter recommended in your waffle maker's instructions. Watch the batters closely as sweet batters will burn easily.

Savory muffins are great with most any meal. I serve them with bacon, sausage and eggs for breakfast, with soup and salads for a quick lunch or for dinner instead of rolls.

Cheddar Pepper Muffins

Makes about 18 muffins

2 1/2 cups all purpose flour
2 tbs. baking powder
1/2 tsp. salt
1/4 cup plain yellow cornmeal
1/4 cup granulated sugar
1/4 tsp. cayenne pepper
3/4 cup shredded sharp cheddar cheese
1/4 cup finely chopped onion
3 tbs. finely chopped green bell pepper
2 oz. jar diced red pimentos, drained
2 beaten eggs
1 1/2 cups whole milk
1/4 cup vegetable oil

In a mixing bowl, add the all purpose flour, baking powder, salt, cornmeal, granulated sugar, cayenne pepper, cheddar cheese, onion, green bell pepper and red pimentos. Stir until combined.

Add the eggs, milk and vegetable oil to a small bowl. Whisk until combined and add to the dry ingredients. Mix only until the batter is moistened and combined. Spray your muffin tins with non stick cooking spray. Spoon the batter into the muffin cups filling them about 2/3 full.

Preheat the oven to 400°. Bake for 20 minutes or until a toothpick inserted in the center of the muffins comes out clean. Remove the muffins from the oven and immediately remove the muffins from the pan. Serve hot.

Bacon Cheddar Cornbread Muffins

Makes 1 dozen

2 cups self rising white cornmeal
1 tbs. granulated sugar
1 1/2 cups buttermilk
1 egg
4 tbs. melted unsalted butter
6 bacon slices, cooked and crumbled
1 cup shredded cheddar cheese

Preheat the oven to 425°. Spray a 12 count muffin tin with non stick cooking spray. In a mixing bowl, add the cornmeal, granulated sugar, buttermilk, egg and butter. Mix until well combined. Add the bacon and cheddar cheese. Stir until combined.

Spoon the batter into the muffin cups filling them about 3/4 full. Bake for 15 minutes or until the muffins are golden brown. Remove the muffins from the oven and cool the muffins in the pans for 10 minutes. Remove the muffins from the pans and serve.

Bacon Cornbread Muffins

Makes 1 dozen

2 tbs. bacon drippings
1 3/4 cup plain white cornmeal
1 tsp. salt
1 tsp. granulated sugar
1 tsp. baking powder
1/2 tsp. baking soda
1 beaten egg
1 1/2 cups buttermilk
4 bacon slices, cooked and crumbled

Preheat the oven to 450°. Add the bacon drippings to a 12 count muffin tin. Place the muffin tin in the oven until the bacon drippings melt and the muffin tin is sizzling hot.

In a mixing bowl, add the cornmeal, salt, granulated sugar, baking powder and baking soda. Whisk until combined. Add the egg, buttermilk and bacon. Mix until well combined.

Spoon the batter into the muffin cups filling them about 3/4 full. Bake for 15 minutes or until the muffins are golden brown. Remove the muffins from the oven and cool the muffins in the pan for 10 minutes. Remove the muffins from the pan and serve.

Bacon Cheddar Muffins

Makes 1 dozen

2 cups all purpose flour
3/4 cup granulated sugar
2 tsp. baking powder
1/2 tsp. baking soda
1/2 tsp. salt
3/4 cup plus 2 tbs. whole milk
1/3 cup melted unsalted butter
1 egg
1 cup shredded cheddar cheese
6 bacon slices, cooked crisp and crumbled

Preheat the oven to 350°. Spray a 12 count muffin tin with non stick cooking spray. In a mixing bowl, add the all purpose flour, granulated sugar, baking powder, baking soda and salt. Stir until combined. Add the milk, butter and egg. Mix until well combined. Add the bacon and cheddar cheese. Stir until combined.

Spoon the batter into the muffin cups filling them about 3/4 full. Bake for 15 minutes or until a toothpick inserted in the center of the muffins comes out clean. Remove the muffins from the oven and cool the muffins in the pan for 2 minutes. Remove the muffins from the pan and serve.

Onion Cheddar Muffins

Makes 6 muffins

1 1/2 cups Bisquick
3/4 cup shredded cheddar cheese
1 egg
1/2 cup whole milk
1/3 cup finely chopped onion
1 tbs. unsalted butter
1 tbs. toasted sesame seeds

In a mixing bowl, add the Bisquick and 1/2 cup cheddar cheese. Stir until combined. In a small bowl, add the egg and milk. Whisk until combined. In a small skillet, add the onion and butter. Saute the onion for 3 minutes or until the onion is tender. Remove the skillet from the heat and add the onions to the egg mixture. Whisk until combined and add to the dry ingredients. Mix only until the batter is moistened and combined.

Spray a 6 count muffin tin with non stick cooking spray. Spoon the batter into the muffin cups filling them about 3/4 full. Sprinkle 1/4 cup cheddar cheese over the batter. Sprinkle the sesame seeds over the batter.

Preheat the oven to 400°. Bake for 20 minutes or until a toothpick inserted in the center of the muffins comes out clean. Remove the muffins from the oven and cool the muffins in the pan for 10 minutes. Remove the muffins from the pan and serve.

Garlic Cheddar Muffins

Makes 1 dozen

2 cups self rising flour
1 cup whole milk
1 cup shredded cheddar cheese
3 garlic cloves, minced
1/4 cup mayonnaise
2 tbs. granulated sugar
2 tbs. melted unsalted butter

Preheat the oven to 375°. Spray a 12 count muffin tin with non stick cooking spray. In a mixing bowl, add the self rising flour, milk, cheddar cheese, garlic, mayonnaise and granulated sugar. Whisk until the batter is moistened and combined.

Spoon the batter into the muffin cups filling them about 2/3 full. Bake for 18 minutes or until the muffins are golden brown. Remove the muffins from the oven and brush the tops of the muffins with the melted butter. Remove the muffins from the pan and serve.

Caraway Cheddar Muffins

Makes 1 dozen

1 1/4 cups all purpose flour
1/2 cup rye flour
2 tbs. granulated sugar
2 1/2 tsp. baking powder
1/2 tsp. salt
1 cup shredded cheddar cheese
1 1/2 tsp. caraway seeds
1 cup whole milk
1/4 cup vegetable oil
1 egg

Preheat the oven to 400°. Spray a 12 count muffin tin with non stick cooking spray. In a mixing bowl, add the all purpose flour, rye flour, granulated sugar, baking powder, salt, cheddar cheese and caraway seeds. Whisk until combined.

In a small bowl, add the milk, vegetable oil and egg. Whisk until combined and add to the dry ingredients. Mix only until the batter is moistened and combined.

Spoon the batter into the muffin cups filling them about 2/3 full. Bake for 20 minutes or until the muffins are golden brown and a toothpick inserted in the center of the muffins comes out clean. Remove the muffins from the oven and immediately remove the muffins from the pan. Cool the muffins for 10 minutes and serve.

Rye & Wheat Muffins

Makes 1 dozen

1 cup medium rye flour
1 cup whole wheat flour
1 tsp. baking soda
1/2 tsp. salt
1 tsp. grated orange zest
1/3 cup vegetable oil
2 tbs. honey
1 cup plain yogurt
2 eggs

Preheat the oven to 350°. Spray a 12 count muffin tin with non stick cooking spray. In a mixing bowl, add the rye flour, whole wheat flour, baking soda, salt and orange zest. Whisk until combined.

In a small bowl, add the vegetable oil, honey, yogurt and eggs. Whisk until combined and add to the dry ingredients. Mix only until the batter is moistened and combined.

Spoon the batter into the muffin cups filling them about 2/3 full. Bake for 15-20 minutes or until the muffins are golden brown and a toothpick inserted in the center of the muffins comes out clean. Remove the muffins from the oven and immediately remove the muffins from the pan. Cool the muffins for 10 minutes and serve.

Ham & Swiss Corn Muffins

Makes 1 dozen

2 cups self rising white cornmeal
1 tbs. granulated sugar
1 1/2 cups buttermilk
1 egg
2 tbs. Dijon mustard
3 tbs. melted unsalted butter
1 cup cooked diced ham
1 cup shredded Swiss cheese

Preheat the oven to 425°. Spray a 12 count muffin tin with non stick cooking spray. In a mixing bowl, add the cornmeal, granulated sugar, buttermilk, egg, Dijon mustard and butter. Mix until well combined. Add the ham and Swiss cheese. Stir until combined.

Spoon the batter into the muffin cups filling them about 3/4 full. Bake for 15 minutes or until the muffins are golden brown. Remove the muffins from the oven and cool the muffins in the pan for 10 minutes. Remove the muffins from the pan and serve.

Southwestern Chile Cheese Corn Muffins

Makes 1 dozen

2 cups self rising white cornmeal
1 tbs. granulated sugar
1 1/2 cups buttermilk
1 egg
4 tbs. melted unsalted butter
4 oz. can diced green chiles, drained
1 cup shredded Pepper Jack

Preheat the oven to 425°. Spray a 12 count muffin tin with non stick cooking spray. In a mixing bowl, add the cornmeal, granulated sugar, buttermilk, egg and butter. Mix until well combined. Add the green chiles and Pepper Jack cheese. Stir until combined.

Spoon the batter into the muffin cups filling them about 3/4 full. Bake for 15 minutes or until the muffins are golden brown. Remove the muffins from the oven and cool the muffins in the pan for 10 minutes. Remove the muffins from the pan and serve.

Curry Cornbread Muffins

Makes 1 dozen

1/4 cup chopped green onion
3 tbs. vegetable oil
1 1/4 cups plain white cornmeal
3/4 cup all purpose flour
3/4 tsp. salt
1 tbs. baking powder
2 tbs. granulated sugar
1 tbs. curry powder
1 beaten egg
1 cup whole milk

Preheat the oven to 425°. Spray a 12 count muffin tin with non stick cooking spray. In a small skillet, add the green onion and vegetable oil. Saute the green onions for 5 minutes. Remove the skillet from the heat.

In a mixing bowl, add the cornmeal, all purpose flour, salt, baking powder, granulated sugar and curry powder. Whisk until combined. Add the green onions with any remaining oil, egg and milk. Whisk until the batter is moistened and combined.

Spoon the batter into the muffin cups filling them about 2/3 full. Bake for 15 minutes or until a toothpick inserted in the center of the muffins comes out clean and the muffins are golden brown. Remove the muffins from the oven and immediately remove the muffins from the pan. Serve hot.

Cheese Cornmeal Muffins

Makes 1 dozen

1 cup self rising flour
1 cup self rising white cornmeal
1/4 cup granulated sugar
2/3 cup shredded cheese (use your favorite flavor)
1 cup whole milk
1 egg
2 tbs. melted vegetable shortening

Preheat the oven to 400°. Spray a 12 count muffin tin with non stick cooking spray. In a mixing bowl, add the self rising flour, cornmeal, granulated sugar and cheese. Whisk until combined. Add the milk, egg and vegetable shortening. Whisk until the batter is moistened and combined.

Spoon the batter into the muffin cups filling them about 2/3 full. Bake for 20 minutes or until a toothpick inserted in the center of the muffins comes out clean and the muffins are golden brown. Remove the muffins from the oven and immediately remove the muffins from the pan. Serve hot.

Maple Cornbread Muffins

Makes 1 dozen

2 tbs. vegetable shortening
1 beaten egg
1/3 cup whole milk
2 tbs. maple syrup
1/2 cup plain yellow cornmeal
3/4 cup all purpose flour
1 1/2 tsp. baking powder
1/4 tsp. salt
3 tbs. melted unsalted butter

Preheat the oven to 425°. Add the vegetable shortening to a 12 count muffin tin. Place the muffin tin in the oven until the shortening melts and the muffin tin is sizzling hot.

In a mixing bowl, add the egg, milk and maple syrup. Whisk until combined. Add the cornmeal, all purpose flour, baking powder and salt. Whisk until combined. Add the butter and mix until the batter is well blended.

Spoon the batter into the muffin cups filling them a little more than 1/2 full. Bake for 15 minutes or until a toothpick inserted in the center of the muffins comes out clean and the muffins are golden brown. Remove the muffins from the oven and immediately remove the muffins from the pan. Serve hot.

Mayonnaise Cornmeal Muffins

Makes 1 dozen

2 tbs. vegetable shortening
2 cups plain white or yellow cornmeal
1 tsp. baking powder
1 tsp. salt
1 egg
1 tbs. mayonnaise
1 1/2 cups whole milk

Preheat the oven to 400°. Add the vegetable shortening to a 12 count muffin tin. Place the muffin tin in the oven until the shortening melts and the muffin tin is sizzling hot.

In a mixing bowl, add the cornmeal, baking powder and salt. Whisk until combined. Add the egg, mayonnaise and milk. Whisk until the batter is moistened and combined.

Spoon the batter into the muffin cups filling them about 2/3 full. Bake for 25 minutes or until a toothpick inserted in the center of the muffins comes out clean and the muffins are golden brown. Remove the muffins from the oven and immediately remove the muffins from the pan. Serve hot.

Italian Parmesan Muffins

Makes 1 dozen

2 cups all purpose flour
3/4 cup grated Parmesan cheese
2 tsp. granulated sugar
2 tsp. baking powder
2 tsp. dried Italian seasoning
2 tsp. dried basil
2 tsp. dried parsley flakes
2 tsp. dried cilantro flakes
1/2 tsp. baking soda
1/2 tsp. salt
1 egg
1 1/4 cups whole milk
1/4 cup vegetable oil

Preheat the oven to 400°. Spray a 12 count muffin tin with non stick cooking spray. In a mixing bowl, add the all purpose flour, Parmesan cheese, granulated sugar, baking powder, Italian seasoning, basil, parsley flakes, cilantro flakes, baking soda and salt. Whisk until combined.

In a small bowl, add the egg, milk and vegetable oil. Whisk until combined and add to the dry ingredients. Mix only until the batter is moistened and combined. Spoon the batter into the muffin cups filling them about 2/3 full. Bake for 20 minutes or until a toothpick inserted in the center of the muffins comes out clean. Remove the muffins from the oven and cool the muffins in the pans for 5 minutes. Remove the muffins from the pan and serve.

Parmesan Cheese Muffins

Makes 1 dozen

2 cups self rising flour
3/4 cup shredded Parmesan cheese
2 tbs. granulated sugar
1 cup whole milk
1/4 cup vegetable oil
2 eggs

Preheat the oven to 400°. Spray a 12 count muffin tin with non stick cooking spray. In a mixing bowl, add the self rising flour, Parmesan cheese and granulated sugar. Whisk until combined.

In a small bowl, add the milk, vegetable oil and eggs. Whisk until combined and add to the dry ingredients. Mix only until the batter is moistened and combined.

Spoon the batter into the muffin cups filling them about 2/3 full. Bake for 20 minutes or until a toothpick inserted in the center of the muffins comes out clean and the muffins are golden brown. Remove the muffins from the oven and cool the muffins in the pan for 5 minutes. Remove the muffins from the pan and serve.

Note: You can add 1 cup cooked pork sausage, bacon, ground beef or your favorite ground meat to the recipe for a different flavor. Add the meat to the dry ingredients and stir until the meat is coated in the dry ingredients. Mix and bake as directed above. You may need to add a tablespoon or two of additional milk to the batter.

You can add 1 teaspoon of your favorite dried herbs, garlic or seasonings for a different flavor. You may need to add a tablespoon of additional milk to the batter.

Rosemary Lemon Muffins

Makes 1 dozen

1 cup whole milk
2 tbs. minced fresh rosemary
2 tsp. grated lemon zest
2 cups all purpose flour
1 1/2 tsp. baking powder
1/4 tsp. salt
2 eggs
1/2 cup melted unsalted butter
2 tbs. granulated sugar

Preheat the oven to 375°. Spray a 12 count muffin tin with non stick cooking spray. In a sauce pan over low heat, add the milk, rosemary and lemon zest. Stir until combined and simmer for 2 minutes. Remove the pan from the heat and cool for 10 minutes.

In a mixing bowl, add the all purpose flour, baking powder and salt. Whisk until combined. Add the eggs, butter and granulated sugar to the rosemary mixture. Whisk until combined and add to the dry ingredients. Mix only until the batter is moistened and combined.

Spoon the batter into the muffin cups filling them about 2/3 full. Bake for 20 minutes or until a toothpick inserted in the center of the muffins comes out clean. Remove the muffins from the oven and cool the muffins in the pan for 5 minutes. Remove the muffins from the pan and serve.

Cheese Grits & Chive Muffins

Makes 2 dozen

1 1/2 cups all purpose flour
1 tsp. baking powder
1/2 tsp. baking soda
1/2 tsp. salt
2 eggs
3/4 cup buttermilk
1/2 cup melted unsalted butter
1 cup cooked grits
1 cup shredded sharp cheddar cheese
1 tbs. chopped fresh chives
1/8 tsp. cayenne pepper

Preheat the oven to 350°. Spray your muffin tins with non stick cooking spray. In a mixing bowl, add the all purpose flour, baking powder, baking soda and salt. Stir until combined.

In a separate bowl, add the eggs, buttermilk, butter and grits. Whisk until smooth and combined. Add to the dry ingredients and mix only until the batter is moistened. Add the cheddar cheese, chives and cayenne pepper. Mix only until combined.

Spoon the batter into the muffin cups filling them about 3/4 full. Bake for 30 minutes or until the muffins are golden brown and begin to pull away from the sides of the pan. Remove the muffins from the oven and cool the muffins in the pans for 5 minutes. Remove the muffins from the pans and serve.

Ham & Cheddar Muffins

Makes 1 dozen

2 cups self rising flour
1/2 tsp. baking soda
1 cup whole milk
1/2 cup mayonnaise
1/2 cup finely chopped cooked ham
1/2 cup shredded cheddar cheese

Preheat the oven to 425°. Spray a 12 count muffin tin with non stick cooking spray. In a mixing bowl, add the self rising flour and baking soda. In a separate bowl, add the milk, mayonnaise, ham and cheddar. Mix until combined and add to the dry ingredients. Stir until the batter is moistened and combined.

Spoon the batter into the muffin cups filling them about 2/3 full. Bake for 16 minutes or until the muffins are golden brown. Remove the muffins from the oven and cool the muffins in the pan for 5 minutes. Remove the muffins from the pan and serve.

Green Tomato Corn Muffins

Makes 2 dozen

2 cups diced green tomatoes
1/2 cup granulated sugar
1/2 cup melted unsalted butter
2 cups self rising white cornmeal
2 tsp. grated lemon zest
5 eggs
2 cups sour cream

Preheat the oven to 450°. In a skillet over medium heat, add the green tomatoes, 2 tablespoons granulated sugar and 2 tablespoons melted butter. Saute the tomatoes for 10 minutes or until the tomatoes are lightly browned. Remove the skillet from the heat.

In a mixing bowl, add the cornmeal, lemon zest and remaining granulated sugar. Stir until combined. In a small bowl, add the eggs, sour cream and remaining melted butter. Whisk until combined and add to the dry ingredients. Mix only until the batter is moistened and combined. Fold in the green tomatoes.

Spray your muffin tins with non stick cooking spray. Spoon the batter into the muffin cups filling them about 2/3 full. Bake for 15 minutes or until a toothpick inserted in the center of the muffins comes out clean. Remove the muffins from the oven and cool the muffins in the pans for 10 minutes. Remove the muffins from the pans and serve.

Mayonnaise Sesame Muffins

Makes 1 dozen

2 tsp. mayonnaise
2 cups self rising flour
2 tsp. granulated sugar
1 cup whole milk
2 tbs. toasted sesame seed

Preheat the oven to 400°. Spray a 12 count muffin tin with non stick cooking spray. In a mixing bowl, add the mayonnaise, self rising flour, granulated sugar and milk. Stir until combined.

Spoon the batter into the muffin cups filling them about 2/3 full. Sprinkle the sesame seeds over the top of the batter. Bake for 20 minutes or until the muffins are golden brown. Remove the muffins from the oven and cool the muffins in the pan for 5 minutes. Remove the muffins from the pan and serve.

Beer Pimento Cheese Muffins

Makes 18 muffins

12 oz. bottle beer, at room temperature
4 oz. jar diced red pimento, drained
1 egg
1 tsp. finely grated onion
4 cups Bisquick
2 cups shredded sharp cheddar cheese
1 cup crushed cheese crackers

Preheat the oven to 400°. Spray your muffin tins with non stick cooking spray. In a mixing bowl, add the beer, red pimento, egg and onion. Stir until combined. Add the Bisquick and mix only until combined. Add the cheddar cheese and mix until combined.

Spoon the batter into the muffin cups filling them about 3/4 full. Sprinkle the cheese crackers over the top of the batter. Bake for 15 minutes or until the muffins are lightly browned. Remove the muffins from the oven and cool the muffins in the pans for 10 minutes. Remove the muffins from the pans and serve.

Sausage Cheddar Muffins

Makes 2 dozen

1 lb. ground hot pork sausage
10.75 oz. can condensed cheddar cheese soup
1/2 cup whole milk
2 tsp. rubbed sage
3 cups Bisquick

In a skillet over medium heat, add the sausage. Stir frequently to break the sausage into crumbles as it cooks. Cook for 8 minutes or until the sausage is well browned and no longer pink. Remove the skillet from the heat and drain all the excess grease from the skillet.

Add the sausage to a mixing bowl. Add the cheddar cheese soup, milk and sage. Stir until combined. Add the Bisquick and mix only until the batter is moistened and combined.

Spray two 12 count muffin tins with non stick cooking spray. Spoon the batter into the muffin cups filling them about 2/3 full. Bake for 15 minutes or until a toothpick inserted in the center of the muffins comes out clean. Remove the muffins from the oven and cool for 5 minutes in the pans. Remove the muffins from the pans and serve.

Smoked Salmon Muffins

Makes 24 miniature muffins

1/2 cup Bisquick
1/2 cup whole milk
1/4 cup sour cream
1/2 tsp. Worcestershire sauce
2 eggs
2/3 cup shredded cheddar cheese
1/3 cup chopped smoked salmon
2 green onions, sliced

Preheat the oven to 400°. Spray a 24 count miniature muffin pan with non stick cooking spray. In a mixing bowl, add the Bisquick, milk, sour cream and Worcestershire sauce. Stir until combined. Add the eggs and mix until combined. Fold in the cheddar cheese, salmon and green onions.

Spoon about 1 tablespoon batter into each muffin cup. Bake for 15 minutes or until the muffins are golden brown. Remove the muffins from the oven and cool the muffins for 5 minutes in the pan. Remove the muffins from the pan and serve.

Corn Dog Muffins

Makes about 18 muffins

8 oz. pkg. corn muffin mix, 8 oz. size
2 tbs. light brown sugar
2 eggs
1 cup whole milk
11 oz. can whole kernel corn, drained
5 hot dogs, chopped

Preheat the oven to 400°. Spray your muffin tins with non stick cooking spray. In a mixing bowl, add the corn muffin mix, brown sugar, eggs and milk. Mix until the batter is moistened and combined. Add the corn and hot dogs to the batter. Stir until combined. The batter will be thin.

Pour the batter into the muffin cups filling them about 3/4 full. Bake for 15 minutes or until the muffins are done and golden brown. Remove the muffins from the oven and immediately remove the muffins from the pan. Serve hot.

Bell Pepper Biscuit Muffins

Not really a biscuit but a cross between a biscuit and a muffin.

Makes 10 muffins

1/2 cup unsalted butter, cubed
1/3 cup finely chopped green onion
1/3 cup chopped red bell pepper
1/3 cup chopped yellow bell pepper
2 eggs
2/3 cup sour cream
1 1/2 cups all purpose flour
2 tbs. granulated sugar
1 1/2 tsp. baking powder
3/4 tsp. salt
1/2 tsp. dried basil
1/4 tsp. baking soda
1/4 tsp. dried tarragon

In a skillet over medium heat, add the butter. When the butter melts, add the green onion, red bell pepper and yellow bell pepper. Saute the vegetables for 5 minutes. Remove the skillet from the heat.

In a small bowl, add the eggs and sour cream. Whisk until combined. Add the vegetables from the skillet and stir until combined. In a mixing bowl, add the all purpose flour, granulated sugar, baking powder, salt, basil, baking soda and tarragon. Whisk until combined and add to the sour cream mixture. Whisk only until the batter is moistened and combined.

Spray your muffin tin with non stick cooking spray. Spoon the batter into the muffin cups filling them about 2/3 full. These muffins will not rise much. Preheat the oven to 350°. Bake for 20 minutes or until a toothpick inserted in the muffins comes out clean. Remove the muffins from the oven and cool for 2 minutes in the pan. Remove the muffins from the pan and serve.

Buttermilk Rosemary Muffins

Makes 1 dozen

2 1/4 cups all purpose flour
2 tbs. granulated sugar
1 tbs. baking powder
2 tsp. minced fresh rosemary
3/4 tsp. salt
1/2 cup plus 1 tbs. vegetable shortening
3/4 cup buttermilk
1/4 cup melted unsalted butter

Preheat the oven to 400°. Spray a 12 count muffin tin with non stick cooking spray. In a mixing bowl, add the all purpose flour, granulated sugar, baking powder, rosemary and salt. Whisk until combined. Add the vegetable shortening to the bowl. Using a pastry blender, cut the shortening into the dry ingredients until you have coarse crumbs.

Add the buttermilk to the bowl. Mix only until the batter is combined. The batter will be crumbly. Spoon the batter into the muffin cups filling them about 3/4 full. Brush the melted butter over the batter. Bake for 10-12 minutes or until a toothpick inserted in the center of the muffins comes out clean. Remove the muffins from the oven and cool for 5 minutes in the pan. Remove the muffins from the pan and serve.

Sausage Pizza Muffins

Makes about 20 muffins

8 oz. ground pork sausage
1 1/2 cups chopped fresh mushrooms
1/2 cup chopped pepperoni
1/4 cup chopped black olives
2 1/3 cups Bisquick
2 tsp. dried Italian seasoning
1 tsp. dried minced onion
1/4 tsp. garlic powder
3 beaten eggs
1/4 cup whole milk
3/4 cup shredded pizza cheese blend
14 oz. can diced tomatoes, drained

Preheat the oven to 375°. Spray your muffin tins with non stick cooking spray. In a skillet over medium heat, add the sausage, mushrooms, pepperoni and black olives. Stir frequently to break the sausage into crumbles as it cooks. Cook for 5 minutes or until the sausage is well browned and no longer pink. Remove the skillet from the heat and drain off any excess grease.

In a mixing bowl, add the Bisquick, Italian seasoning, minced onion and garlic powder. Whisk until combined. Add the sausage and vegetables, eggs, milk, pizza cheese blend and tomatoes with juice. Stir only until the batter is moistened and combined.

Spoon the batter into the muffin cups filling them about 3/4 full. Bake for 20 minutes or until a toothpick inserted in the center of the muffins comes out clean and the muffins are lightly browned. Remove the muffins from the oven and cool for 5 minutes in the pan. Remove the muffins from the pan and serve.

Pizza Muffins

Makes 1 dozen

1/4 cup finely chopped onion
1 garlic clove, minced
6 tbs. olive oil
2 cups all purpose flour
1 cup shredded mozzarella cheese
1/4 cup diced pepperoni
2 1/4 tsp. baking powder
1 tsp. dried oregano
3/4 tsp. salt
1 cup tomato juice
1 egg
1/2 cup freshly grated Parmesan cheese

In a small skillet over medium heat, add the onion, garlic and 2 tablespoons olive oil. Saute for 4 minutes. Remove the skillet from the heat. In a mixing bowl, add the all purpose flour, mozzarella cheese, pepperoni, baking powder, oregano and salt. Whisk until combined.

Add the tomato juice, egg and 4 tablespoons olive oil to the skillet. Whisk until combined and add to the dry ingredients. Mix only until the batter is moistened and combined.

Preheat the oven to 400°. Spray a 12 count muffin tin with non stick cooking spray. Spoon the batter into the muffin cups filling them about 3/4 full. Sprinkle the Parmesan cheese over the top of the batter. Bake for 20 minutes or until a toothpick inserted in the center of the muffins comes out clean. Remove the muffins from the oven and cool for 5 minutes in the pan. Remove the muffins from the pan and serve.

Hushpuppy Muffins

Makes about 18 muffins

2/3 cup plain white cornmeal
1/3 cup all purpose flour
1 tsp. baking powder
1/2 tsp. salt
1/2 cup minced onion
1/3 cup whole milk
1 beaten egg
1 tbs. vegetable oil
1/8 tsp. black pepper

Preheat the oven to 450°. Spray a 12 count muffin tin with non stick cooking spray. In a mixing bowl, add the cornmeal, all purpose flour, baking powder and salt. Whisk until combined.

In a small bowl, add the onion, milk, egg, vegetable oil and black pepper. Whisk until combined and add to the dry ingredients. Mix only until the batter is moistened and combined.

Spoon the batter into the muffin cups filling them about 3/4 full. Bake for 12-15 minutes or until the muffins are done and golden brown. Remove the muffins from the oven and immediately remove the muffins from the pan. Serve hot.

Mushroom Muffins

Makes 1 dozen

4 oz. can chopped mushrooms
1 tsp. unsalted butter
2 cups all purpose flour
1/4 cup granulated sugar
1 tsp. salt
3 tsp. baking powder
1 beaten egg
3/4 cup whole milk
1/2 cup shredded American cheese
1/4 cup vegetable oil

Drain the mushrooms but reserve 1/4 cup liquid. Add the mushrooms and butter to a small skillet over medium heat. Saute the mushrooms for 3 minutes. Remove the skillet from the heat.

In a mixing bowl, add the all purpose flour, granulated sugar, salt and baking powder. Whisk until combined. Add the egg, milk, American cheese, mushrooms, 1/4 cup mushroom liquid and vegetable oil. Whisk until the batter is moistened and combined.

Spray a 12 count muffin tin with non stick cooking spray. Spoon the batter into the muffin cups filling them about 2/3 full. Preheat the oven to 450°. Bake for 20 minutes or until a toothpick inserted in the center of the muffins comes out clean. Remove the muffins from the oven and immediately remove the muffins from the pan. Serve immediately.

Apple Cheddar Muffins

Makes 1 dozen

1 cup whole wheat flour
1 cup all purpose flour
2 tbs. granulated sugar
1 tbs. baking powder
1/2 tsp. salt
1 cup peeled apple, chopped
1 cup freshly shredded cheddar cheese
2 eggs
1 cup whole milk
4 tbs. melted unsalted butter

In a mixing bowl, add the whole wheat flour, all purpose flour, granulated sugar, baking powder and salt. Stir until combined. Add the apple and cheddar cheese. Stir until combined.

Add the eggs, milk and melted butter to a small bowl. Whisk until combined and add to the dry ingredients. Mix only until the batter is moistened and combined.

Spray a 12 count muffin tin with non stick cooking spray. Spoon the batter into the muffin cups filling them about 2/3 full. Preheat the oven to 400°. Bake for 20 minutes or until a toothpick inserted in the center of the muffins comes out clean. Remove the muffins from the oven and immediately remove the muffins from the pan. Serve warm.

Golden Apple Cheese Muffins

Makes 1 dozen

1 1/2 cups finely chopped peeled apple
2 tbs. unsalted butter
1/2 cup cottage cheese
2 tbs. granulated sugar
1 tsp. dried minced onion
1 egg
2 cups Bisquick

Preheat the oven to 400°. Spray a 12 count muffin tin with non stick cooking spray. In a small skillet over medium heat, add the apples and butter. Saute the apples for 5 minutes or until the apples are tender. Remove the skillet from the heat.

In a mixing bowl, add the cottage cheese, granulated sugar and onion. Using a mixer on medium speed, beat until smooth and combined. Add the egg and mix until combined. Turn the mixer off. Add the apples with any butter to the bowl. Stir until combined. Add the Bisquick and mix only until the batter is moistened and combined.

Spoon the batter into the muffin cups filling them almost to the top of the muffin cups. Bake for 25 minutes or until a toothpick inserted in the center of the muffins comes out clean. Remove the muffins from the oven and immediately remove the muffins from the pan. Serve warm.

Apple Cornmeal Muffins

Makes 1 dozen

1/2 cup all purpose flour
1 cup plain white cornmeal
1/2 tsp. salt
1 tbs. granulated sugar
2 1/2 tsp. baking powder
1 beaten egg
2/3 cup whole milk
2 tbs. melted unsalted butter
1/2 cup finely chopped apple

Preheat the oven to 400°. Spray a 12 count muffin tin with non stick cooking spray. In a mixing bowl, add the all purpose flour, cornmeal, salt, granulated sugar and baking powder. Whisk until combined. Add the egg, 1/2 cup whole milk, butter and apple. Whisk until well combined. Every cornmeal absorbs liquids differently. Add the remaining milk if needed to make a batter the consistency of pancake batter.

Spoon the batter into the muffin cups filling them a little more than 1/2 full. Bake for 20 minutes or until a toothpick inserted in the center of the muffins comes out clean. Remove the muffins from the oven and immediately remove the muffins from the pan. Serve warm.

Herb Cornbread Muffins

Makes 1 dozen

2 tbs. vegetable shortening
2 cups self rising white cornmeal
1/2 tsp. salt
1/4 tsp. dried thyme
1/2 tsp. celery seed
1 beaten egg
2 tsp. grated onion
1/2 cup sour cream
2 tbs. vegetable oil

Preheat the oven to 450°. Add the vegetable shortening to a 12 cup muffin tin. Place the muffin tin in the oven until the shortening melts and the muffin tin is sizzling hot.

In a mixing bowl, add the cornmeal, salt, thyme and celery seed. Whisk until combined. In a small bowl, add the egg, onion, sour cream and vegetable oil. Whisk until combined and add to the dry ingredients. Mix only until the batter is moistened and combined.

Spoon the batter into the muffin cups filling them about 2/3 full. Bake for 20 minutes or until the cornbread is done and golden brown. Remove the muffins from the oven and serve.

Parmesan Pepper Cornbread Biscotti

You don't think about biscotti being made from a quick bread but making biscotti from a quick bread is very easy and tasty.

Makes about 18 biscotti

2 pkgs. buttermilk cornbread muffin mix, 6 oz. size
1 cup freshly grated Parmesan cheese
2 tsp. black pepper
3/4 tsp. chopped fresh rosemary
1/4 cup cold unsalted butter, cubed
3 eggs
1/4 cup buttermilk

Preheat the oven to 350°. Add the cornbread mix, 3/4 cup Parmesan cheese, black pepper, rosemary and butter to a food processor. Process about 5 times or until crumbly.

In a small bowl, add 2 eggs and the buttermilk. Whisk until combined. With the food processor running, slowly add the egg mixture. Mix until the dough is moistened and thick.

Place a 12" x 4" piece of parchment paper on a large baking sheet. Lightly spray your hands with non stick cooking spray. Spread the dough over the parchment paper. Add 1 egg to a small bowl. Whisk until combined and brush over the top of the dough. Sprinkle 1/4 cup Parmesan cheese over the top of the dough.

Bake for 20 minutes or until the biscotti is light golden brown and firm. Remove the pan from the oven and let the biscotti cool for 10 minutes on the baking pan. Reduce the oven temperature to 300°.

Slide the biscotti with the parchment paper off the baking pan. Cut into 1/2" slices using a serrated knife. Place the slices, cut side down, on the baking sheet. Bake for 20 minutes or until both sides of the biscotti are golden brown. Remove the biscotti from the oven and cool for 10 minutes. Serve the biscotti warm. The cooled biscotti will keep about 3 days in an airtight container.

Jalapeno Pepper Jack Cornbread Biscotti

Makes about 18 biscotti

2 pkgs. buttermilk cornbread muffin mix, 6 oz. size
1 cup shredded Pepper Jack cheese
1 jalapeno pepper, seeded and chopped
1/4 cup cold unsalted butter, cubed
3 eggs
1/4 cup whole milk

Preheat the oven to 350°. Add the cornbread mix, 3/4 cup Pepper Jack cheese, jalapeno pepper and butter to a food processor. Process about 5 times or until crumbly.

In a small bowl, add 2 eggs and the milk. Whisk until combined. With the food processor running, slowly add the egg mixture. Mix until the dough is moistened and thick.

Place a 12" x 4" piece of parchment paper on a large baking sheet. Lightly spray your hands with non stick cooking spray. Spread the dough over the parchment paper. Add 1 egg to a small bowl. Whisk until combined and brush over the top of the dough. Sprinkle 1/4 cup Pepper Jack cheese over the top of the dough.

Bake for 20 minutes or until the biscotti is light golden brown and firm. Remove the pan from the oven and let the biscotti cool for 10 minutes on the baking pan. Reduce the oven temperature to 300°.

Slide the biscotti with the parchment paper off the baking pan. Cut into 1/2" slices using a serrated knife. Place the slices, cut side down, on the baking sheet. Bake for 20 minutes or until both sides of the biscotti are golden brown. Remove the biscotti from the oven and cool for 10 minutes. Serve the biscotti warm. The cooled biscotti will keep about 3 days in an airtight container.

Bacon Cheddar & Chive Cornbread Biscotti

Makes about 18 biscotti

2 pkgs. buttermilk cornbread muffin mix, 6 oz. size
1 cup freshly shredded cheddar cheese
1 tbs. chopped fresh chives
4 bacon slices, cooked and crumbled
1/4 cup cold unsalted butter, cubed
3 eggs
1/4 cup buttermilk

Preheat the oven to 350°. Add the cornbread mix, 3/4 cup cheddar cheese, chives, bacon and butter to a food processor. Process about 5 times or until crumbly.

In a small bowl, add 2 eggs and the buttermilk. Whisk until combined. With the food processor running, slowly add the egg mixture. Mix until the dough is moistened and thick.

Place a 12" x 4" piece of parchment paper on a large baking sheet. Lightly spray your hands with non stick cooking spray. Spread the dough over the parchment paper. Add 1 egg to a small bowl. Whisk until combined and brush over the top of the dough. Sprinkle 1/4 cup cheddar cheese over the top of the dough.

Bake for 20 minutes or until the biscotti is light golden brown and firm. Remove the pan from the oven and let the biscotti cool for 10 minutes on the baking pan. Reduce the oven temperature to 300°.

Slide the biscotti with the parchment paper off the baking pan. Cut into 1/2" slices using a serrated knife. Place the slices, cut side down, on the baking sheet. Bake for 20 minutes or until both sides of the biscotti are golden brown. Remove the biscotti from the oven and cool for 10 minutes. Serve the biscotti warm. The cooled biscotti will keep about 3 days in an airtight container.

Parmesan Garlic Cornbread Biscotti

Makes about 18 biscotti

2 pkgs. buttermilk cornbread muffin mix, 6 oz. size
1 cup freshly grated Parmesan cheese
1 garlic clove, minced
1/4 tsp. salt
1/4 cup cold unsalted butter, cubed
2 eggs
1/4 cup buttermilk
1/4 cup melted unsalted butter

Preheat the oven to 350°. Add the cornbread mix, 3/4 cup Parmesan cheese, garlic, salt and cold cubed butter to a food processor. Process about 5 times or until crumbly.

In a small bowl, add the eggs and buttermilk. Whisk until combined. With the food processor running, slowly add the egg mixture. Mix until the dough is moistened and thick.

Place a 12" x 4" piece of parchment paper on a large baking sheet. Lightly spray your hands with non stick cooking spray. Spread the dough over the parchment paper. Brush 1/4 cup melted butter over the top of the dough. Sprinkle 1/4 cup Parmesan cheese over the top of the dough.

Bake for 20 minutes or until the biscotti is light golden brown and firm. Remove the pan from the oven and let the biscotti cool for 10 minutes on the baking pan. Reduce the oven temperature to 300°.

Slide the biscotti with the parchment paper off the baking pan. Cut into 1/2" slices using a serrated knife. Place the slices, cut side down, on the baking sheet. Bake for 20 minutes or until both sides of the biscotti are golden brown. Remove the biscotti from the oven and cool for 10 minutes. Serve the biscotti warm. The cooled biscotti will keep about 3 days in an airtight container.

Savory Herb Shortbread

Makes 24 shortbread

1/2 cup freshly shredded Parmesan cheese
1/2 cup freshly shredded sharp cheddar cheese
1/4 cup cold unsalted butter, cubed
2/3 cup all purpose flour
1/2 tsp. dried sage
1/4 tsp. ground mustard
1/4 tsp. black pepper
1/4 cup chopped walnuts

Preheat the oven to 425°. In a food processor, add the Parmesan cheese, cheddar cheese and butter. Pulse until a crumb mixture forms. Add the all purpose flour, sage, ground mustard, black pepper and walnuts. Pulse until the dough forms and the ingredients are combined.

Divide the dough into 4 equal pieces. Pat each piece into a 5" circle. Cut each circle into 6 wedges. Place the wedges on an ungreased baking sheet. Bake for 6-8 minutes or until the shortbread are golden brown. Remove the shortbread from the oven and immediately remove the shortbread from the baking sheet. Serve warm or at room temperature. Store the shortbread in an airtight container up to 2 days.

Old South Spoon Bread

Makes 6 servings

1 1/2 cups boiling water
1 cup self rising white cornmeal
1 tbs. unsalted butter, softened
3 eggs, separated and at room temperature
1 cup buttermilk
1 tsp. granulated sugar
1/4 tsp. baking soda

Preheat the oven to 375°. Spray a 2 quart casserole dish with non stick cooking spray. Add the boiling water and cornmeal to a mixing bowl. Stir until combined and cool for 5 minutes. Add the butter and egg yolks to the bowl. Whisk until smooth and combined. Add the buttermilk, granulated sugar and baking soda. Whisk until well combined.

In a mixing bowl, add the egg whites. Using a mixer on medium speed, beat until soft peaks form. Fold the egg whites into the batter. Spoon the batter into the casserole dish. Bake for 45 minutes or until a toothpick inserted off center of the bread comes out clean. Remove the bread from the oven and serve.

Southern Spoonbread

Makes 12 servings

3 cups boiling water
2 cups plain white or yellow cornmeal
2 tsp. salt
1/2 cup unsalted butter, cut into small pieces
2 cups whole milk
4 beaten eggs
1 tbs. baking powder

Preheat the oven to 375°. Spray a 9 x 13 baking pan with non stick cooking spray. Add the boiling water and cornmeal to a mixing bowl. Stir until smooth and combined. Add the salt and butter to the bowl. Whisk until smooth and combined. Let the batter sit for 10 minutes. Whisk constantly and add the milk and eggs. Whisk until well combined. Add the baking powder and whisk until combined.

Spoon the batter into the baking pan. Bake for 45 minutes or until the bread is lightly browned and firm. Remove the bread from the oven and serve.

Tomato Spoon Bread

Makes 4 servings

1 cup plain white cornmeal
1 cup tomato juice
2 cups scalded whole milk
1/4 cup unsalted butter
1/3 cup grated onion
1 tsp. baking powder
3/4 tsp. salt
3 eggs, separated and at room temperature

Preheat the oven to 375°. Spray a 1 1/2 quart casserole dish with non stick cooking spray. In a sauce pan over low heat, add the cornmeal, tomato juice and milk. Stir constantly and cook until the cornmeal thickens. Remove the pan from the heat and add the butter, onion, baking powder and salt. Whisk until the butter melts and the batter is smooth. Add the egg yolks and mix until well combined.

In a mixing bowl, add the egg whites. Using a mixer on medium speed, beat until stiff peaks form. Fold the egg whites into the batter. Spoon the batter into the casserole dish. Bake for 40 minutes or until a toothpick inserted off center of the bread comes out clean. Remove the bread from the oven and serve.

Vegetable Spoonbread

Makes 6 servings

1 cup plain white cornmeal
1 1/2 tsp. salt
1 cup cold whole milk
1 1/2 cups scalded whole milk
1 tbs. unsalted butter
15 oz. can mixed vegetables, drained
5 bacon slices, cooked and crumbled
4 eggs, separated and at room temperature

Preheat the oven to 375°. Spray a 2 quart casserole dish with non stick cooking spray. In a sauce pan over low heat, add the cornmeal, salt and cold milk. Stir constantly and cook until the cornmeal thickens. Remove the pan from the heat and add the scalded whole milk, butter, mixed vegetables and bacon. Whisk until the butter melts and the batter is combined. Add the egg yolks and mix until well combined.

In a mixing bowl, add the egg whites. Using a mixer on medium speed, beat until stiff peaks form. Fold the egg whites into the batter. Spoon the batter into the casserole dish. Bake for 50 minutes or until a toothpick inserted off center of the bread comes out clean. Remove the bread from the oven and serve.

3 SWEET BREADS

Sweet breads are great for breakfast, desserts or snacks. They are easy to make and come in a wide variety of flavors. You can also make pancakes and waffles from muffin batters. Use 1/4 cup batter for each pancake and use the amount of batter recommended in your waffle maker's instructions. Watch the batters closely as sweet batters will burn easily.

Chocolate Chai Loaves

Makes 3 small loaves

2 oz. semisweet chocolate, chopped
1/2 cup water
1/2 cup plus 1 tbs. unsalted butter, softened
1 cup light brown sugar
2 eggs
1 1/2 tsp. vanilla extract
1 1/2 cups all purpose flour
4 tbs. chai tea latte mix
1 tsp. baking soda
1/2 tsp. salt
1/2 cup sour cream
1 cup powdered sugar
5 tsp. whole milk

Preheat the oven to 350°. Spray three 6" x 3" x 2" loaf pans with non stick cooking spray. In a microwavable bowl, add the chocolate and water. Stir every 30 seconds. Microwave for 1 minute or until the chocolate melts. Remove the bowl from the microwave and stir until smooth and combined.

In a mixing bowl, add 1/2 cup butter and brown sugar. Using a mixer on medium speed, beat for 3 minutes. Add the eggs and beat for 3 minutes. Add the melted chocolate and 1 teaspoon vanilla extract. Mix until the batter is smooth and combined.

In a separate bowl, add the all purpose flour, 3 tablespoons chai tea latte mix, baking soda and salt. Stir until combined. Add the dry ingredients to the mixing bowl along with the sour cream. Mix only until the batter is combined. Spoon the batter into the prepared pans.

Bake for 35 minutes or until a toothpick inserted in the loaves comes out clean. Remove the loaves from the oven and cool the bread in the pans for 10 minutes. Remove the loaves from the pan and cool completely before frosting.

Add 1 tablespoon butter, 1/2 teaspoon vanilla extract, 1 tablespoon chai tea latte mix, powdered sugar and 4 teaspoons milk to a mixing bowl. Using a mixer on medium speed, beat until smooth and fluffy. Add the remaining teaspoon milk if needed to make a fluffy frosting. Spread the frosting over the loaves and serve.

Sweet Potato Bread with Pineapple Butter

Makes one loaf

1 3/4 cups all purpose flour
1 1/2 cups granulated sugar
1 1/2 tsp. ground cinnamon
1 tsp. ground nutmeg
1/2 tsp. baking soda
1/2 tsp. baking powder
1/2 tsp. salt
2 eggs
1 cup mashed sweet potatoes
1/2 cup vegetable oil
1/3 cup water
1/2 cup unsalted butter, softened
8 oz. can crushed pineapple, drained

Preheat the oven to 350°. Spray a 9 x 5 loaf pan with non stick cooking spray. In a mixing bowl, add the all purpose flour, granulated sugar, cinnamon, nutmeg, baking soda, baking powder and salt. Stir until combined.

In a separate bowl, add the eggs, sweet potatoes, vegetable oil and water. Whisk until combined and add to the dry ingredients. Stir only until the batter is moistened and combined. Spoon the batter into the prepared pan.

Bake for 50 minutes or until a toothpick inserted in the center of the bread comes out clean. Remove the bread from the oven and cool the bread in the pan for 10 minutes. Remove the bread from the pan and cool for 10 minutes.

Add the butter and pineapple to a small bowl. Stir until well combined. Spread on slices of the warm bread. Serve the bread warm or at room temperature.

Coconut Bread

Makes one loaf

3 cups all purpose flour
1 cup granulated sugar
3 tsp. baking powder
3/4 tsp. salt
1 egg
1 1/2 cups whole milk
3/4 tsp. vanilla extract
1/4 tsp. almond extract
1 cup toasted sweetened flaked coconut

Preheat the oven to 350°. Spray a 9 x 5 loaf pan with non stick cooking spray. In a mixing bowl, add the all purpose flour, granulated sugar, baking powder and salt. Stir until combined.

In a separate bowl, add the egg, milk, vanilla extract and almond extract. Whisk until combined. Add to the dry ingredients. Stir only until the batter is moistened and combined. Gently fold in the coconut. Spoon the batter into the prepared pan.

Bake for 40 minutes or until a toothpick inserted in the center of the bread comes out clean. Remove the bread from the oven and cool the bread in the pan for 10 minutes. Remove the bread from the pan and cool completely before slicing.

Orange Sally Lunn Quick Bread

Makes one loaf

15 oz. can mandarin oranges
2 cups all purpose flour
3/4 cup granulated sugar
1 tbs. baking powder
1/4 tsp salt
2 beaten eggs
1/4 cup whole milk
1/2 cup orange juice
2 tbs. melted unsalted butter

Drain the mandarin oranges but save 1/4 cup juice. Preheat the oven to 350°. Spray an 8 x 4 loaf pan with non stick cooking spray. In a mixing bowl, add the all purpose flour, 1/2 cup granulated sugar, baking powder and salt. Whisk until combined.

In a small bowl, add 1/4 cup mandarin orange juice, eggs, milk, orange juice and butter. Whisk until combined and add to the dry ingredients. Mix only until the batter is moistened and combined. Spoon the batter into the prepared pan. Sprinkle 1/4 cup granulated sugar over the top of the batter.

Bake for 45 minutes or until a toothpick inserted in the center of the bread comes out clean. Remove the pan from the oven and remove the bread from the pan. Cool the bread completely before slicing.

Peanut Butter Bread With Ginger Cream

Makes one loaf

3/4 cup light brown sugar
1/2 cup creamy peanut butter
3 tbs. cold unsalted butter, cut into small pieces
2 eggs
1 cup all purpose flour
1/2 cup whole wheat flour
2 tsp. baking powder
1/2 tsp. ground cinnamon
1/4 tsp. salt
1/4 tsp. ground nutmeg
1/4 tsp. ground allspice
2/3 cup whole milk
1/2 tsp. vanilla extract
1 cup chopped peanuts
3 oz. softened cream cheese
2 tbs. softened unsalted butter
2 tbs. honey
1/8 tsp. ground ginger

Preheat the oven to 325°. Spray an 8 x 4 loaf pan with non stick cooking spray. In a food processor, add the brown sugar, peanut butter and 3 tablespoons cold butter. Process until smooth. Add the eggs and process until well combined. Add the all purpose flour, whole wheat flour, baking powder, cinnamon, salt, nutmeg and allspice. Pulse until well combined.

Add the milk and vanilla extract to the food processor. Process until well combined. Add the peanuts and pulse until combined. Do not over mix the batter or the bread will be tough.

Pour the batter into the prepared pan. Bake for 1 hour or until a toothpick inserted in the center of the bread comes out clean. Remove the bread from the oven and cool the bread in the pan for 10 minutes. Remove the bread from the pan and cool completely before slicing.

In a mixing bowl, add the cream cheese, 2 tablespoons softened butter, honey and ginger. Whisk until smooth and creamy. Spread on slices of the cooled bread.

Peanut Butter Chocolate Chip Bread

Makes 2 loaves

3 cups all purpose flour
1 1/2 tsp. baking powder
1 tsp. baking soda
1 tsp. salt
1 cup creamy peanut butter
1/2 cup softened unsalted butter
1/2 cup granulated sugar
1/2 cup light brown sugar
2 eggs
1 1/2 cups whole milk
2 tsp. vanilla extract
1 cup miniature semisweet chocolate chips

Spray two 8 x 4 loaf pans with non stick cooking spray. Preheat the oven to 350°. In a mixing bowl, add the all purpose flour, baking powder, baking soda and salt. Whisk until combined and set aside.

In a separate mixing bowl, add the peanut butter, butter, granulated sugar and brown sugar. Using a mixer on medium speed, beat until light and fluffy. Add the eggs and mix until well combined. Add the milk and vanilla extract to the bowl. Mix only until combined. Add the dry ingredients to the wet ingredients. Mix only until the batter is moistened and combined. Turn the mixer off and stir in the chocolate chips.

Pour the batter into the prepared pans. Bake for 45 minutes or until a toothpick inserted in the center of the loaves comes out clean. Remove the bread from the oven and cool the loaves in the pans for 10 minutes. Remove the loaves from the pans and cool completely before slicing.

Cinnamon Coffee Cake Loaf

Makes 1 loaf

2 cups all purpose flour
1 1/4 cups granulated sugar
3 tsp. baking powder
3 1/2 tsp. ground cinnamon
1 1/4 tsp. salt
2 eggs
1 cup whole milk
1/3 cup vegetable oil
2 tsp. vanilla extract
3 tbs. melted unsalted butter

Preheat the oven to 350°. Spray a 9 x 5 loaf pan with non stick cooking spray. In a mixing bowl, add the all purpose flour, 1 cup granulated sugar, baking powder, 1 1/2 teaspoons cinnamon and salt. Whisk until combined.

In a small bowl, add the eggs, milk, vegetable oil and vanilla extract. Whisk until combined and add to the dry ingredients. Mix only until the batter is moistened and combined. Spread half the batter into the prepared pan.

In a small bowl, add 1/4 cup granulated sugar, 2 teaspoons cinnamon and butter. Stir until combined. Sprinkle half the mixture over the batter. Using a knife, swirl the cinnamon through out the batter. Spread the remaining batter in the pan. Sprinkle the remaining cinnamon mixture over the batter. Swirl the cinnamon through the batter with a knife.

Bake for 55 minutes or until a toothpick inserted in the center of the loaf comes out clean. Remove the loaf from the oven and cool for 10 minutes in the pan. Remove the loaf from the pan and cool completely before serving.

Cinnamon Swirl Bread

Makes one loaf

1 1/2 cups granulated sugar
1 tbs. ground cinnamon
2 cups all purpose flour
1 tsp. baking soda
1/2 tsp. salt
1 cup buttermilk
1 egg
1/4 cup vegetable oil
1/4 cup powdered sugar
2 tsp. whole milk

In a small bowl, add 1/2 cup granulated sugar and cinnamon. Stir until combined. In a mixing bowl, add the all purpose flour, baking soda and salt. Whisk until combined. In a small bowl, add the buttermilk, egg and vegetable oil. Whisk until combined and add to the dry ingredients. Mix only until the batter is moistened and combined.

Preheat the oven to 350°. Spray a 9 x 5 loaf pan with non stick cooking spray. Spread half the batter into the pan. Sprinkle half the cinnamon sugar over the batter. Spread the remaining batter over the cinnamon sugar. Sprinkle the remaining cinnamon sugar over the top.

Bake for 45 minutes or until a toothpick inserted in the center of the bread comes out clean. Remove the bread from the oven and cool the bread for 10 minutes in the pan. Remove the bread from the pan and cool completely.

In a small bowl, add the powdered sugar and milk. Whisk until combined. Drizzle the glaze over the cooled bread and serve.

Spice Bread with Maple Butter

Makes one loaf

3/4 cup unsalted butter, softened
3/4 cup granulated sugar
2 eggs
1/2 tsp. vanilla extract
1 cup all purpose flour
1/2 cup whole wheat flour
2 tsp. baking powder
1 1/2 tsp. ground cinnamon
1/4 tsp. ground nutmeg
1/4 tsp. ground allspice
1/4 tsp. salt
1/3 cup whole milk
1/2 cup chopped walnuts
2 tbs. maple syrup

In a mixing bowl, add 1/4 cup butter and granulated sugar. Using a mixer on medium speed, beat for 3 minutes. Add the eggs and vanilla extract. Beat for 3 minutes.

In a separate bowl, add the all purpose flour, whole wheat flour, baking powder, 1 teaspoon cinnamon, nutmeg, allspice and salt. Stir until combined and add to the wet ingredients. Add the milk to the wet ingredients. Mix only until the batter is moistened and combined. Turn the mixer off and stir in the walnuts.

Preheat the oven to 350°. Spray an 8 x 4 loaf pan with non stick cooking spray. Spoon the batter into the pan. Bake for 40 minutes or until a toothpick inserted in the center of the bread comes out clean. Remove the bread from the oven and cool the bread in the pan for 10 minutes. Remove the bread from the pan and cool completely before slicing.

Add 1/2 cup butter, maple syrup and 1/2 teaspoon cinnamon to a small bowl. Stir until combined and spread on the bread. Serve the bread warm or at room temperature.

Orange Nut Bread With Orange Cream Cheese

Makes 3 small loaves

1/3 cup unsalted butter, softened
2/3 cup granulated sugar
2 eggs
1/2 tsp. orange extract
1/2 tsp. vanilla extract
2 cups all purpose flour
1 tsp. baking powder
1/2 tsp. salt
1/4 tsp. baking soda
1 cup plus 2 tbs. orange juice
1 cup chopped walnuts
8 oz. cream cheese, softened
1 tbs. powdered sugar
1 tsp. grated orange zest

In a mixing bowl, add the butter and granulated sugar. Using a mixer on medium speed, beat for 3 minutes. Add the eggs, orange extract and vanilla extract. Beat for 3 minutes.

In a separate bowl, add the all purpose flour, baking powder, salt and baking soda. Stir until combined and add to the wet ingredients. Add 1 cup orange juice to the wet ingredients. Mix only until the batter is moistened and combined. Turn the mixer off and stir in the walnuts.

Preheat the oven to 350°. Spray three 6 x 3 x 2 loaf pans with non stick cooking spray. Spoon the batter into the pans. Bake for 35 minutes or until a toothpick inserted in the center of the loaves comes out clean. Remove the loaves from the oven and cool in the pans for 10 minutes. Remove the loaves from the pans and cool completely before slicing.

Add the cream cheese, 2 tablespoons orange juice, powdered sugar and orange zest to a mixing bowl. Using a mixer on medium speed, beat until smooth and combined. Spread on the bread. Serve the bread warm or at room temperature.

Orange Peanut Bread

Makes one loaf

2 1/4 cups all purpose flour
3 tsp. baking powder
1/2 tsp. salt
1/3 cup granulated sugar
1/2 cup peanut butter
1 beaten egg
1 cup whole milk
1 1/2 tsp. grated orange zest
1/4 cup chopped salted peanuts

Preheat the oven to 350°. Spray a 9 x 5 loaf pan with non stick cooking spray. In a mixing bowl, add the all purpose flour, baking powder, salt and granulated sugar. Whisk until combined. Add the peanut butter to the bowl. Using a pastry blender, cut the peanut butter into the dry ingredients until you have coarse crumbs.

In a small bowl, add the egg, milk and orange zest. Whisk until combined and add to the dry ingredients. Whisk until the batter is moistened and combined. Gently fold in the peanuts.

Bake for 35 minutes or until a toothpick inserted in the center of the bread comes out clean. Remove the bread from the oven and cool the bread for 10 minutes in the pan. Remove the bread from the pan and cool completely.

Chocolate Peanut Butter Banana Bread

Makes two loaves

2 3/4 cups all purpose flour
1/2 cup light brown sugar
1/4 cup creamy peanut butter
1 1/2 tsp. ground cinnamon
1/2 cup unsalted butter, softened
8 oz. cream cheese, softened
1 1/4 cups granulated sugar
2 eggs
1 cup mashed ripe bananas
1 tsp. vanilla extract
1 1/2 tsp. baking powder
1/2 tsp. baking soda
1 1/2 cups semisweet chocolate chips

In a small bowl, add 1/2 cup all purpose flour, brown sugar, peanut butter and 1/2 teaspoon cinnamon. Stir until combined. In a mixing bowl, add the butter, cream cheese and granulated sugar. Using a mixer on medium speed, beat for 4 minutes. Add the eggs and beat for 2 minutes. Add the bananas and vanilla extract. Mix until combined. Add 2 1/4 cups all purpose flour, baking powder, baking soda and 1 teaspoon cinnamon. Mix only until the batter is combined.

Preheat the oven to 350°. Spray two 8 x 4 loaf pans with non stick cooking spray. Spoon half the batter into the prepared pans. Sprinkle half the peanut butter mixture over the batter. Sprinkle the chocolate chips over the batter. Spoon the remaining batter over the chocolate chips. Spread the remaining peanut butter mixture over the batter.

Bake for 45 minutes or until a toothpick inserted in the center of the bread comes out clean. Remove the bread from the oven and cool the bread in the pans for 10 minutes. Remove the bread from the pans and cool completely before slicing.

Strawberry Banana Nut Bread

Makes 1 loaf

1 1/2 cups all purpose flour
1 tsp. ground cinnamon
1/2 tsp. baking soda
1/2 tsp. salt
1/4 tsp. ground nutmeg
2 eggs
1 cup granulated sugar
1/4 cup vegetable oil
3/4 cup mashed ripe fresh strawberries
1/2 cup mashed ripe banana
1/2 cup chopped walnuts

Preheat the oven to 350°. Spray a 9 x 5 loaf pan with non stick cooking spray. In a mixing bowl, add the all purpose flour, cinnamon, baking soda, salt and nutmeg. Whisk until combined.

In a mixing bowl, add the eggs, granulated sugar and vegetable oil. Whisk until combined. Add the strawberries, banana and walnuts. Stir only until combined and add to the dry ingredients. Mix only until the batter is moistened and combined. Spoon the batter into the prepared pan.

Bake for 1 hour or until a toothpick inserted in the center of the bread comes out clean. Remove the bread from the oven and cool the bread in the pan for 10 minutes. Remove the bread from the pan and cool completely before slicing.

Chocolate Chip Banana Nut Bread

Makes 2 loaves

1 1/2 cups mashed ripe bananas
1 1/4 cups granulated sugar
3 eggs
1/3 cup vegetable oil
1 tbs. vanilla extract
2 1/4 cups all purpose flour
3/4 cup dry quick cooking oats
2 tsp. ground cinnamon
1 tsp. baking powder
1 tsp. baking soda
1 tsp. salt
1/4 tsp. ground nutmeg
1 cup semisweet chocolate chips
3/4 cup chopped walnuts

Preheat the oven to 350°. Spray two 8 x 4 loaf pans with non stick cooking spray. In a mixing bowl, add the bananas, granulated sugar, eggs, vegetable oil and vanilla extract. Whisk until well combined.

In a mixing bowl, add the all purpose flour, oats, cinnamon, baking powder, baking soda, salt and nutmeg. Whisk until combined and add to the wet ingredients. Mix only until the batter is moistened and combined. Fold in the chocolate chips and walnuts. Spoon the batter into the prepared pans.

Bake for 55 minutes or until a toothpick inserted in the center of the loaves comes out clean. Remove the bread from the oven and cool the bread in the pans for 10 minutes. Remove the bread from the pans and cool completely before slicing.

Pecan Cream Cheese Banana Bread

Makes one loaf

2 cups all purpose flour
2 tsp. baking powder
1/2 tsp. baking soda
1 tsp. grated lemon zest
1/2 cup toasted chopped pecans
5 tbs. unsalted butter, softened
3/4 cup granulated sugar
3 eggs
1 1/3 cups mashed ripe banana
6 oz. cream cheese, softened
1/3 cup granulated sugar
1/2 tsp. vanilla extract

Preheat the oven to 350°. Spray a 9 x 5 loaf pan with non stick cooking spray. In a mixing bowl, add the all purpose flour, baking powder, baking soda, lemon zest and pecans. Stir until combined.

In a mixing bowl, add the butter and 3/4 cup granulated sugar. Using a mixer on medium speed, beat until smooth and creamy. Add 2 eggs and the banana. Mix until well combined. Add the dry ingredients to the bowl. Mix only until the batter is moistened and combined.

In a mixing bowl, add the cream cheese, 1/3 cup granulated sugar, 1 egg and vanilla extract. Using a mixer on medium speed, beat until smooth and creamy. Spoon half the banana batter into the prepared pan. Spoon the cream cheese batter over the top. Spoon the remaining banana batter over the top. Using a knife, swirl the batters to create a marble effect.

Bake for 1 hour or until a toothpick inserted in the center of the bread comes out clean and the bread is golden brown. Remove the bread from the oven and cool the bread in the pan for 10 minutes. Remove the bread from the pan and cool completely before slicing.

Pineapple Carrot Bread

Makes two loaves

3 cups all purpose flour
1 tsp. baking soda
1 tsp. ground cinnamon
2 cups granulated sugar
3/4 tsp. salt
1 cup chopped pecans
3 beaten eggs
2 cups grated carrot
1 cup vegetable oil
8 oz. can crushed pineapple, drained
2 tsp. vanilla extract

Preheat the oven to 350°. Spray two 8 x 4 loaf pans with non stick cooking spray. In a mixing bowl, add the all purpose flour, baking soda, cinnamon, granulated sugar, salt and pecans. Stir until combined.

In a separate bowl, add the eggs, carrot, vegetable oil, pineapple and vanilla extract. Whisk until combined and add to the dry ingredients. Stir only until the batter is moistened and combined. Spoon the batter into the prepared pans.

Bake for 1 hour or until a toothpick inserted in the center of the bread comes out clean. Remove the bread from the oven and cool the bread in the pans for 10 minutes. Remove the bread from the pans and cool completely before slicing.

Golden Lemon Bread

Makes 1 loaf

1/2 cup vegetable shortening
1 cup granulated sugar
2 eggs
1 1/2 cups all purpose flour
1 tsp. baking powder
1/2 tsp. salt
3/4 cup whole milk
1/2 cup powdered sugar
2 tsp. grated lemon zest
3 tbs. lemon juice

Preheat the oven to 350°. Spray an 8 x 4 loaf pan with non stick cooking spray. In a mixing bowl, add the vegetable shortening and granulated sugar. Using a mixer on medium speed, beat for 3 minutes. Add the eggs and beat for 2 minutes.

Add the all purpose flour, baking powder, salt and milk. Mix only until the batter is moistened and combined. Spoon the batter into the prepared pan. Bake for 50 minutes or until a toothpick inserted in the center of the loaf comes out clean. Remove the pan from the oven and cool the bread in the pan. Cool the bread for 10 minutes.

In a small bowl, add the powdered sugar, lemon zest and lemon juice. Whisk until combined and pour over the bread. Cool the bread completely. Remove the bread from the pan and serve.

Lemon Cake Mix Bread

Makes two loaves

18 oz. box lemon cake mix
4 serving size instant lemon pudding mix
4 eggs
1/2 cup vegetable oil
1 cup cold water

Preheat the oven to 350°. Spray two 9 x 5 loaf pans with non stick cooking spray. In a mixing bowl, add the lemon cake mix, lemon pudding mix, eggs, vegetable oil and cold water. Whisk until the batter is smooth and combined. Spoon the batter into the prepared pans.

Bake for 45 minutes or until a toothpick inserted in the center of the loaves comes out clean. Remove the loaves from the oven and cool the loaves in the pans for 10 minutes. Remove the loaves from the pans and cool completely before serving.

You can add 1-2 tablespoons poppy seeds or 3/4 cup chopped pecans to the batter if desired.

Lemon Tea Bread

Makes two loaves

3 cups all purpose flour
3 3/4 tsp. baking powder
1 cup chopped toasted walnuts
1 tsp. salt
4 eggs
3 cups granulated sugar
1 cup plus 2 tbs. vegetable oil
5 tbs. grated lemon zest
1 cup plus 2 tbs. whole milk
6 tbs. melted unsalted butter
1/2 cup fresh lemon juice

Preheat the oven to 350°. Spray two 9 x 5 loaf pans with non stick cooking spray. In a mixing bowl, add the all purpose flour, baking powder, walnuts and salt. Whisk until combined.

In a mixing bowl, add the eggs, 2 1/4 cups granulated sugar, vegetable oil and 3 tablespoons lemon zest. Using a mixer on medium speed, beat until smooth and creamy. Turn the mixer off. Add the dry ingredients and milk to the bowl. Mix until the batter is moistened and combined. Add the butter to the batter and stir until combined.

Spoon the batter into the prepared pans. Bake for 50 minutes or until a toothpick inserted in the center of the loaves comes out clean and the loaves are golden brown. Remove the pans from the oven.

In a small bowl, add 3/4 cup granulated sugar, lemon juice and 2 tablespoons lemon zest. Whisk until combined and pour over the hot loaves. Cool the loaves in the pans for 10 minutes. Remove the loaves from the pans and cool completely before slicing.

Sweet Tropical Bread

Makes 2 loaves

18 oz. box yellow cake mix
8 oz. can crushed pineapple
1 cup evaporated milk
2 eggs
1/2 tsp. ground nutmeg
1/2 cup sweetened flaked coconut
1 1/2 cups powdered sugar
2 tbs. whole milk
1/8 tsp. coconut extract
2 tbs. toasted sweetened flaked coconut

Preheat the oven to 325°. Spray two 8 x 4 loaf pans with non stick cooking spray. In a mixing bowl, add the yellow cake mix, pineapple with juice, evaporated milk, eggs and nutmeg. Using a mixer on medium speed, beat for 3 minutes. Turn the mixer off and stir in 1/2 cup sweetened flaked coconut.

Pour the batter into the prepared pans. Bake for 45 minutes or until a toothpick inserted in the center of the bread comes out clean. Remove the bread from the oven and cool the loaves for 10 minutes in the pan. Remove the loaves from the pans and cool completely.

In a mixing bowl, add the powdered sugar, whole milk and coconut extract. Whisk until combined and spread over the top of the loaves. Sprinkle 2 tablespoons toasted flaked coconut over the top and serve.

Lemon Pecan Poppy Seed Loaves

Makes two loaves

2 tbs. poppy seeds
1 cup hot water
18 oz. box yellow cake mix
4 serving size pkg. coconut cream instant pudding mix
4 eggs
1/2 cup vegetable oil
1/2 cup toasted chopped pecans

Preheat the oven to 350°. Spray two 8 x 4 loaf pans with non stick cooking spray. In a mixing bowl, add the poppy seeds, water, yellow cake mix, coconut cream pudding mix, eggs and vegetable oil. Using a mixer on medium speed, beat for 2 minutes. Add the pecans and mix until combined.

Spread the batter into the prepared pans. Bake for 45 minutes or until a toothpick inserted in the center of the loaves comes out clean. Remove the loaves from the oven and cool for 10 minutes in the pans. Remove the loaves from the pans and cool completely before slicing.

Orange Poppy Seed Bread

Makes 2 loaves

3 cups all purpose flour
2 1/2 cups granulated sugar
1 1/2 cups whole milk
1 1/2 cups vegetable oil
3 eggs
1 1/2 tbs. poppy seeds
1 tbs. grated orange zest
1 1/2 tsp. baking powder
1 1/2 tsp. salt
2 tsp. vanilla extract

Preheat the oven to 350°. Spray two 8 x 4 loaf pans with non stick cooking spray. In a mixing bowl, add all the ingredients. Using a mixer on medium speed, beat until well combined and creamy.

Spread the batter into the prepared pans. Bake for 1 hour or until a toothpick inserted in the center of the loaves comes out clean. Remove the loaves from the oven and cool for 10 minutes in the pans. Remove the loaves from the pans and cool completely before slicing.

Pineapple Zucchini Bread

Makes 3 loaves

4 cups all purpose flour
3 cups granulated sugar
2 tsp. baking powder
1 1/2 tsp. salt
4 eggs
1 1/2 cups vegetable oil
1 tsp. coconut extract
1 tsp. rum extract
1 tsp. vanilla extract
3 cups shredded zucchini
1 cup canned crushed pineapple, drained
1/2 cup chopped pecans

Line three 8 x 4 loaf pans with waxed paper on the bottom of the pans. Spray the waxed paper with non stick cooking spray. Do not skip this step or the bread will stick to the bottom of the pan.

In a mixing bowl, add the all purpose flour, granulated sugar, baking powder and salt. Stir until combined. In a separate bowl, add the eggs, vegetable oil, coconut extract, rum extract and vanilla extract. Whisk until combined and add to the dry ingredients. Mix only until the batter is moistened and combined.

Fold in the zucchini, pineapple and pecans. Spoon the batter into the prepared pans. Preheat the oven to 350°. Bake for 45 minutes or until a toothpick inserted off center of the loaves comes out clean. Remove the bread from the oven and cool the bread in the pans for 10 minutes. Remove the bread from the pans and cool completely before slicing.

Zucchini Honey Bread

Makes two loaves

3 cups all purpose flour
1 tsp. baking powder
1 tsp. baking soda
1 tsp. salt
1 tbs. ground cinnamon
1 cup chopped pecans
2 cups shredded zucchini
2 beaten eggs
1 1/2 cups granulated sugar
3/4 cup honey
1 cup vegetable oil
2 tsp. vanilla extract

Preheat the oven to 350°. Spray two 8 x 4 loaf pans with non stick cooking spray. In a mixing bowl, add the all purpose flour, baking powder, baking soda, salt, cinnamon and pecans. Stir until combined.

In a separate bowl, add the zucchini, eggs, granulated sugar, honey, vegetable oil and vanilla extract. Whisk until combined and add to the dry ingredients. Stir only until the batter is moistened and combined. Spoon the batter into the prepared pans.

Bake for 1 hour or until a toothpick inserted in the center of the bread comes out clean. Remove the bread from the oven and cool the bread in the pans for 10 minutes. Remove the bread from the pans and cool completely before slicing.

Lemon Poppy Seed Zucchini Bread

Makes 3 small loaves

1/2 cup unsalted butter, softened
1 1/2 cups granulated sugar
3 eggs
1 1/2 cups all purpose flour
1/2 tsp. salt
1/8 tsp. baking soda
2/3 cup sour cream
1 cup shredded zucchini
1 tbs. grated lemon zest
2 tsp. poppy seeds

Preheat the oven to 425°. Spray three 5 x 3 loaf pans with non stick cooking spray. In a mixing bowl, add the butter. Using a mixer on medium speed, beat until the butter is creamy. Add the granulated sugar and beat for 3 minutes. Add the eggs and beat for 2 minutes.

Add the all purpose flour, salt, baking soda and sour cream. Mix only until the batter is moistened and combined. Turn the mixer off and stir in the zucchini, lemon zest and poppy seeds.

Spoon the batter into the prepared pans. Bake for 40 minutes or until a toothpick inserted in the center of the bread comes out clean. Remove the bread from the oven and cool the bread in the pans for 10 minutes. Remove the bread from the pans and cool completely before slicing.

Cranberry Zucchini Bread

Makes 2 loaves

3 cups all purpose flour
2 cups granulated sugar
2 1/2 tsp. ground cinnamon
1 1/4 tsp. salt
1 tsp. baking soda
1/2 tsp. baking powder
1/4 tsp. ground nutmeg
3 eggs
1 1/2 cups shredded zucchini
1 cup vegetable oil
1 tbs. vanilla extract
1 cup chopped fresh or frozen cranberries
1/2 cup chopped walnuts

Preheat the oven to 350°. Spray two 9 x 5 loaf pans with non stick cooking spray. In a mixing bowl, add the all purpose flour, granulated sugar, cinnamon, salt, baking soda, baking powder and nutmeg. Whisk until combined.

In a separate bowl, add the eggs, zucchini, vegetable oil and vanilla extract. Whisk until combined and add to the dry ingredients. Mix only until the batter is moistened and combined. Fold in the cranberries and walnuts.

Spoon the batter into the prepared pans. Bake for 50 minutes or until a toothpick inserted in the center of the loaves comes out clean. Remove the loaves from the oven and cool the bread for 10 minutes in the pans. Remove the loaves from the pans.

Lemon Zucchini Bread

Makes two loaves

4 cups all purpose flour
1 1/2 cups granulated sugar
4 serving size pkg. instant lemon pudding mix
1 1/2 tsp. baking soda
1 tsp. baking powder
1 tsp. salt
4 eggs
1 1/4 cups whole milk
1 cup vegetable oil
3 tbs. lemon juice
1 tsp. lemon extract
2 cups shredded zucchini
2 tsp. grated lemon zest

Preheat the oven to 350°. Spray two 9 x 5 loaf pans with non stick cooking spray. In a mixing bowl, add the all purpose flour, granulated sugar, dry pudding mix, baking soda and salt. Stir until combined.

In a separate bowl, add the eggs, milk, vegetable oil, lemon juice and lemon extract. Whisk until combined and add the zucchini and lemon zest. Add to the dry ingredients and stir only until the batter is moistened and combined. Spoon the batter into the prepared pans.

Bake for 50 minutes or until a toothpick inserted in the center of the bread comes out clean. Remove the bread from the oven and cool the bread in the pans for 10 minutes. Remove the bread from the pans and cool completely before slicing.

Zucchini Chocolate Chip Bread

Makes two loaves

3 cups all purpose flour
2 cups granulated sugar
1 tsp. baking soda
1 tsp. salt
1 tsp. ground nutmeg
1/2 tsp. ground cinnamon
1/4 tsp. baking powder
3 eggs
1/2 cup unsweetened applesauce
1/2 cup vegetable oil
1 tbs. grated orange zest
2 tsp. vanilla extract
2 cups shredded zucchini
1 cup chopped walnuts
1 cup semisweet chocolate chips

Preheat the oven to 350°. Spray two 9 x 5 loaf pans with non stick cooking spray. In a mixing bowl, add the all purpose flour, granulated sugar, baking soda, salt, nutmeg, cinnamon and baking powder. Whisk until combined.

In a mixing bowl, add the eggs, applesauce, vegetable oil, orange zest and vanilla extract. Whisk until combined and add to the dry ingredients. Mix only until the batter is moistened and combined. Add the zucchini, walnuts and chocolate chips. Gently fold until combined. Spoon the batter into the prepared pans.

Bake for 50 minutes or until a toothpick inserted in the center of the bread comes out clean. Remove the bread from the oven and cool the bread in the pans for 10 minutes. Remove the bread from the pans and cool completely before slicing.

Cocoa Bread With Stewed Peaches

Makes 6 servings

1 cup boiling water
1/2 cup melted unsalted butter
1/2 cup molasses
1 1/4 cups granulated sugar
2 beaten eggs
2 cups self rising flour
1/2 tsp. baking soda
1/4 cup unsweetened baking cocoa
1 tsp. ground cinnamon
6 cups sliced peeled peaches
1/2 cup cold water

Preheat the oven to 350°. Spray an 8" square baking pan with non stick cooking spray. In a mixing bowl, add the boiling water, butter, molasses and 1/2 cup granulated sugar. Whisk until smooth and combined.

Add the self rising flour, baking soda, cocoa and cinnamon. Whisk until the batter is smooth and combined. Pour the batter into the prepared pan. Bake for 30 minutes or until a toothpick inserted in the center of the bread comes out clean. Remove the pan from the oven.

In a sauce pan over medium heat, add the peaches, 3/4 cup granulated sugar and cold water. Stir until well combined and bring the peaches to a boil. Reduce the heat to low and simmer for 10 minutes or until the peaches are tender. Remove the pan from the heat.

Serve the bread warm. Spoon the peaches over each serving.

Spiced Peach Carrot Bread

Makes one loaf

2 1/2 cups all purpose flour
1 cup granulated sugar
1 tsp. ground cinnamon
3/4 tsp. baking soda
1/2 tsp. baking powder
1/2 tsp. salt
1/4 tsp. ground nutmeg
1 1/2 cups peeled fresh peaches, chopped
3/4 cup freshly grated carrots
2/3 cup vegetable oil
1/2 cup whole milk
2 eggs, beaten
3/4 cup toasted chopped pecans

Preheat the oven to 350°. Spray a 9 x 5 loaf pan with non stick cooking spray. In a mixing bowl, add the all purpose flour, granulated sugar, cinnamon, baking soda, baking powder, salt and nutmeg. Stir until combined.

In a separate bowl, add the peaches, carrots, vegetable oil, milk, eggs and pecans. Whisk until combined and add to the dry ingredients. Stir only until the batter is moistened and combined. Spoon the batter into the prepared pan.

Bake for 1 hour or until a toothpick inserted in the center of the bread comes out clean. Remove the bread from the oven and cool the bread in the pan for 10 minutes. Remove the bread from the pan and cool completely before slicing.

Strawberry Bread

Makes two loaves

3 cups all purpose flour
2 cups granulated sugar
1 tsp. baking soda
1 tsp. salt
1 tsp. ground cinnamon
4 beaten eggs
1 1/4 cups vegetable oil
2 pkgs. thawed chopped frozen strawberries, 10 oz. size

Preheat the oven to 350°. Spray two 8 x 4 loaf pans with non stick cooking spray. In a mixing bowl, add the all purpose flour, granulated sugar, baking soda, salt and cinnamon. Whisk until combined.

In a small bowl, add the eggs, vegetable oil and strawberries. Whisk until combined and add to the dry ingredients. Mix only until the batter is moistened and combined.

Spoon the batter into the prepared pans. Bake for 1 hour or until a toothpick inserted in the center of the loaves comes out clean. Remove the pans from the oven and cool the loaves in the pans for 10 minutes. Remove the loaves from the pans and cool completely before slicing.

Pumpkin Pecan Bread

Makes 2 loaves

3 1/2 cups all purpose flour
3 cups granulated sugar
1 tbs. pumpkin pie spice
1 tsp. baking soda
1 tsp. salt
15 oz. can pumpkin
1 cup vegetable oil
4 eggs
2 cups toasted pecans, chopped

Preheat the oven to 350°. Spray two 9 x 5 loaf pans with non stick cooking spray. In a mixing bowl, add the all purpose flour, granulated sugar, pumpkin pie spice, baking soda and salt. Whisk until combined.

In a separate bowl, add the pumpkin, vegetable oil and eggs. Whisk until smooth and combined. Add to the dry ingredients. Mix only until the batter is moistened and combined. Fold in the pecans.

Spoon the batter into the pans. Bake for 1 hour or until a toothpick inserted in the center of the loaves comes out clean. Remove the loaves from the oven and cool the loaves for 10 minutes in the pans. Remove the loaves from the pans and cool completely before slicing.

Caramel Glazed Pumpkin Pecan Bread

Makes 2 loaves

3 1/3 cups all purpose flour
3 1/4 cups granulated sugar
2 tsp. baking soda
1 1/2 tsp. salt
1 tsp. ground cinnamon
1 tsp. ground nutmeg
15 oz. can pumpkin
1 cup vegetable oil
4 beaten eggs
2/3 cup water
1/2 cup chopped pecans
1/4 cup unsalted butter
1/4 cup light brown sugar
1/4 cup whipping cream
2/3 cup powdered sugar
1 tsp. vanilla extract

Preheat the oven to 350°. Spray two 9 x 5 loaves with non stick cooking spray. In a mixing bowl, add the all purpose flour, 3 cups granulated sugar, baking soda, salt, cinnamon and nutmeg. Whisk until combined.

In a separate bowl, add the pumpkin, vegetable oil, eggs and water. Whisk until combined and add to the dry ingredients. Mix only until the batter is moistened and combined. Stir in the pecans. Spoon the batter into the prepared pans.

Bake for 1 hour or until a toothpick inserted in the center of the loaves comes out clean. Remove the loaves from the oven and cool the loaves in the pans for 10 minutes. Remove the loaves from the pans and cool completely.

In a sauce pan over medium heat, add the butter, 1/4 cup granulated sugar, brown sugar and whipping cream. Stir constantly and cook until the sugars dissolve. Remove the pan from the heat and cool for 20 minutes. Add the powdered sugar and vanilla extract to the pan. Whisk until you have a smooth glaze. Drizzle the glaze over the cooled loaves.

Pumpkin Honey Beer Bread

Makes 2 loaves

2 cups granulated sugar
1 cup vegetable oil
2/3 cup beer, at room temperature
1/4 cup honey
4 eggs
15 oz. can pumpkin
3 1/2 cups all purpose flour
2 tsp. salt
2 tsp. baking soda
1 tsp. baking powder
1 tsp. pumpkin pie spice
2 tbs. vegetable shortening

Preheat the oven to 350°. In a mixing bowl, add the granulated sugar, vegetable oil, beer and honey. Using a mixer on medium speed, beat until smooth and combined. Add the eggs and beat until well combined. Turn the mixer to low and add the pumpkin. Mix until well combined.

In a separate bowl, add the all purpose flour, salt, baking soda, baking powder and pumpkin pie spice. Stir until combined and add to the wet ingredients. Mix only until the batter is moistened and combined.

Grease two 9 x 5 loaf pans with the vegetable shortening. Make sure you get the shortening into the corners or the bread will stick. Spoon the batter into the pans. Preheat the oven to 350°. Bake for 45 minutes or until a toothpick inserted in the center of the bread comes out clean. The bread tends to brown fast so lightly cover the top of the bread with aluminum foil if needed .

Remove the bread from the oven and cool the bread in the pans for 10 minutes. Remove the bread from the pans and cool for 30 minutes before slicing.

Pumpkin Crunch Bread

Makes one loaf

1/2 cup whole milk
3 tbs. vegetable oil
1 egg
3/4 cup canned pumpkin
1 1/4 cups plus 1 tbs. all purpose flour
1/2 cup whole wheat flour
1/2 cup light brown sugar
1/4 cup dry rolled oats
1/4 cup plus 2 tbs. granulated sugar
2 tsp. baking powder
1/4 tsp. salt
1/8 tsp. ground cinnamon
1/8 tsp. ground nutmeg
2 tbs. chopped walnuts
1/4 cup whole wheat cereal flakes
1 tsp. unsalted butter

Preheat the oven to 400°. Spray a 9 x 5 loaf pan with non stick cooking spray. In a mixing bowl, add the milk, vegetable oil, egg and pumpkin. Whisk until smooth and combined.

In a separate bowl, add 1 1/4 cups all purpose flour, whole wheat flour, brown sugar, oats, 1/4 cup granulated sugar, baking powder, salt, cinnamon, nutmeg and walnuts. Whisk until combined and add to the wet ingredients. Mix only until the batter is moistened and combined.

Spoon the batter into the prepared pan. In a food processor, add the whole wheat cereal flakes, 1 tablespoon all purpose flour, 2 tablespoons granulated sugar and butter. Pulse until combined and you have coarse crumbs. Sprinkle the crumbs over the top of the batter.

Bake for 50-60 minutes or until a toothpick inserted near the center of the bread comes out clean. Remove the pan from the oven and cool the bread for 10 minutes in the pan. Remove the bread from the pan and cool completely before slicing.

Sweet Potato Bread

Makes one loaf

1 3/4 cups all purpose flour
1 1/2 cups granulated sugar
1 tsp. baking soda
1 tsp. ground cinnamon
1 tsp. ground nutmeg
3/4 tsp. salt
1/4 tsp. ground allspice
1/4 tsp. ground cloves
2 eggs
1 1/2 cups cooked mashed sweet potatoes
1/2 cup vegetable oil
6 tbs. orange juice
1/2 cup chopped pecans

Preheat the oven to 350°. Spray a 9 x 5 loaf pan with non stick cooking spray.
In a mixing bowl, add the all purpose flour, granulated sugar, baking soda, cinnamon, nutmeg, salt, allspice and cloves. Whisk until combined.

In a separate bowl, add the eggs, sweet potatoes, vegetable oil and orange juice. Whisk until smooth and combined and add to the dry ingredients. Mix only until the batter is moistened and combined. Fold in the pecans.

Spoon the batter into the prepared pan. Bake for 1 hour or until a toothpick inserted near the center of the bread comes out clean. Remove the pan from the oven and cool the bread for 10 minutes in the pan. Remove the bread from the pan and cool completely before slicing.

White Chocolate Iced Blueberry Loaf

Makes one loaf

2 1/2 cups all purpose flour
1 cup granulated sugar
3 tsp. baking powder
1/2 tsp. salt
1/4 tsp. ground allspice, optional
1 cup buttermilk
1/4 cup melted unsalted butter
2 eggs
1 1/2 cups frozen blueberries
1/2 cup chopped pecans
1/4 cup white chocolate baking chips
3 tbs. powdered sugar
2 tbs. whole milk

Preheat the oven to 350°. Spray a 9 x 5 loaf pan with non stick cooking spray. In a mixing bowl, add the all purpose flour, granulated sugar, baking powder, salt and allspice. Whisk until combined.

In a small bowl, add the buttermilk, butter and eggs. Whisk until combined and add to the dry ingredients. Whisk only until the batter is moistened and combined. Gently fold in the blueberries and pecans. Spoon the batter into the prepared pan.

Bake for 1 1/4 hours or until a toothpick inserted near the center of the bread comes out clean. Remove the pan from the oven and cool the bread for 10 minutes in the pan. Remove the bread from the pan and cool completely before icing.

In a microwavable bowl, add the white chocolate baking chips. White chocolate burns easily in the microwave. Microwave on 50% powder for 30 seconds or until the white chocolate melts. Remove the bowl from the microwave and add the powdered sugar. Whisk until combined. Add 1 or 2 tablespoons milk to the bowl until a smooth icing forms. Drizzle the icing over the top of the cooled bread. Let the icing sit for 1 hour before slicing.

Blueberry Crunch Bread

Makes one loaf

3/4 cup whole milk
3 tbs. vegetable oil
1 egg
1 1/4 cups plus 1 tbs. all purpose flour
1/2 cup whole wheat flour
1/2 cup light brown sugar
1/4 cup dry rolled oats
1/4 cup plus 2 tbs. granulated sugar
2 tsp. baking powder
1/4 tsp. salt
1/8 tsp. ground cinnamon
1 cup fresh blueberries
1/4 cup whole wheat cereal flakes
1 tsp. unsalted butter

Preheat the oven to 400°. Spray a 9 x 5 loaf pan with non stick cooking spray. In a mixing bowl, add the milk, vegetable oil and egg. Whisk until smooth and combined.

In a separate bowl, add 1 1/4 cups all purpose flour, whole wheat flour, brown sugar, oats, 1/4 cup granulated sugar, baking powder, salt and cinnamon. Whisk until combined and add to the wet ingredients. Mix only until the batter is moistened and combined. Gently fold in the blueberries.

Spoon the batter into the prepared pan. In a food processor, add the whole wheat cereal flakes, 1 tablespoon all purpose flour, 2 tablespoons granulated sugar and butter. Pulse until combined and you have coarse crumbs. Sprinkle the crumbs over the top of the batter.

Bake for 50-60 minutes or until a toothpick inserted near the center of the bread comes out clean. Remove the pan from the oven and cool the bread for 10 minutes in the pan. Remove the bread from the pan and cool completely before slicing.

Orange Cranberry Raisin Bread

Makes one loaf

2 cups plus 3 tbs. all purpose flour
3/4 cup granulated sugar
1 1/2 tsp. baking powder
1 tsp. salt
1/2 tsp. baking soda
1/4 cup plus 2 tbs. cold unsalted butter
1 egg
3/4 cup plus 2 tsp. orange juice
2 tsp. grated orange zest
1 cup chopped fresh cranberries
1/2 cup golden raisins
1/3 cup light brown sugar
1/2 cup powdered sugar

Preheat the oven to 350°. Spray an 8 x 4 loaf pan with non stick cooking spray. In a mixing bowl, add 2 cups all purpose flour, granulated sugar, baking powder, salt and baking soda. Stir until combined. Add 1/4 cup butter to the bowl. Using a pastry blender, cut the butter into the dry ingredients until you have coarse crumbs.

In a small bowl, add the egg and 3/4 cup orange juice. Whisk until combined and add to the dry ingredients. Add the orange zest to the dry ingredients. Whisk only until the batter is moistened and combined. Fold in the cranberries and raisins. Spoon the batter into the prepared pan.

In a small bowl, add the brown sugar, 3 tablespoons all purpose flour and 2 tablespoons butter. Using a fork, mix until you have coarse crumbs. Sprinkle the topping over the batter in the pan. Bake for 55 minutes or until a toothpick inserted off center of the bread comes out clean. Remove the bread from the oven and cool the bread in the pan for 10 minutes. Remove the bread from the pan and cool completely before glazing.

To make the glaze, add the powdered sugar and 2 teaspoons orange juice to a small bowl. Stir until combined and drizzle over the top of the loaf.

Cranberry Gingerbread Loaf

Makes one loaf

2 cups all purpose flour
1/4 cup granulated sugar
2 tsp. baking powder
1 1/2 tsp. ground ginger
1 1/2 tsp. ground cinnamon
1 tsp. baking soda
1/2 tsp. salt
1/4 tsp. ground nutmeg
1/4 tsp. ground cloves
1/2 cup molasses
1/2 cup whole milk
1/4 cup vegetable oil
2 eggs
1 tsp. vanilla extract
1 cup sweet dried cranberries

Preheat the oven to 325°. Spray a 9 x 5 loaf pan with non stick cooking spray. In a mixing bowl, add the all purpose flour, granulated sugar, baking powder, ginger, cinnamon, baking soda, salt, nutmeg and cloves. Whisk until combined.

In a separate bowl, add the molasses, milk, vegetable oil, eggs and vanilla extract. Whisk until combined and add to the dry ingredients. Mix only until the batter is moistened and combined. Fold in the cranberries.

Spoon the batter into the prepared pan. Bake for 50-60 minutes or until a toothpick inserted near the center of the bread comes out clean. Remove the pan from the oven and cool the bread for 10 minutes in the pan. Remove the bread from the pan and cool completely before slicing.

White Chocolate Cranberry Bread

Makes one loaf

1/2 cup butter flavored shortening
1 cup granulated sugar
3 eggs
1/2 cup whole milk
3 tbs. orange juice
1 tsp. grated lemon zest
1 tsp. vanilla extract
1/2 cup melted white chocolate
2 1/4 cups all purpose flour
1/2 tsp. salt
1/4 tsp. baking soda
1 cup dried cranberries

Preheat the oven to 350°. Spray a 9 x5 loaf pan with non stick cooking spray. In a mixing bowl, add the butter flavored shortening and granulated sugar. Using a mixer on medium speed, beat for 3 minutes. Add the eggs and beat for 3 minutes. Add the milk, orange juice. lemon zest, vanilla extract and white chocolate. Mix until combined.

Add the all purpose flour, salt and baking soda. Mix only until the batter is moistened and combined. Turn the mixer off and stir in the cranberries. Spoon the batter into the prepared pan.

Bake for 55 minutes or until a toothpick inserted in the center of the bread comes out clean. Remove the bread from the oven and cool the bread in the pan for 10 minutes. Remove the bread from the pan and cool completely before slicing.

Cranberry Cocoa Bread With Cranberry Cream Cheese Spread

Makes one loaf

16 oz. can whole berry cranberry sauce
1 1/2 cups raisins
2 tbs. grated orange zest
3 tbs. unsalted butter, softened
1 cup granulated sugar
1 egg
1/3 cup whole milk
3 cups all purpose flour
2 tsp. baking soda
1 tsp. salt
1/4 cup unsweetened baking cocoa
1 tsp. ground cinnamon
1/2 tsp. ground nutmeg
1 cup chopped walnuts
8 oz. pkg. cream cheese, softened
1/4 cup cranberry juice

Preheat the oven to 350°. Spray a 9 x 5 loaf pan with non stick cooking spray. In a sauce pan over low heat, add the cranberry sauce, raisins and orange zest. Stir constantly and cook for 5 minutes or until the cranberry sauce melts. Remove the pan from the heat and cool completely.

In a mixing bowl, add the butter. Using a mixer on medium speed, beat until the butter is light and fluffy. Add the granulated sugar and mix until light and fluffy. Add the egg and milk to the bowl. Mix until combined.

In a separate bowl, add the all purpose flour, baking soda, salt, baking cocoa, cinnamon, nutmeg and walnuts. Whisk until combined and add to the wet ingredients. Mix only until the batter is moistened and combined. Spoon the batter into the prepared pan.

Bake for 45 minutes or until a toothpick inserted in the center of the bread comes out clean. Remove the bread from the oven and cool the bread for 10 minutes in the pan. Remove the bread from the pan and cool completely.

In a small bowl, add the cream cheese and cranberry juice. Whisk until smooth and fluffy. Serve with slices of the cooled bread.

Honey Almond Cranberry Bread

Makes two loaves

2 cups fresh cranberries
6 cups Bisquick
1 tsp. ground allspice
2 tbs. orange zest
1 cup chopped almonds
2 beaten eggs
1 cup honey
1/2 cup whole milk
1/2 cup orange juice

Preheat the oven to 350°. Spray two 9 x 5 loaf pans with non stick cooking spray. In a mixing bowl, add the cranberries, Bisquick, allspice, orange zest and almonds. Whisk until combined.

In a separate bowl, add the eggs, honey, milk and orange juice. Whisk until combined and add to the dry ingredients. Mix only until the batter is moistened and combined.

Spoon the batter into the prepared pans. Bake for 50 minutes or until a toothpick inserted in the center of the loaves comes out clean. Remove the bread from the oven and cool the loaves for 10 minutes in the pans. Remove the loaves from the pans and cool completely.

Friendship Bread

Makes two loaves

4 tsp. cinnamon sugar
1 cup vegetable oil
1 1/2 cups granulated sugar
1 tsp. vanilla extract
3 eggs
1/2 tsp. salt
2 tsp. ground cinnamon
2 1/2 cups all purpose flour
1 1/4 cups whole milk
1/2 tsp. baking soda
4 serving size pkg. instant vanilla pudding mix
1 1/2 tsp. baking powder
1/3 cup chopped walnuts, optional

Preheat the oven to 325°. Spray two 9 x 5 loaf pans with non stick cooking spray. Sprinkle the bottom of each pan with 1 teaspoon cinnamon sugar. In a mixing bowl, add the vegetable oil, granulated sugar, vanilla extract, eggs, salt and cinnamon. Whisk until well combined.

Add the all purpose flour, milk, baking soda, dry vanilla pudding mix, baking powder and walnuts. Whisk until the batter is moistened and combined.

Spoon the batter into the prepared pans. Sprinkle 1 teaspoon cinnamon sugar over the top of each loaf. Bake for 50 minutes or until a toothpick inserted in the center of the loaves comes out clean. Remove the bread from the oven and cool the loaves for 10 minutes in the pan. Remove the loaves from the pans and cool completely.

Pear Walnut Bread

Makes one loaf

1/2 cup vegetable oil
1 cup granulated sugar
2 eggs
1/4 cup sour cream
1 tsp. vanilla extract
2 cups all purpose flour
1/2 tsp. salt
1 tsp. baking soda
1/4 tsp. ground cinnamon
1/4 tsp. ground nutmeg
1/2 cup chopped walnuts
1 cup chopped & peeled pears

Preheat the oven to 350°. Spray a 9 x 5 loaf pan with non stick cooking spray. In a mixing bowl, add the vegetable oil and granulated sugar. Using a mixer on medium speed, beat until well blended. Add the eggs, sour cream and vanilla extract to the bowl. Mix until smooth and combined.

In a separate bowl, add the all purpose flour, salt, baking soda, cinnamon, nutmeg, walnuts and pears. Whisk until combined and add to the wet ingredients. Mix only until the batter is moistened and combined.

Spoon the batter into the prepared pan. Bake for 1 hour or until a toothpick inserted in the center of the bread comes out clean. Remove the bread from the oven and cool the bread for 10 minutes in the pan. Remove the bread from the pan and cool completely.

Spiced Pear Bread

Makes 4 small loaves

3 cans sliced pears, 15 oz. size
1 cup granulated sugar
1/4 cup unsweetened applesauce
1/4 cup canola oil
3 eggs
3 1/4 cups all purpose flour
3 tsp. ground cinnamon
1 tsp. baking soda
1 tsp. baking powder
1 tsp. ground cloves
1/2 tsp. salt

Preheat the oven to 350°. Add the pears to a mixing bowl. Mash the pears with a fork. Add the granulated sugar, applesauce, canola oil and eggs to the bowl. Whisk until well combined.

In a separate bowl, add the all purpose flour, cinnamon, baking soda, baking powder, cloves and salt. Whisk until combined and add to the wet ingredients. Mix only until the batter is moistened and combined.

Spray four 5 x 3 loaf pans with non stick cooking spray. Spoon the batter into the prepared pans. Bake for 50 minutes or until a toothpick inserted in the bread comes out clean. Remove the pans from the oven and cool the bread in the pans for 10 minutes. Remove the bread from the pans and cool completely before slicing.

Christmas Eggnog Bread

Makes one loaf

1/4 cup melted unsalted butter
3/4 cup granulated sugar
2 beaten eggs
2 1/4 cups all purpose flour
2 tsp. baking powder
1 tsp. salt
1 cup eggnog
1/2 cup chopped pecans
1/2 cup raisins
1/2 cup red candied cherries, chopped
1/2 cup green candied cherries, chopped

In a mixing bowl, add the butter and granulated sugar. Using a mixer on medium speed, beat until light and fluffy. Add the eggs and mix until well combined. Add the all purpose flour, baking powder, salt and eggnog. Mix only until the batter is moistened and combined. Turn the mixer off and stir in the pecans, raisins, red cherries and green cherries.

Spray an 8 x 4 loaf pan with non stick cooking spray. Preheat the oven to 350°. Spoon the batter into the pan. Bake for 1 hour or until a toothpick inserted in the center of the bread comes out clean. Remove the bread from the oven and cool the bread for 10 minutes in the pan. Remove the bread from the pan and cool completely before slicing.

Cinnamon Crunch Walnut Loaf

Makes one loaf

1 1/2 cups chopped walnuts
1 tbs. melted unsalted butter
1 cup granulated sugar
2 tsp. ground cinnamon
3 cups all purpose flour
4 1/2 tsp. baking powder
1 1/2 tsp. salt
1/4 cup vegetable shortening
1 egg
1 1/4 cups whole milk

Preheat the oven to 350°. Spray a 9 x 5 loaf pan with non stick cooking spray. In a small bowl, add the walnuts and butter. Toss until the walnuts are coated in the butter. Add 1/4 cup granulated sugar and cinnamon to the walnuts. Toss until the walnuts are coated in the cinnamon sugar.

In a mixing bowl, add 3/4 cup granulated sugar, all purpose flour, baking powder and salt. Whisk until combined. Add the vegetable shortening to the dry ingredients. Using a pastry blender, cut the shortening into the dry ingredients until you have coarse crumbs.

In a small bowl, whisk together the egg and milk. Add to the dry ingredients and mix only until the batter is moistened and combined. Reserve 1/4 cup walnut mixture and set aside. Add the remaining walnut mixture to the batter and stir until combined.

Spoon the batter into the prepared pan. Sprinkle the reserved 1/4 cup walnut mixture over the top of the batter. Let the batter sit for 15 minutes. Bake for 1 hour or until a toothpick inserted in the center of the bread comes out clean. Remove the bread from the oven and cool the bread in the pan for 10 minutes. Remove the bread from the pan and cool completely before slicing.

Banana Nut Cranberry Bread

Makes two loaves

8 oz. cream cheese, softened
3/4 cup unsalted butter, softened
2 cups granulated sugar
2 eggs
3 cups all purpose flour
1/2 tsp. baking powder
1/2 tsp. baking soda
1/2 tsp. salt
1 1/2 cups mashed ripe bananas
3/4 cup chopped fresh cranberries
1/2 tsp. vanilla extract
1/2 cup toasted pecans, chopped
1 cup powdered sugar
1 tsp. grated orange zest
3 tbs. orange juice

Preheat the oven to 350°. Spray two 8 x 4 loaf pans with non stick cooking spray. In a mixing bowl, add the cream cheese and butter. Using a mixer on medium speed, beat for 4 minutes. Add the granulated sugar and beat for 3 minutes. Add the eggs and mix until combined.

In a separate bowl, add the all purpose flour, baking powder, baking soda and salt. Stir until combined. Turn the mixer to low speed and add the dry ingredients. Mix only until the batter is moistened and combined. Turn the mixer off and stir in the bananas, cranberries, vanilla extract and pecans.

Spoon the batter into the prepared pans. Bake for 1 hour or until a toothpick inserted in the center of the loaves comes out clean. Remove the loaves from the oven and cool the bread for 10 minutes in the pans. Remove the loaves from the pans.

In a small bowl, add the powdered sugar, orange zest and 2 tablespoons orange juice. Whisk until smooth and combined. You should have a pourable glaze. Add the remaining tablespoon orange juice if needed to make the glaze. Pour the glaze over the warm loaves. Cool for 30 minutes before serving.

Cranberry Almond Banana Bread

Makes one loaf

1 egg
1 cup granulated sugar
1/2 cup melted unsalted butter
3 large ripe bananas, peeled and mashed
1/2 tsp. almond extract
1 1/2 cups all purpose flour
1 tsp. baking soda
1/8 tsp. salt
1/2 cup chopped almonds
1/2 cup dried sweet cranberries

Preheat the oven to 350°. Spray a 9 x 5 loaf pan with non stick cooking spray. In a mixing bowl, add the egg. Using a mixer on medium speed, beat until foamy. Add the granulated sugar, butter, bananas and almond extract. Mix until well blended. Add the all purpose flour, baking soda and salt. Mix until the batter is moistened and combined. Turn the mixer off and stir in the almonds and cranberries.

Spoon the batter into the prepared pan. Bake for 1 hour or until a toothpick inserted in the center of the bread comes out clean. Remove the bread from the oven and cool the bread for 10 minutes in the pan. Remove the bread from the pan and cool completely before slicing.

Honey Raisin Quick Bread

Makes one loaf

1 1/2 cups all purpose flour
2/3 cup light brown sugar
2 1/2 tsp. baking powder
1/2 tsp. salt
1 cup bran cereal flakes
1 cup whole milk
1 beaten egg
1/4 cup honey
2 tbs. melted unsalted butter
1 cup raisins

Preheat the oven to 350°. Spray an 8 x 4 loaf pan with non stick cooking spray. In a mixing bowl, add the all purpose flour, brown sugar, baking powder and salt. Whisk until combined. In a small bowl, add the bran flakes and milk. Let the cereal sit for 5 minutes. Add the egg, honey, butter and raisins to the cereal. Whisk until combined and add to the dry ingredients. Mix only until the batter is moistened and combined.

Spoon the batter into the prepared pan. Bake for 1 hour or until a toothpick inserted in the center of the loaf comes out clean. Remove the loaf from the oven and cool the bread for 10 minutes in the pan. Remove the loaf from the pan and cool completely before serving.

Applesauce Raisin Oatmeal Bread

Makes one loaf

1/3 cup vegetable shortening
1/2 cup plus 1 1/2 tsp. light brown sugar
4 egg whites
1 cup chunky applesauce
2 tbs. water
1 1/2 cups plus 2 tbs. dry quick oats
1 1/4 cups all purpose flour
1 3/4 tsp. ground cinnamon
1 tsp. baking soda
1 tsp. baking powder
1/4 tsp. salt
1 cup raisins
1 tbs. chopped almonds

Preheat the oven to 375°. Spray a 9 x 5 loaf pan with non stick cooking spray. In a mixing bowl, add the vegetable shortening and 1/2 cup brown sugar. Using a mixer on medium speed, beat until smooth and creamy. With the mixer running, add the egg whites, applesauce and water. Mix until smooth and combined.

In a separate bowl, add 1 1/2 cups oats, all purpose flour, 1 1/2 teaspoons cinnamon, baking soda, baking powder and salt. Whisk until combined. Add the raisins and mix until combined. Add to the wet ingredients and mix only until the batter is moistened and combined. Spoon the batter into the prepared pan.

In a small bowl, add 2 tablespoons oats, 1 1/2 teaspoons brown sugar, 1/4 teaspoon cinnamon and almonds. Stir until combined. Sprinkle over the top of the batter. Bake for 50 minutes or until a toothpick inserted in the center of the bread comes out clean. Remove the bread from the oven and cool the bread in the pan for 10 minutes. Remove the bread from the pan and cool completely before slicing.

Cinnamon Apple Tea Bread

Makes one loaf

1 1/4 cups boiling water
4 cinnamon apple herbal tea bags
1/2 cup raisins
1/2 cup plus 2 tbs. honey
2 tbs. unsalted butter
1 egg
3 cups all purpose flour
1 tbs. baking powder
1/2 tsp. salt
1/2 cup chopped walnuts
1/2 cup powdered sugar

In a teapot, add the boiling water and tea bags. Steep for 5 minutes. Remove the tea bags and discard. Remove 2 tablespoons tea and set aside. Add the raisins, 1/2 cup honey and butter to a bowl. Pour the remaining tea in the pot over the raisins. Do not stir and cool completely before using. When the tea is cool, whisk in the egg.

Preheat the oven to 350°. Spray a 9 x 5 loaf pan with non stick cooking spray. In a mixing bowl, add the all purpose flour, baking powder, salt and walnuts. Whisk until combined. Add the raisin mixture and mix only until the batter is moistened and combined. Spoon the batter into the prepared pan.

Bake for 1 hour or until a toothpick inserted in the center of the bread comes out clean. Remove the bread from the oven and cool the bread in the pan for 10 minutes. Remove the bread from the pan and set aside to cool.

In a small bowl, add 2 tablespoons reserved tea, 2 tablespoons honey and powdered sugar. Whisk until combined and drizzle over the warm bread. Cool completely before slicing.

Applesauce Pecan Bread

Makes one loaf

1/4 cup vegetable shortening
1/2 cup granulated sugar
1 egg
2/3 cup unsweetened applesauce
2 cups all purpose flour
1/2 tsp. baking powder
1/2 tsp. baking soda
1/4 tsp. salt
3 tbs. buttermilk
1/2 cup chopped pecans

In a mixing bowl, add the vegetable shortening and granulated sugar. Using a mixer on medium speed, beat until smooth and fluffy. Add the egg and applesauce. Mix until well combined.

In a separate bowl, add the all purpose flour, baking powder, baking soda and salt. Whisk until combined and add to the wet ingredients. Add the buttermilk to the bowl and mix only until the batter is moistened and combined. Turn the mixer off and stir in the pecans.

Bake for 45 minutes or until a toothpick inserted in the center of the bread comes out clean. Remove the bread from the oven and cool the bread for 10 minutes in the pan. Remove the bread from the pan and cool completely.

Prune Nut Bread

Makes one loaf

3/4 cup prune juice
1/4 cup water
3/4 cup chopped pitted prunes
3 tbs. unsalted butter
1 egg, beaten
3/4 tsp. vanilla extract
1 1/2 cups all purpose flour
1 tsp. baking soda
1/8 tsp. salt
1/2 cup granulated sugar
1/2 cup chopped pecans

In a sauce pan over medium heat, add the prune juice and water. Bring the juice to a boil and remove the pan from the heat. Add the prunes and butter to the pan. Stir until the butter melts. Cool the mixture to lukewarm.

Add the egg and vanilla extract to the pan. Stir until well combined. In a mixing bowl, add the all purpose flour, baking soda, salt, granulated sugar and pecans. Stir until combined. Add the prunes to the bowl. Stir only until the batter is moistened and combined.

Preheat the oven to 325°. Spray an 8 x 4 loaf pan with non stick cooking spray. Spoon the batter into the prepared pan. Bake for 50 minutes or until a toothpick inserted in the center of the bread comes out clean. Remove the bread from the oven and cool the bread in the pan for 10 minutes. Remove the bread from the pan and cool completely before slicing.

Spice Prune Loaf

Makes one loaf

1 cup chopped pitted prunes
1/2 cup prune juice
1 cup all purpose flour
1 cup whole wheat flour
1 tsp. baking powder
3/4 tsp. ground cinnamon
1/2 tsp. baking soda
1/4 tsp. ground ginger
1/8 tsp. salt
2 egg whites
1/3 cup molasses
3 tbs. vegetable oil
1/4 tsp. vanilla extract

Preheat the oven to 350°. Spray an 8 x 4 loaf pan with non stick cooking spray. In a sauce pan over medium heat, add the prunes and prune juice. Bring the prunes to a boil and remove the pan from the heat. Let the prunes sit for 5 minutes.

In a mixing bowl, add the all purpose flour, whole wheat flour, baking powder, cinnamon, baking soda, ginger and salt. Whisk until combined. Add the egg whites, molasses, vegetable oil and vanilla extract. Whisk until combined. Add the prunes and any remaining liquid to the batter. Mix only until the batter is moistened and combined.

Spoon the batter into the prepared pan. Bake for 55 minutes or until a toothpick inserted in the center of the bread comes out clean. Remove the bread from the oven and cool the bread in the pan for 10 minutes. Remove the bread from the pan and cool completely before slicing.

Nutty Wheat Loaf

Makes one loaf

1 1/4 cups all purpose flour
1 cup whole wheat flour
2 tsp. baking powder
3/4 tsp. salt
1/2 cup honey crunch wheat germ
1 cup dark brown sugar
1 tsp. ground cinnamon
1/2 tsp. ground nutmeg
1/2 cup chopped walnuts
2 beaten eggs
1 1/4 cups whole milk
1/2 cup melted unsalted butter

Preheat the oven to 325°. Spray a 9 x 5 loaf pan with non stick cooking spray. In a mixing bowl, add the all purpose flour, whole wheat flour, baking powder, salt, wheat germ, brown sugar, cinnamon, nutmeg and walnuts. Stir until combined.

In a separate bowl, add the eggs, milk and butter. Whisk until combined and add to the dry ingredients. Stir only until the batter is moistened and combined. Spoon the batter into the prepared pan.

Bake for 1 1/4 hours or until a toothpick inserted in the center of the bread comes out clean. Remove the bread from the oven and cool the bread in the pan for 10 minutes. Remove the bread from the pan and cool completely before slicing.

Apricot Nut Bread

Makes one loaf

1 1/2 cups chopped dried apricots
1 cup water
2 1/2 cups all purpose flour
3/4 cup granulated sugar
4 tsp. baking powder
1 tsp. salt
1/2 tsp. baking soda
2/3 cup chopped pecans
1 beaten egg
1 cup buttermilk
3 tablespoons vegetable shortening, melted

Preheat the oven to 350°. Spray a 9 x 5 loaf pan with non stick cooking spray. In a sauce pan over medium heat, add the apricots and water. Bring the apricots to a boil. When the apricots are boiling, reduce the heat to low. Simmer the apricots for 10 minutes. Remove the pan from the heat. Cool completely before using.

In a mixing bowl, add the all purpose flour, granulated sugar, baking powder, salt, baking soda, pecans and apricots. Stir until combined. In a separate bowl, add the egg, buttermilk and melted vegetable shortening. Whisk until combined and add to the dry ingredients. Stir only until the batter is moistened and combined. Spoon the batter into the prepared pan.

Bake for 1 hour or until a toothpick inserted in the center of the bread comes out clean. Remove the bread from the oven and cool the bread in the pan for 10 minutes. Remove the bread from the pan and cool completely before slicing.

Sweet Anise Bread

Makes one loaf

3 cups all purpose flour
4 1/2 tsp. baking powder
1/2 tsp. salt
1/2 cup granulated sugar
2 beaten eggs
2 cups whole milk
2 tbs. melted unsalted butter
5 tsp. anise seed

Spray two 8 x 4 loaf pans with non stick cooking spray. Preheat the oven to 350°. In a mixing bowl, add the all purpose flour, baking powder, salt and granulated sugar. Whisk until combined. Add the eggs, milk, butter and anise seeds. Whisk until the batter is moistened and combined.

Spoon the batter into the prepared pan. Bake for 35 minutes or until a toothpick inserted in the center of the bread comes out clean. Remove the bread from the oven and cool the bread in the pan for 10 minutes. Remove the bread from the pan and cool completely before slicing.

Fruit & Nut Loaf

Makes one loaf

3/4 cup mixed dried fruit
1/4 cup chopped pecans
1 1/2 cups plus 1 tbs. all purpose flour
1/2 cup whole wheat flour
1/4 cup granulated sugar
1 tbs. baking powder
3/4 tsp. baking soda
1/4 tsp. salt
3 eggs
3/4 cup orange juice
1/4 cup vegetable oil
1/4 cup water
1 tbs. grated orange zest
1/2 tsp. vanilla extract

Preheat the oven to 350°. Spray an 8 x 4 loaf pan with non stick cooking spray. In a mixing bowl, add the dried fruit, pecans, all purpose flour, whole wheat flour, granulated sugar, baking powder, baking soda and salt. Stir until combined.

In a separate bowl, add the eggs, orange juice, vegetable oil. water, orange zest and vanilla extract. Whisk until combined and add to the dry ingredients. Stir only until the batter is moistened and combined. Spoon the batter into the prepared pan.

Bake for 35 minutes or until a toothpick inserted in the center of the bread comes out clean. Remove the bread from the oven and cool the bread in the pan for 10 minutes. Remove the bread from the pan and cool completely before slicing.

Pork & Bean Bread

Makes three loaves

1 cup raisins
1 cup boiling water
15 oz. can pork & beans
2 cups granulated sugar
3 beaten eggs
1 cup vegetable oil
1 tsp. vanilla extract
3 cups all purpose flour
1 tsp. ground cinnamon
1/2 tsp. baking powder
1 tsp. baking soda
1 cup chopped walnuts

In a small bowl, add the raisins and boiling water. Let the raisins sit while you prepare the batter. Add the pork & beans with liquid to a mixing bowl. Mash with a fork until smooth. Add the granulated sugar, eggs, vegetable oil and vanilla extract. Whisk until well combined.

In a separate bowl, add the all purpose flour, cinnamon, baking powder, baking soda and walnuts. Whisk until combined and add to the wet ingredients. Mix only until the batter is moistened and combined. Drain the raisins of all liquid and stir into the batter.

Preheat the oven to 325°. Spray three 8 x 4 loaf pans with non stick cooking spray. Spoon the batter into the prepared pans. Bake for 50 minutes or until a toothpick inserted in the center of the bread comes out clean. Remove the bread from the oven and cool the bread in the pans for 10 minutes. Remove the bread from the pans and cool completely before slicing.

Old Fashioned Boston Brown Bread

Makes one loaf

1/2 cup plain white cornmeal
1/2 cup whole wheat flour
1/2 cup rye flour
1/2 tsp. baking powder
1/2 tsp. baking soda
1/4 tsp. salt
1 cup buttermilk
1/3 cup molasses
2 tbs. light brown sugar
1 tbs. vegetable oil
3 tbs. chopped toasted walnuts
3 tbs. raisins
Boiling water

Preheat the oven to 350°. Spray an 8 x 4 loaf pan with non stick cooking spray. In a mixing bowl, add the cornmeal, whole wheat flour, rye flour, baking powder, baking soda and salt. Stir until combined.

Add the buttermilk, molasses, brown sugar and vegetable oil. Stir only until the batter is moistened and combined. Gently fold in the raisins and walnuts. Spoon the batter into the prepared pan.

Place the loaf pan in a 9 x 13 baking pan. Pour the boiling water to a depth of 1" on the loaf pan. Cover the pans with aluminum foil. Bake for 40 minutes or until a toothpick inserted off center of the bread comes out clean. Remove the bread from the oven and cool the bread in the pan for 10 minutes. Do not remove the loaf pan from the water and keep the aluminum foil on the pans while the bread is cooling for 10 minutes. Remove the bread from the pan and cool completely before slicing.

Add boiling water as needed to keep the 1" depth in the pan while baking.

Carrot Brown Bread

Makes 3 loaves

2 eggs
1/2 cup molasses
2 cups buttermilk
2 cups graham flour
1/3 cup melted unsalted butter
1/2 cup granulated sugar
1 1/2 cups all purpose flour
2 1/2 tsp. baking soda
1 tsp. salt
1 cup raisins
1 cup shredded carrots

Preheat the oven to 350°. Spray three 8 x 4 loaf pans with non stick cooking spray. In a mixing bowl, add the eggs, molasses and buttermilk. Whisk until smooth and combined. Add the graham flour and butter. Mix until well combined.

Add the granulated sugar, all purpose flour, baking soda, salt, raisins and carrots to the bowl. Mix until the batter is well combined. Spoon the batter into the prepared pans.

Bake for 45 minutes or until a toothpick inserted in the center of the bread comes out clean. Remove the bread from the oven and cool the bread for 10 minutes in the pans. Remove the bread from the pans and cool completely.

Georgia Peach Bread

Makes two loaves

3 cups sliced & peeled fresh peaches
1 1/2 cups plus 6 tbs. granulated sugar
2 cups all purpose flour
1 tsp. baking soda
1/4 tsp. salt
1 tsp. ground cinnamon
1/2 cup vegetable shortening
2 eggs
1 tsp. vanilla extract
1 cup finely chopped pecans

Add the peaches and 6 tablespoons granulated sugar to a blender. Process until pureed. You need 2 1/4 cups puree for this recipe.

Preheat the oven to 325°. Spray two 8 x 4 loaf pans with non stick cooking spray. In a mixing bowl, add the all purpose flour, baking soda, salt and cinnamon. Whisk until combined.

In a separate bowl, add 1 1/2 cups granulated sugar and the vegetable shortening. Using a mixer on medium speed, beat for 3 minutes. Add the eggs and vanilla extract. Mix until combined. Add the dry ingredients and peach puree to the bowl. Mix only until the batter is moistened and combined. Turn the mixer off and stir in the pecans.

Spoon the batter into the prepared pans. Bake for 50 minutes or until a toothpick inserted in the center of the bread comes out clean. Remove the bread from the oven and cool the bread for 10 minutes in the pans. Remove the bread from the pans and cool completely.

4 SWEET MUFFINS

I like to serve sweet muffins with breakfast and as a snack. Muffin are easy to make and are excellent for brunch. You can also make pancakes and waffles from muffin batters. Use 1/4 cup batter for each pancake and use the amount of batter recommended in your waffle maker's instructions. Watch the batters closely as sweet batters will burn easily.

Upside Down Peach Cornbread Muffins

Makes 8 muffins

1/4 cup unsalted butter
1/2 cup light brown sugar
1 fresh peach, thinly sliced
2 pkgs. cornbread mix, 8 oz. size
2 eggs
1/2 cup whole milk
2 tbs. vegetable oil
1 1/2 cups diced fresh or thawed frozen peaches

Preheat the oven to 400°. Spray 8 jumbo muffin cups with non stick cooking spray. Place the muffin tin on a baking sheet. The muffin cups will be full and may spill over while baking. Place 1 1/2 teaspoons butter and 1 tablespoon brown sugar in the bottom of each muffin cup. Place the fresh peach slices in the muffin cups.

In a mixing bowl, add the cornbread mixes, eggs, milk and vegetable oil. Whisk until well combined. Add 1 1/2 cups diced peaches and stir until combined. Spoon about 3/4 cup batter into each muffin cup.

Bake for 20 minutes or until the muffins are golden brown and a toothpick inserted in the center of the muffins comes out clean. Remove the muffins from the oven and cool the muffins in the pan for 5 minutes. Run a knife around the edges of the muffins to loosen them from the pan. Invert the pan onto a serving platter. Serve warm.

Buttermilk Oat Muffins

Makes 8 muffins

1 cup quick cooking oats
1 cup buttermilk
1 egg
1/2 cup light brown sugar
1/4 cup vegetable oil
1 cup all purpose flour
1 tsp. baking powder
1/2 tsp. baking soda
1/2 tsp. salt

In a mixing bowl, add the oats and buttermilk. Soak the oats for 10 minutes. Add the egg, brown sugar and vegetable oil. Whisk until the batter is well combined. Add the all purpose flour, baking powder, baking soda and salt. Whisk only until the batter is moistened and combined.

Preheat the oven to 400°. Spray 8 muffin cups with non stick cooking spray. Spoon the batter into the muffin cups filling them about 3/4 full. Bake for 16 minutes or until a toothpick inserted in the center of the muffins comes out clean. Remove the muffins from the oven and cool the muffins in the pan for 5 minutes. Remove the muffins from the pan and serve warm or at room temperature.

Miniature Orange Tea Muffins

Makes 5 dozen

3/4 cup fresh orange juice
1 3/4 cups plus 2 tbs. granulated sugar
1 cup unsalted butter, softened
2 eggs
1 tsp. baking soda
3/4 cup buttermilk
3 cups all purpose flour
1 tbs. grated orange zest
1 tsp. lemon extract
1 cup currants

In a small sauce pan over medium heat, add 1/2 cup orange juice and 1 cup plus 2 tablespoons granulated sugar. Stir constantly and cook until the sauce boils and the sugar dissolves. Remove the pan from the heat and refrigerate until chilled.

In a mixing bowl, add the butter. Using a mixer on medium speed, beat until the butter is light and fluffy. Add 3/4 cup granulated sugar and beat for 3 minutes. Add the eggs and beat until well combined.

In a small bowl, add the baking soda and buttermilk. Stir until combined and add to the bowl. Mix only until combined. Add the all purpose flour, orange zest, lemon extract and currants. Mix only until the batter is moistened and combined.

Spray your miniature muffin pans with non stick cooking spray. Spoon the batter into the muffin cups filling them about 3/4 full. Preheat the oven to 400°. Bake for 10 minutes or until the muffins are lightly browned. Remove the muffins from the oven and immediately remove the muffins from the pans.

Remove the sauce from the refrigerator. Dip the top and sides of the muffins in the sauce. Place the muffins on wire racks to drain.

Miniature Lemon Tea Muffins: Substitute fresh lemon juice and lemon zest for the orange juice and orange zest. Mix and bake as directed above.

French Breakfast Muffins

Makes 1 dozen

1/3 cup vegetable shortening
1 cup granulated sugar
1 egg
1 1/2 cups all purpose flour
1 1/2 tsp. baking powder
1/2 tsp. salt
1/4 tsp. ground nutmeg
1/2 cup whole milk
1 tsp. ground cinnamon
6 tbs. melted unsalted butter

Preheat the oven to 350°. Spray a 12 count muffin tin with non stick cooking spray. In a mixing bowl, add the vegetable shortening and 1/2 cup granulated sugar. Using a mixer on medium speed, beat until light and fluffy. Add the egg and mix until combined.

Add the all purpose flour, baking powder, salt, nutmeg, milk and 1/2 teaspoon cinnamon. Mix only until the batter is moistened and combined. Spoon the batter into the muffin cups filling them about 2/3 full. Bake for 20 minutes or until a toothpick inserted in the center of the muffins comes out clean. Remove the muffins from the oven.

Immediately remove the muffins from the muffin tin. In a small bowl, add 1/2 cup granulated sugar and 1/2 teaspoon cinnamon. Stir until combined. Add the melted butter to a small bowl. Dip the top and sides of the muffins in the melted butter. Roll the muffins in the cinnamon sugar and serve.

Peanut Orange Breakfast Muffins

Makes 1 dozen

2 cups all purpose flour
1 tbs. baking powder
1 tsp. salt
1/2 cup granulated sugar
1 beaten egg
1 cup whole milk
1/4 cup vegetable oil
1/2 cup chopped salted peanuts
1 tsp. grated orange zest
1/4 cup melted unsalted butter

Preheat the oven to 350°. Spray a 12 count muffin tin with non stick cooking spray. In a mixing bowl, add the all purpose flour, baking powder, salt and 1/4 cup granulated sugar. Whisk until combined.

In a small bowl, add the egg, milk and vegetable oil. Whisk until combined and add to the dry ingredients. Add the peanuts and mix until the batter is moistened and combined.

Spoon the batter into the muffin cups filling them about 2/3 full. Bake for 15 minutes or until a toothpick inserted in the center of the muffins comes out clean and the tops of the muffins are lightly browned. Remove the muffins from the oven.

Immediately remove the muffins from the muffin tin. In a small bowl, add 1/4 cup granulated sugar and orange zest. Stir until combined. Add the melted butter to a small bowl. Dip the tops of the muffins in the melted butter. Roll the muffins in the orange sugar and serve.

Applesauce Breakfast Puffs

Makes 12 muffins

1/2 cup granulated sugar
1 1/4 tsp. ground cinnamon
2 cups Bisquick
1/2 cup applesauce
1/4 cup whole milk
1 beaten egg
2 tbs. vegetable oil
2 tbs. melted unsalted butter

In a small bowl, add 1/4 cup granulated sugar and 1/4 teaspoon cinnamon. Whisk until combined and set aside. Preheat the oven to 400°. Spray a 12 count muffin tin with non stick cooking spray.

In a mixing bowl, add the Bisquick and 1/4 cup granulated sugar. Whisk until combined. Add the applesauce, milk, egg and vegetable oil. Whisk until the batter is moistened and combined.

Spoon the batter into the muffin cups filling them about 3/4 full. Bake for 12-15 minutes or until a toothpick inserted in the center of the muffins comes out clean. Remove the muffins from the oven and cool the muffins in the pan for 5 minutes.

Remove the muffins from the pan. Add the melted butter to a small bowl. Dip the top of the muffins in the butter. Dip the tops of the muffins in the cinnamon sugar and serve.

Apple Cinnamon Muffins

Makes 1 dozen

1 1/2 cups plus 1 tbs. all purpose flour
1/2 cup granulated sugar
1 3/4 tsp. baking powder
1/2 tsp. salt
1/2 tsp. ground cinnamon
1/8 tsp. ground nutmeg
1 egg
1/2 cup whole milk
3 tbs. vegetable oil
3 tbs. applesauce
1 apple, peeled, cored and grated
1/4 cup light brown sugar
2 tbs. cold unsalted butter
1/2 cup old fashioned oats
1/4 cup finely chopped pecans

Preheat the oven to 400°. Spray a 12 count muffin tin with non stick cooking spray. In a mixing bowl, add 1 1/2 cups all purpose flour, granulated sugar, baking powder, salt, cinnamon and nutmeg. Whisk until combined.

In a separate bowl, add the egg, milk, vegetable oil, applesauce and apple. Whisk until combined and add to the dry ingredients. Mix only until the batter is moistened and combined.

Spoon the batter into the muffin cups filling them about 3/4 full. In a small bowl, add the brown sugar and butter. Using a fork, cut the butter into the brown sugar until you have coarse crumbs. Add the oats and pecans to the bowl. Stir until combined and sprinkle over the top of the muffins.

Bake for 12-15 minutes or until a toothpick inserted in the center of the muffins comes out clean. Remove the muffins from the oven and cool the muffins in the pan for 5 minutes.

Sweet Potato Muffins

Makes 2 dozen

2 cups all purpose flour
3/4 cup chopped walnuts
3/4 cup golden raisins
1/2 cup light brown sugar
1 tbs. baking powder
1 tsp. ground cinnamon
1/2 tsp. salt
1/2 tsp. baking soda
1/4 tsp. ground nutmeg
1 cup mashed cooked sweet potato
3/4 cup whole milk
1/2 cup melted unsalted butter
1 1/2 tsp. vanilla extract

Preheat the oven to 400°. Spray two 12 count muffin tins with non stick cooking spray. In a mixing bowl, add the all purpose flour, walnuts, raisins, brown sugar, baking powder, cinnamon, salt, baking soda and nutmeg. Whisk until combined.

In a separate bowl, add the sweet potato, milk, butter and vanilla extract. Whisk until combined and add to the dry ingredients. Mix only until the batter is moistened and combined.

Spoon the batter into the muffin cups filling them about 3/4 full. Bake for 15 minutes or until a toothpick inserted in the center of the muffins comes out clean. Remove the muffins from the oven and cool the muffins in the pans for 5 minutes. Remove the muffins from the pans and cool completely.

Snickerdoodle Muffins

Makes 1 dozen

3 cups all purpose flour
1 1/4 cups granulated sugar
2 1/2 tsp. baking powder
3/4 tsp. salt
1/2 tsp. ground nutmeg
2 eggs
1 1/4 cups whole milk
1/3 cup melted unsalted butter
1/4 cup melted unsalted butter
3/4 tsp. ground cinnamon

Preheat the oven to 350°. Spray a 12 count muffin tin with non stick cooking spray. In a mixing bowl, add the all purpose flour, 1 cup granulated sugar, baking powder and salt. Whisk until combined.

In a separate bowl, add the eggs, milk and 1/3 cup butter. Whisk until combined and add to the dry ingredients. Mix only until the batter is moistened and combined.

Spoon the batter into the muffin cups filling them about 3/4 full. Bake for 25 minutes or until the muffins are golden brown. Remove the muffins from the oven and remove the muffins from the pan.

In a small bowl, add 1/4 cup melted butter. In a separate small bowl, add 1/4 cup granulated sugar and the cinnamon. Stir until combined. Dip the top of each muffin in the butter and then in the cinnamon sugar. Serve warm.

Blueberry Muffins with Lemon Cream Cheese Glaze

Makes about 16 muffins

3 1/2 cups plus 1 tbs. all purpose flour
1 cup granulated sugar
1 tbs. baking powder
1 1/2 tsp. salt
3 eggs
1 1/2 cups whole milk
1/2 cup melted unsalted butter
2 cups frozen blueberries
3 oz. cream cheese, softened
1 tsp. grated lemon zest
1 tbs. fresh lemon juice
1/4 tsp. vanilla extract
1 1/2 cups powdered sugar

Preheat the oven to 450°. Spray your muffin tins with non stick cooking spray. In a mixing bowl, add 3 1/2 cups all purpose flour, granulated sugar, baking powder and salt. Whisk until combined.

In a separate bowl, add the eggs, milk and butter. Whisk until combined and add to the dry ingredients. Mix only until the batter is moistened and combined. In a small bowl, add 1 tablespoon all purpose flour and the blueberries. Toss until the blueberries are coated in the flour. Fold the blueberries into the batter.

Spoon the batter into the muffin cups filling them about 3/4 full. Bake for 15 minutes or until the muffins are golden brown. Remove the muffins from the oven and cool for 10 minutes in the pan. Remove the muffins from the pan.

In a mixing bowl, add the cream cheese. Using a mixer on medium speed, beat until light and fluffy. Add the lemon zest, lemon juice, vanilla extract and powdered sugar. Beat until smooth and combined. Drizzle the glaze over the warm muffins and serve.

Blueberry Spice Whole Wheat Muffins

Makes 1 dozen

1/4 cup light brown sugar
1 cup plus 1 tbs. all purpose flour
3 tbs. chopped pecans
1 tbs. melted unsalted butter
1 cup whole wheat flour
1/4 cup granulated sugar
3/4 tsp. baking powder
3/4 tsp. baking soda
1/2 tsp. ground cinnamon
1/4 tsp. ground allspice
1 egg
1 1/4 cups buttermilk
1 1/2 tbs. vegetable oil
1 cup fresh or frozen blueberries

In a small bowl, add the brown sugar, 1 tablespoon all purpose flour and pecans. Stir until combined. Add the melted butter and stir until combined.

In a mixing bowl, add 1 cup all purpose flour, whole wheat flour, granulated sugar, baking powder, baking soda, cinnamon and allspice. Whisk until combined. In a small bowl, add the egg, buttermilk and vegetable oil. Whisk until combined and add to the dry ingredients. Mix only until the batter is moistened and combined. Gently fold in the blueberries.

Preheat the oven to 375°. Spray a 12 count muffin tin with non stick cooking spray. Spoon 1/3 cup batter into each muffin cup. Sprinkle the brown sugar streusel over the top. Bake for 18-20 minutes or until the muffins are golden brown. Remove the muffins from the oven and cool for 5 minutes in the pan. Remove the muffins from the pan and serve.

Berry Cheesecake Muffins

Makes about 20 muffins

1/3 cup unsalted butter, softened
3/4 cup granulated sugar
3 eggs
1/3 cup whole milk
1 3/4 cups all purpose flour
1 1/2 tsp. baking powder
1 1/2 tsp. ground cinnamon
6 oz. cream cheese, softened
1/3 cup granulated sugar
3/4 cup fresh raspberries
3/4 cup fresh blueberries
2 tbs. light brown sugar
1 tbs. cold unsalted butter

Preheat the oven to 375°. Spray your muffin tins with non stick cooking spray. In a mixing bowl, add 1/3 cup softened butter and 3/4 cup granulated sugar. Using a mixer on medium speed, beat until light and fluffy. Add 2 eggs and beat until well combined. Add the milk and mix until combined.

Add 1 1/2 cups all purpose flour, baking powder and 1 teaspoon cinnamon to the bowl. Mix only until the batter is moistened and combined. Spoon the batter into the muffin cups filling them 1/3 full.

In a mixing bowl, add the cream cheese, 1/3 cup granulated sugar and 1 egg. Using a mixer on medium speed, beat until smooth and combined. Turn the mixer off and fold in the raspberries and blueberries. Spoon the cream cheese filling in the center of the batter in the muffin tin. The muffins should be almost full at this point.

In a small bowl, add 1/4 cup all purpose flour, brown sugar and 1/2 teaspoon cinnamon. Stir until combined. Add 1 tablespoon cold butter. Using a fork, mix until you have small crumbs. Sprinkle the mixture over the top of the muffin batter. The muffin cups will be full. I place my muffin tins on a baking sheet to prevent spillage.

Bake for 25 minutes or until a toothpick inserted in the center of the muffins comes out clean. Remove the muffins from the oven and cool for 5 minutes in the pan. Remove the muffins from the pans. Serve the muffins warm.

Blueberry Yogurt Muffins

Makes 1 dozen

2 cups dry oat bran hot cereal
1/4 cup light brown sugar
2 tsp. baking powder
1 cup plain yogurt
2 egg whites, beaten until foamy
1/4 cup whole milk
1/4 cup honey
2 tbs. vegetable oil
1 tsp. grated lemon zest
1/2 cup fresh blueberries

Preheat the oven to 425°. Spray a 12 count muffin tin with non stick cooking spray. In a mixing bowl, add the oat bran cereal, brown sugar and baking powder. Whisk until combined.

In a small bowl, add the yogurt, egg whites, milk, honey, vegetable oil and lemon zest. Whisk until combined and add to the dry ingredients. Mix only until the batter is moistened and combined. Gently fold in the blueberries.

Spoon the batter into the muffin cups filling them about 3/4 full. Bake for 18 minutes or until the muffins are golden brown. Remove the muffins from the oven and cool for 10 minutes in the pan. Remove the muffins from the pan and serve.

Almond Berry Muffins

Makes 18 muffins

1 1/4 cups sliced almonds
1 egg white, beaten until foamy
1 1/2 cups granulated sugar
1/4 cup vegetable shortening
1/4 cup softened unsalted butter
2 eggs
1 tsp. vanilla extract
1/2 tsp. almond extract
2 cups all purpose flour
1 tsp. baking powder
1/2 tsp. salt
1/4 tsp. baking soda
3/4 cup buttermilk
1 1/4 cups fresh strawberries, chopped

Preheat the oven to 350°. Spray a 15 x 10 x 1 jelly roll pan with non stick cooking spray. In a mixing bowl, add 1 cup almonds, egg white and 1/2 cup granulated sugar. Toss until combined and spread on the jelly roll pan. Bake for 9 minutes or until the almonds are golden brown. Stir occasionally while the almonds are cooking to prevent them from burning. Remove the pan from the oven and cool while you prepare the batter.

In a mixing bowl, add the vegetable shortening, butter and 1 cup granulated sugar. Using a mixer on medium speed, beat until light and creamy. Add the eggs, vanilla extract and almond extract. Mix until smooth and combined.

In a separate bowl, add the all purpose flour, baking powder, salt and baking soda. Whisk until combined and add to the wet ingredients. Add the buttermilk and mix only until the batter is moistened and combined. Turn the mixer off and stir in the strawberries and 1/4 cup uncooked almonds.

Spray your muffin tins with non stick cooking spray. Spoon the batter into the muffin cups filling them about 3/4 full. Sprinkle the baked almonds over the batter. Bake for 20 minutes or until a toothpick inserted in the center of the muffins comes out clean. Remove the muffins from the oven and cool for 5 minutes in the pans. Remove the muffins from the pans and serve warm or at room temperature.

Strawberry Jam Muffins

Makes 1 dozen

2 cups all purpose flour
1 cup granulated sugar
1 tsp. baking soda
1 tsp. ground cinnamon
1/2 tsp. salt
1/2 tsp. ground nutmeg
1/2 cup whole milk
1/2 cup unsweetened applesauce
3 egg whites
1/2 cup strawberry jam

Preheat the oven to 350°. Spray a 12 count muffin tin with non stick cooking spray. In a mixing bowl, add the all purpose flour, granulated sugar, baking soda, cinnamon, salt and nutmeg. Whisk until combined.

In a small bowl, add the milk, applesauce and egg whites. Whisk until combined and add to the dry ingredients. Mix only until the batter is moistened and combined. Gently fold in the strawberry jam.

Spoon the batter into the muffin cups filling them about 3/4 full. Bake for 18 minutes or until the muffins are golden brown. Remove the muffins from the oven and cool for 10 minutes in the pan. Remove the muffins from the pan. Serve the muffins warm or at room temperature.

Glazed Strawberry Lemon Muffins

Makes 1 dozen

1/4 cup chopped pecans
1/4 cup light brown sugar
1 1/2 cups plus 2 tbs. all purpose flour
1 1/2 tsp. ground cinnamon
1 1/2 tsp. grated lemon zest
1/2 cup granulated sugar
2 tsp. baking powder
1/4 tsp. salt
1/2 cup melted unsalted butter
1 egg
1 1/2 cups chopped fresh strawberries
1/2 cup powdered sugar
1 tbs. fresh lemon juice

Preheat the oven to 375°. Spray a 12 count muffin tin with non stick cooking spray. In a small bowl, add the pecans, brown sugar, 2 tablespoons all purpose flour, 1/2 teaspoon cinnamon and 1/2 teaspoon lemon zest. Whisk until combined and set the topping aside.

In a mixing bowl, add 1 1/2 cups all purpose flour, 1 teaspoon cinnamon, 1 teaspoon lemon zest, granulated sugar, baking powder and salt. Whisk until combined. In a small bowl, add the butter and egg. Whisk until combined and add to the dry ingredients. Mix only until the batter is moistened and combined. Gently fold in the strawberries.

Spoon the batter into the muffin cups filling them about 3/4 full. Sprinkle the topping over the top of the batter. Bake for 20 minutes or until a toothpick inserted in the center of the muffins comes out clean. Remove the muffins from the oven and cool for 10 minutes in the pan. Remove the muffins from the pan and glaze.

To make the glaze, add the powdered sugar and lemon juice to a small bowl. Whisk until combined and drizzle over the top of the muffins. Serve warm or at room temperature.

Cranberry Lemon Muffins

Makes about 15 muffins

2 cups all purpose flour
1/2 cup granulated sugar
1 tsp. baking powder
1/2 tsp. salt
1/2 tsp. baking soda
1/2 cup golden raisins
1/2 cup sweetened dried cranberries
1/4 cup melted unsalted butter
2 tsp. grated lemon zest
1/4 cup lemon juice

Preheat the oven to 400°. Spray your muffin tins with non stick cooking spray. In a mixing bowl, add the all purpose flour, granulated sugar, baking powder, salt and baking soda. Whisk until combined. Add the raisins and cranberries to the bowl. Toss until the raisins and cranberries are coated in the dry ingredients.

In a small bowl, add the butter, lemon zest and lemon juice. Whisk until combined and add to the dry ingredients. Mix only until the batter is moistened and combined.

Spoon the batter into the muffin cups filling them about 3/4 full. Bake for 15-18 minutes or until a toothpick inserted in the center of the muffins comes out clean. Remove the muffins from the oven and cool for 10 minutes in the pan. Cool completely before serving.

Strawberry Rhubarb Spring Muffins

Makes 1 dozen

2 cups all purpose flour
1/2 cup plus 2 tsp. granulated sugar
1 tbs. baking powder
1/2 tsp. salt
1 egg
3/4 cup whole milk
1/3 cup vegetable oil
1/2 cup sliced fresh strawberries
1/2 cup sliced fresh rhubarb
6 fresh strawberries, hulled and halved

Preheat the oven to 375°. Spray a 12 count muffin tin with non stick cooking spray. In a mixing bowl, add the all purpose flour, 1/2 cup granulated sugar, baking powder and salt. Whisk until combined.

In a small bowl, add the egg, milk and vegetable oil. Whisk until combined and add to the dry ingredients. Mix only until the batter is moistened and combined. Gently fold in the sliced strawberries and rhubarb.

Spoon the batter into the muffin cups filling them about 3/4 full. Place a strawberry half in the center of each muffin. Sprinkle 2 teaspoons granulated sugar over the top of the batter. Bake for 20 minutes or until a toothpick inserted in the center of the muffins comes out clean. Remove the muffins from the oven and cool for 10 minutes in the pan. Serve warm or at room temperature.

Strawberry Muffin Ice Cream Cones

Makes 15 muffins

2 cups all purpose flour
1/2 cup granulated sugar
2 tsp. baking powder
1/2 tsp. baking soda
1/2 tsp. salt
2 eggs
6 oz. carton strawberry yogurt
1/2 cup vegetable oil
1 cup chopped fresh strawberries
15 cake ice cream cones, 3" tall
1 cup semisweet chocolate chips
1 tbs. vegetable shortening
Sprinkles to taste

In a mixing bowl, add the all purpose flour, granulated sugar, baking powder, baking soda and salt. Whisk until combined. In a separate mixing bowl, add the eggs, strawberry yogurt, vegetable oil and strawberries. Whisk until combined and add to the dry ingredients. Mix only until the batter is moistened and combined.

Preheat the oven to 375°. Place the ice cream cones in muffin cups. Spoon about 3 tablespoons batter in each ice cream cone. Bake for 20 minutes or until a toothpick inserted in the center of each muffin comes out clean. Remove the muffins from the oven and cool completely.

In a sauce pan over low heat, add the chocolate chips and vegetable shortening. Stir constantly and cook until the chocolate melts. Dip the top of the muffin cones in the melted chocolate. Roll in sprinkles as desired. Let the chocolate sit for 10 minutes before serving.

If you do not want to cook the muffins in the ice cream cones, use a 12 count muffin tin for the ice cream cones. Spoon the batter into the muffin cups filling them about 2/3 full. Bake and frost as directed above.

Pecan Rhubarb Muffins

Makes 1 dozen

1 cup light brown sugar
1/2 cup buttermilk
1/2 cup vegetable oil
1 egg
1 tsp. vanilla extract
2 cups all purpose flour
1/2 tsp. baking soda
1/2 tsp. salt
1 cup diced fresh rhubarb
3/4 cup chopped pecans
1/2 tsp. ground cinnamon

Preheat the oven to 375°. Spray a 12 count muffin tin with non stick cooking spray. In a mixing bowl, add 3/4 cup brown sugar, buttermilk, vegetable oil, egg and vanilla extract. Whisk until well combined.

In a separate bowl, add the all purpose flour, baking soda and salt. Whisk until combined and add to the wet ingredients. Mix only until the batter is moistened and combined. Stir in the rhubarb and 1/2 cup pecans.

Spoon the batter into the muffin cups filling them about 3/4 full. In a small bowl, add 1/4 cup brown sugar, 1/4 cup pecans and the cinnamon. Stir until combined and sprinkle over the top of the batter. Bake for 20 minutes or until a toothpick inserted in the center of the muffins comes out clean. Remove the muffins from the oven and cool for 10 minutes in the pan. Serve warm or at room temperature.

Spicy Plum Muffins

Makes 1 dozen

4 fresh plums, chopped
1 cup granulated sugar
1/2 cup vegetable oil
1 egg
1 1/2 cups all purpose flour
1/2 cup oat bran
2 tsp. baking soda
2 tsp. ground cinnamon
1/2 tsp. ground cloves

Preheat the oven to 375°. Spray a 12 count muffin tin with non stick cooking spray. In a mixing bowl, add the plums, granulated sugar, vegetable oil and egg. Whisk until combined.

In a separate bowl, add the all purpose flour, oat bran, baking soda, cinnamon and cloves. Whisk until combined and add to the wet ingredients. Mix only until the batter is moistened and combined.

Spoon the batter into the muffin cups filling them about 3/4 full. Bake for 20 minutes or until a toothpick inserted in the center of the muffins comes out clean. Remove the muffins from the oven and cool for 10 minutes in the pan. Remove the muffins from the pan and serve.

Tropical Muffins

Makes 1 dozen

2 cups Bisquick
2/3 cup granulated sugar
1 cup whole milk
1 egg
8 oz. can crushed pineapple
1 tsp. vanilla extract
1/4 tsp. almond extract
1/8 tsp. salt
1/2 cup chopped macadamia nuts
1/4 cup sweetened flaked coconut

Preheat the oven to 400°. Spray a 12 count muffin tin with non stick cooking spray. In a mixing bowl, add the Bisquick and granulated sugar. Whisk until combined.

In a small bowl, add the milk, egg, pineapple with juice, vanilla extract, almond extract and salt. Whisk until combined and add to the dry ingredients. Mix only until the batter is moistened and combined. Fold in the macadamia nuts and coconut.

Spoon the batter into the muffin cups filling them about 3/4 full. Bake for 15-18 minutes or until a toothpick inserted in the center of the muffins comes out clean. Remove the muffins from the oven and cool for 10 minutes in the pan. Cool completely before serving.

Morning Glory Muffins

Makes about 18 muffins

1 cup whole wheat flour
3/4 cup granulated sugar
1/2 cup oat bran
1/2 cup all purpose flour
2 tsp. baking soda
1/2 tsp. salt
3 eggs
3/4 cup applesauce
1/4 cup vegetable oil
1/4 cup molasses
2 tsp. vanilla extract
1/4 tsp. orange extract
2 cups grated carrots
1/2 cup raisins
1/2 cup chopped walnuts
1/2 cup sweetened flaked coconut
1 apple, peeled, cored and shredded

Preheat the oven to 350°. Spray your muffin tins with non stick cooking spray. In a mixing bowl, add the whole wheat flour, granulated sugar, oat bran, all purpose flour, baking soda and salt. Whisk until combined.

In a separate bowl, add the eggs, applesauce, vegetable oil, molasses, vanilla extract and orange extract. Whisk until combined and add to the dry ingredients. Mix only until the batter is moistened and combined. Stir in the carrots, raisins, walnuts, coconut and apple.

Spoon the batter into the muffin cups filling them about 3/4 full. Bake for 25 minutes or until a toothpick inserted in the center of the muffins comes out clean. Remove the muffins from the oven and cool the muffins in the pans for 5 minutes. Serve warm or at room temperature.

Cappuccino Muffins With Espresso Cream Cheese

Makes about 14 muffins

4 oz. cream cheese cubed
3/4 cup plus 1 tbs. granulated sugar
2 tbs. plus 1/2 tsp. instant coffee granules
1 1/2 tsp. vanilla extract
1 cup miniature chocolate chips
2 cups all purpose flour
2 1/2 tsp. baking powder
1 tsp. ground cinnamon
1/2 tsp. salt
1 cup whole milk
1/2 cup melted unsalted butter
1 egg

In a food processor, add the cream cheese, 1 tablespoon granulated sugar, 1/2 teaspoon coffee granules, 1/2 teaspoon vanilla extract and 1/4 cup miniature chocolate chips. Process until well blended. The mixture will not be smooth. You should still see chocolate chips in the spread. Spoon the spread into a small bowl and refrigerate for 1 hour before serving.

In a mixing bowl, add the all purpose flour, 3/4 cup granulated sugar, baking powder, cinnamon and salt. Whisk until combined. In a separate bowl, add the milk, 2 tablespoons coffee granules, butter, egg and 1 teaspoon vanilla extract. Whisk until well combined and add to the dry ingredients. Mix only until the batter is moistened and combined. Fold in 3/4 cup miniature chocolate chips.

Spray your muffin tins with non stick cooking spray. Preheat the oven to 375°. Spoon the batter into the muffin cups filling them about 2/3 full. Bake for 17-18 minutes or until a toothpick inserted in the center of the muffins comes out clean. Remove the muffins from the oven and cool the muffins for 5 minutes in the pans. Remove the muffins from the pans and serve with the refrigerated cream cheese spread.

Cappuccino Muffins

Makes 15 muffins

2 cups plus 6 tbs. all purpose flour
1/2 cup granulated sugar
3/4 cup light brown sugar
2 tsp. baking powder
2 tsp. instant coffee granules
1 1/2 tsp. ground cinnamon
1/4 tsp. salt
1 egg
1 cup whole milk
1/2 cup melted unsalted butter
1 tsp. vanilla extract
1 cup miniature semisweet chocolate chips
1/4 cup cold unsalted butter

Preheat the oven to 375°. Spray your muffin tins with non stick cooking spray. In a mixing bowl, add 2 cups all purpose flour, granulated sugar, 1/2 cup brown sugar, baking powder, coffee granules, 1 teaspoon cinnamon and salt. Whisk until combined.

In a small bowl, add the egg, milk, melted butter and vanilla extract. Whisk until combined and add to the dry ingredients. Fold in the chocolate chips. Spoon the batter into the muffin cups filling them about 2/3 full.

In a small bowl, add 6 tablespoons all purpose flour, 1/4 cup brown sugar, 1/2 teaspoon cinnamon and cold butter. Using a fork, cut the butter into the dry ingredients until you have coarse crumbs. Stir until combined. Sprinkle the crumbs over the top of the muffins.

Bake for 22 minutes or until a toothpick inserted in the center of the muffins comes out clean. Remove the muffins from the oven and cool the muffins for 5 minutes in the pans. Remove the muffins from the pans and serve.

White Chocolate Chunk Muffins

Makes 1 dozen jumbo muffins

2 1/2 cups all purpose flour
1 cup light brown sugar
1/3 cup unsweetened baking cocoa
2 tsp. baking soda
1/2 tsp. salt
1 1/2 cups whole milk
6 tbs. melted unsalted butter
2 beaten eggs
1 1/2 tsp. vanilla extract
1 1/2 cups chopped white chocolate

Preheat the oven to 400°. Spray a 12 count jumbo muffin pan with non stick cooking spray. In a mixing bowl, add the all purpose flour, brown sugar, baking cocoa, baking soda and salt. Whisk until combined.

In a small bowl, add the milk, butter, eggs and vanilla extract. Whisk until combined and add to the dry ingredients. Mix only until the batter is moistened and combined. Gently fold in the white chocolate.

Spoon the batter into the muffin cups filling them about 2/3 full. Bake for 25 minutes or until a toothpick inserted in the center of the muffins comes out clean. Remove the muffins from the oven and cool the muffins in the pan for 10 minutes. Remove the muffins from the pan and serve.

Peanut Butter Chocolate Crumb Muffins

Makes 1 dozen

1 1/2 cups chocolate wafer crumbs
1/2 cup plus 2 tbs. granulated sugar
1/2 cup melted unsalted butter
2 cups all purpose flour
1 tbs. baking powder
1/2 tsp. salt
1 egg
3/4 cup whole milk
1/3 cup vegetable oil
1/2 cup creamy peanut butter

Preheat the oven to 400°. In a small bowl, add the chocolate wafer crumbs, 2 tablespoons granulated sugar and butter. Stir until combined and set aside for the moment.

In a mixing bowl, add the all purpose flour, baking powder and salt. Whisk until combined. In a separate bowl, add the egg, milk and vegetable oil. Whisk until combined. In a small bowl, add the peanut butter. Microwave for 20 seconds or until the peanut butter is warm. Remove the peanut butter from the microwave and add to the wet ingredients. Whisk until combined and add to the dry ingredients. Mix only until the batter is moistened and combined.

Press 1 tablespoon chocolate crumbs in the bottom of a 12 count ungreased muffin tin. Spoon the batter into the muffins cups filling them about 3/4 full. Sprinkle the remaining chocolate crumbs over the batter.

Bake for 15 minutes or until a toothpick inserted in the center of the muffins comes out clean. Remove the muffins from the oven and cool the muffins in the pan for 5 minutes. Remove the muffins from the pan and cool completely before serving.

Toffee Crunch Muffins

Makes 3 dozen miniature muffins

1 1/2 cups all purpose flour
1/3 cup light brown sugar
2 tsp. baking powder
1/2 tsp. baking soda
1/2 tsp. salt
1/2 cup whole milk
1/2 cup sour cream
3 tbs. melted unsalted butter
1 beaten egg
1 tsp. vanilla extract
3 chopped Heath toffee candy bars, 1.4 oz. size

Preheat the oven to 400°. Spray your miniature muffin pans with non stick cooking spray. In a mixing bowl, add the all purpose flour, brown sugar, baking powder, baking soda and salt. Whisk until combined.

In a small bowl, add the milk, sour cream, butter, egg and vanilla extract. Whisk until combined and add to the dry ingredients. Mix only until the batter is moistened and combined. Gently fold in 2/3 of the chopped toffee bars.

Spoon the batter into the muffin cups filling them about 3/4 full. Sprinkle the remaining toffee bars over the top. Bake for 15 minutes or until a toothpick inserted in the center of the muffins comes out clean. Remove the muffins from the oven and immediately remove the muffins from the pans. Cool the muffins for 10 minutes before serving.

Mint Chocolate Chip Muffins

Makes 1 dozen large muffins

2 1/3 cups all purpose flour
1 1/4 cups granulated sugar
1/3 cup unsweetened baking cocoa
2 tsp. baking powder
1 tsp. baking soda
1/2 tsp. salt
1 cup sour cream
1/3 cup melted unsalted butter
1/4 cup whole milk
2 beaten eggs
1 cup mint flavored chocolate chips

Preheat the oven to 400°. Spray a 12 count jumbo muffin pan with non stick cooking spray. In a mixing bowl, add the all purpose flour, granulated sugar, baking cocoa, baking powder, baking soda and salt. Whisk until combined.

In a small bowl, add the sour cream, butter, milk and eggs. Whisk until combined and add to the dry ingredients. Mix only until the batter is moistened and combined. Gently fold in the mint chocolate chips.

Spoon the batter into the muffin cups filling them about 1/2 full. Bake for 20 minutes or until a toothpick inserted in the center of the muffins comes out clean. Remove the muffins from the oven and cool the muffins in the pan for 10 minutes. Remove the muffins from the pan and serve.

Pumpkin Cornbread Muffins

Makes 2 dozen

2 cups self rising white cornmeal
1/2 cup granulated sugar
1/2 tsp. pumpkin pie spice
5 eggs
15 oz. can pumpkin
1 cup sour cream
1/2 cup melted unsalted butter

Preheat the oven to 450°. Spray your muffin tins with non stick cooking spray. In a mixing bowl, add the cornmeal, granulated sugar and pumpkin pie spice. Stir until combined.

In a separate bowl, add the eggs, pumpkin, sour cream and butter. Whisk until combined and add to the dry ingredients. Mix only until the batter is moistened and combined.

Spoon the batter into the muffin cups filling them about 2/3 full. Bake for 15 minutes or until the muffins are golden brown. Remove the muffins from the oven and cool for 5 minutes in the pan. Remove the muffins from the pan and serve.

Blackberry Cornbread Muffins

Makes 2 dozen

2 cups self rising white cornmeal
1/2 cup granulated sugar
5 eggs
2 cups sour cream
1/2 cup melted unsalted butter
2 cups frozen blackberries

Preheat the oven to 450°. Spray your muffin tins with non stick cooking spray. In a mixing bowl, add the cornmeal and granulated sugar. Stir until combined.

In a separate bowl, add the eggs, sour cream and butter. Whisk until combined and add to the dry ingredients. Mix only until the batter is moistened and combined. Fold the frozen blackberries into the batter.

Spoon the batter into the muffin cups filling them about 2/3 full. Bake for 15 minutes or until the muffins are golden brown. Remove the muffins from the oven and cool for 5 minutes in the pan. Remove the muffins from the pan and serve.

Banana Cornbread Muffins

Makes 12 large muffins

15 oz. pkg. cornbread muffin mix
1/2 cup granulated sugar
1/4 tsp. baking powder
3 ripe bananas, peeled and mashed
1/4 cup lukewarm water
1 egg

Preheat the oven to 425°. Spray a 12 count jumbo muffin pan with non stick cooking spray. In a mixing bowl, add the cornbread muffin mix, granulated sugar and baking powder. Whisk until combined.

In a small bowl, add the bananas, water and egg. Whisk until combined and add to the dry ingredients. Mix only until the batter is moistened and combined. Spoon them into the muffin cups filling them a little more than 1/2 full. Bake for 15-18 minutes or until a toothpick inserted in the muffins comes out clean and the muffins are lightly browned. Remove the muffins from the oven and cool the muffins in the pan for 10 minutes. Remove the muffins from the pan and serve warm or at room temperature.

Peach Pecan Muffins

Makes 1 dozen

1/2 cup chopped pecans
1/3 cup light brown sugar
1 3/4 cups all purpose flour
1/2 cup plus 2 tbs. melted unsalted butter
2 tsp. ground cinnamon
1/2 cup granulated sugar
2 tsp. baking powder
1/4 tsp. salt
1/4 cup whole milk
1 egg
1 cup frozen peaches, thawed and diced

In a small bowl, add the pecans, brown sugar, 1/4 cup all purpose flour, 2 tablespoons melted butter and 1 teaspoon cinnamon. Stir until combined.

In a mixing bowl, add 1 1/2 cups all purpose flour, granulated sugar, baking powder, 1 teaspoon cinnamon and salt. Stir until combined. In a small bowl, add 1/2 cup melted butter, milk and egg. Whisk until combined and add to the dry ingredients. Mix only until the batter is moistened and combined. Fold in the peaches.

Spray your muffin pan with non stick cooking spray. Spoon the batter into the muffin cups filling them about 2/3 full. Sprinkle the pecan streusel over the top of the batter. Preheat the oven to 400°. Bake for 20 minutes or until the muffins are lightly browned. Remove the muffins from the oven and cool the muffins in the pan for 10 minutes. Remove the muffins from the pan. Serve warm or at room temperature.

Fresh Nectarine Muffins

Makes 1 dozen

1 1/2 cups all purpose flour
3/4 cup toasted wheat germ
1/4 cup granulated sugar
1 tbs. baking powder
1 tsp. ground cinnamon
1/2 tsp. salt
1 cup chopped fresh nectarine
1/2 cup whole milk
1/2 cup raisins
1/4 cup melted unsalted butter
1 egg
1 tsp. grated lemon zest

Preheat the oven to 450°. Spray a 12 count muffin tin with non stick cooking spray. In a mixing bowl, add the all purpose flour, wheat germ, granulated sugar, baking powder, cinnamon and salt. Whisk until combined.

In a separate mixing bowl, add the nectarine, milk, raisins, butter, egg and lemon zest. Using a mixer on medium speed, beat until well blended. Turn the mixer off and add the dry ingredients to the bowl. Stir until the batter is moistened and combined.

Spoon the batter into the muffin cups filling them about 2/3 full. Bake for 15 minutes or until a toothpick inserted in the center of the muffins comes out clean. Remove the muffins from the oven and cool the muffins in the pan for 10 minutes. Remove the muffins from the pan. Serve warm or at room temperature.

Nectarine Pecan Breakfast Muffins

Makes 1 dozen

1 1/2 cups whole wheat flour
1/2 cup chopped pecans
1/4 cup light brown sugar
2 tsp. baking powder
1/2 tsp. salt
1/2 tsp. ground nutmeg
1 cup chopped fresh nectarine
1 cup whole milk
1 beaten egg
3 tbs. vegetable oil
12 pecan halves

Preheat the oven to 400°. Spray a 12 count muffin tin with non stick cooking spray. In a mixing bowl, add the whole wheat flour, pecans, brown sugar, baking powder, salt and nutmeg. Whisk until combined.

In a separate mixing bowl, add the nectarine, milk, egg and vegetable oil. Whisk until well blended. Add to the dry ingredients and stir until the batter is moistened and combined. The batter will be thick and lumpy.

Spoon the batter into the muffin cups filling them about 2/3 full. Place a pecan half in the center of each muffin. Bake for 20 minutes or until a toothpick inserted in the center of the muffins comes out clean. Remove the muffins from the oven and cool the muffins in the pan for 10 minutes. Remove the muffins from the pan. Serve warm or at room temperature.

Nectarine Bran Muffins

Makes 1 dozen

1 cup bran flakes cereal
1/2 cup orange juice
1 cup all purpose flour
1/4 cup granulated sugar
2 1/2 tsp. baking powder
1/2 tsp. salt
1/4 cup vegetable oil
1 egg
1 cup chopped fresh nectarine

Preheat the oven to 400°. Spray a 12 count muffin tin with non stick cooking spray. In a mixing bowl, add the bran flakes cereal and orange juice. Let the cereal sit for 5 minutes. In a separate bowl, all purpose flour, granulated sugar, baking powder and salt. Whisk until combined.

Add the vegetable oil, egg and nectarine to the cereal. Whisk until combined. Add the dry ingredients and whisk until the batter is moistened and combined.

Spoon the batter into the muffin cups filling them about 2/3 full. Bake for 25 minutes or until a toothpick inserted in the center of the muffins comes out clean. Remove the muffins from the oven and cool the muffins in the pan for 10 minutes. Remove the muffins from the pan. Serve warm or at room temperature.

Nectarine Oat Muffins

Makes about 18 muffins

2 cups whole wheat flour
2 cups finely chopped fresh nectarines
1 1/2 cups whole milk
1 cup dry rolled oats
1/2 cup unprocessed bran
1/2 cup light brown sugar
1/4 cup vegetable oil
2 eggs
1 tbs. grated orange zest
1 1/2 tsp. baking soda
1 1/2 tsp. ground cinnamon
1 tsp. salt

Preheat the oven to 400°. Spray your muffin tins with non stick cooking spray. In a mixing bowl, add all the ingredients. Stir until the batter is moistened and combined.

Spoon the batter into the muffin cups filling them about 2/3 full. Bake for 20 minutes or until a toothpick inserted in the center of the muffins comes out clean. Remove the muffins from the oven and cool the muffins in the pan for 10 minutes. Remove the muffins from the pan. Serve warm or at room temperature.

Raspberry Filled Almond Muffins

Makes 1 dozen

2 cups all purpose flour
2/3 cup plus 2 tbs. granulated sugar
2 tsp. baking powder
1/2 tsp. salt
1 cup whole milk
1/2 cup melted unsalted butter
1 beaten egg
1 tsp. vanilla extract
1/2 tsp. almond extract
5 tbs. raspberry preserves
36 whole blanched almonds, toasted

Preheat the oven to 400°. Spray a 12 count brioche tin with non stick cooking spray. In a mixing bowl, add the all purpose flour, 2/3 cup granulated sugar, baking powder and salt. Whisk until combined.

In a separate bowl, add the milk, butter, egg, vanilla extract, almond extract and raspberry preserves. Whisk until combined and add to the dry ingredients. Mix only until the batter is moistened and combined. Spoon the batter into the brioche cups filling them about 1/2 full. Place 3 almonds over the batter in each cup. Sprinkle 2 tablespoons granulated sugar over the top of the batter.

Bake for 15 minutes or until a toothpick inserted in the center of the muffins comes out clean and the muffins are golden brown. Remove the muffins from the oven and cool for 5 minutes in the pan. Remove the muffins from the pan and serve.

Pineapple Bran Muffins

Makes about 18 muffins

1 1/3 cups all purpose flour
2 tsp. baking soda
1 1/3 cups bran cereal
1/3 cup vegetable shortening
1/4 cup granulated sugar
2 eggs
1 cup half and half
1/3 cup honey
8 oz. can crushed pineapple, drained

In a mixing bowl, add the all purpose flour, baking soda and bran cereal. Stir until combined. In a separate mixing bowl, add the vegetable shortening and granulated sugar. Using a mixer on medium speed, beat until smooth and fluffy. Add the eggs, half and half and honey. Mix until well combined.

Turn the mixer off. Add the dry ingredients to the wet ingredients. Stir until the batter is moistened and combined. Add the pineapple and stir until combined.

Spray your muffin tins with non stick cooking spray. Spoon the batter into the muffin cups filling them about 2/3 full. Preheat the oven to 350°. Bake for 20 minutes or until a toothpick inserted in the center of the muffins comes out clean. Remove the muffins from the oven and cool the muffins in the pans for 5 minutes. Remove the muffins from the pans. Serve warm or at room temperature.

Pineapple Raisin Muffins

Makes 1 dozen

1/4 cup finely chopped pecans
1/4 cup light brown sugar
2 cups all purpose flour
1/4 cup granulated sugar
2 1/2 tsp. baking powder
3/4 tsp. salt
1/2 tsp. ground cinnamon
6 tbs. cold unsalted butter
1/2 cup raisins
8 oz. can crushed pineapple
1/3 cup unsweetened pineapple juice
1 egg

Preheat the oven to 400°. Spray a 12 count muffin tin with non stick cooking spray. In a small bowl, add the pecans and brown sugar. Stir until combined.

In a mixing bowl, add the all purpose flour, granulated sugar, baking powder, salt and cinnamon. Whisk until combined. Add the butter to the bowl. Using a pastry blender, cut the butter into the dry ingredients until you have fine crumbs. Add the raisins and stir until combined.

Add the pineapple with juice, pineapple juice and egg to a small bowl. Whisk until combined and add to the dry ingredients. Mix until the batter is moistened and combined.

Spoon the batter into the muffin cups filling them about 2/3 full. Sprinkle the pecan brown sugar mixture over the top of the batter. Bake for 20 minutes or until a toothpick inserted in the center of the muffins comes out clean. Remove the muffins from the oven and cool the muffins in the pan for 5 minutes. Remove the muffins from the pan. Serve warm or at room temperature.

Gingerbread Pear Muffins

Makes 1 dozen

1 3/4 cups all purpose flour
1/3 cup granulated sugar
2 tsp. baking powder
3/4 tsp. ground ginger
1/4 tsp. baking soda
1/4 tsp. salt
1/4 tsp. ground cinnamon
1 cup peeled pear, chopped
1/3 cup whole milk
1/4 cup vegetable oil
1/4 cup mayonnaise
1 egg

Preheat the oven to 375°. Spray a 12 count muffin tin with non stick cooking spray. In a mixing bowl, add the all purpose flour, granulated sugar, baking powder, ginger, baking soda, salt and cinnamon. Whisk until combined. Add the pear and toss until combined.

In a small bowl, add the milk, vegetable oil, mayonnaise and egg. Whisk until combined and add to the dry ingredients. Mix only until the batter is moistened and combined.

Spoon the batter into the muffin cups filling them about 2/3 full. Bake for 25 minutes or until a toothpick inserted in the center of the muffins comes out clean. Remove the muffins from the oven and cool the muffins in the pan for 10 minutes. Remove the muffins from the pan. Serve warm or at room temperature.

Banana Carrot Muffins

Makes 9 large muffins

1 1/2 cups all purpose flour
3/4 cup granulated sugar
1 tsp. baking powder
1 tsp. baking soda
1/2 tsp. salt
1/2 tsp. ground cinnamon
1/4 tsp. ground nutmeg
2 eggs, separated and at room temperature
1 tbs. honey
1/4 tsp. grated orange zest
2 ripe bananas, mashed
1 cup shredded carrots
1/2 cup unsweetened applesauce

Preheat the oven to 350°. Spray your muffin tin with non stick cooking spray. In a mixing bowl, add the all purpose flour, granulated sugar, baking powder, baking soda, salt, cinnamon and nutmeg. Whisk until combined.

In a separate mixing bowl, add the egg yolks. Using a mixer on medium speed, beat for 3 minutes. Add the honey and orange zest to the egg yolks. Mix until combined. Add the dry ingredients and mix only until the batter is moistened and combined. Turn the mixer off and fold in the bananas, carrots and applesauce.

In a small bowl, add the egg whites. Using a mixer on medium speed, beat until stiff peaks form. Gently fold the egg whites into the batter.

Spoon the batter into the muffin cups filling them about 2/3 full. Bake for 25 minutes or until a toothpick inserted in the center of the muffins comes out clean. Remove the muffins from the oven and cool the muffins in the pan for 5 minutes. Remove the muffins from the pan. Serve warm or at room temperature.

Carrot Cake Muffins

Makes 15 muffins

2 cups all purpose flour
3/4 cup granulated sugar
2 tsp. baking soda
1 tsp. ground cinnamon
1 tsp. salt
8 oz. can drained crushed pineapple
1/4 cup vegetable oil
2 eggs
2 egg whites
1 tbs. vanilla extract
3 cups grated carrots
1/2 cup chopped pecans
1/2 cup golden raisins

Preheat the oven to 350°. Spray your muffin tins with non stick cooking spray. In a mixing bowl, add the all purpose flour, granulated sugar, baking soda, cinnamon and salt. Stir until combined.

In a separate mixing bowl, add the pineapple, vegetable oil, eggs, egg whites and vanilla extract. Whisk until combined and add to the dry ingredients. Mix only until the batter is moistened and combined. Fold in the carrots, pecans and raisins.

Spoon the batter into the muffin cups filling them about 2/3 full. Bake for 20 minutes or until a toothpick inserted in the center of the muffins comes out clean. Remove the muffins from the oven and cool for 10 minutes in the muffin tins. Remove the muffins from the pans and cool at least 10 minutes before serving.

Chocolate Chip Cookie Carrot Muffins

Makes 1 dozen

1 1/4 cups crushed Chips Ahoy chocolate chip cookies
1 cup all purpose flour
1 cup grated carrots
1/3 cup chopped walnuts
3 tbs. light brown sugar
1 tbs. baking powder
1 egg
3/4 cup whole milk
1/4 cup melted unsalted butter

Preheat the oven to 400°. Spray a 12 count muffin tin with non stick cooking spray. In a mixing bowl, add the Chips Ahoy cookies, all purpose flour, carrots, walnuts, brown sugar and baking powder. Whisk until combined. In a small bowl, add the egg, milk and butter. Whisk until combined and add to the dry ingredients. Mix only until the batter is moistened and combined.

Spoon the batter into the muffin cups filling them about 2/3 full. Bake for 20 minutes or until a toothpick inserted in the center of the muffins comes out clean. Remove the muffins from the oven and cool for 10 minutes in the muffin tin. Remove the muffins from the pan and cool at least 10 minutes before serving.

Wild Rice & Carrot Muffins

Makes 1 dozen

3/4 cup all purpose flour
3/4 cup whole wheat flour
1/2 cup light brown sugar
2 tsp. baking powder
1 1/4 tsp. ground cinnamon
1/2 tsp. salt
1/2 tsp. ground nutmeg
2 cups cooked wild rice
3/4 cup whole milk
1/3 cup vegetable oil
1 beaten egg
1 cup shredded carrot
1 tbs. granulated sugar
3 oz. cream cheese, softened
1 cup powdered sugar

Preheat the oven to 400°. Spray a 12 count muffin pan with non stick cooking spray. In a mixing bowl, add the all purpose flour, whole wheat flour, brown sugar, baking powder, 1 teaspoon cinnamon and salt. Whisk until combined and stir in the rice.

In a small bowl, add the milk, vegetable oil, egg and carrot. Whisk until combined and add to the dry ingredients. Mix only until the batter is moistened and combined.

Spoon the batter into the muffin cups filling them about 1/2 full. In a small bowl, add the granulated sugar and 1/4 teaspoon ground cinnamon. Stir until combined and sprinkle over the batter.

Bake for 25 minutes or until a toothpick inserted in the center of the muffins comes out clean. Remove the muffins from the oven and cool the muffins in the pan for 10 minutes. Remove the muffins from the pan.

In a mixing bowl, add the cream cheese and powdered sugar. Using a mixer on medium speed, beat until smooth and fluffy. Spread the frosting on the warm muffins. Serve the muffins warm or at room temperature. Store leftover muffins in the refrigerator.

Garden Harvest Muffins

Makes 1 dozen

1 cup granulated sugar
1 cup shredded zucchini
1 cup shredded carrots
1/2 cup raisins
1/2 cup applesauce
1 egg
2 egg whites
2 tbs. vegetable oil
1 tsp. vanilla extract
2 cups all purpose flour
2 tsp. baking powder
1 tsp. salt
1 tsp. grated orange zest
1 tsp. ground nutmeg
1/2 tsp. baking soda

Preheat the oven to 400°. Spray a 12 count muffin pan with non stick cooking spray. In a mixing bowl, add the granulated sugar, zucchini, carrots, raisins, applesauce, egg, egg whites and vegetable oil. Whisk until combined.

In a separate bowl, add the all purpose flour, baking powder, salt, orange zest, nutmeg and baking soda. Whisk until combined and add to the wet ingredients. Mix only until the batter is moistened and combined.

Spoon the batter into the muffin cups filling them about 3/4 full. Bake for 25 minutes or until a toothpick inserted in the center of the muffins comes out clean. Remove the muffins from the oven and cool the muffins in the pan for 10 minutes. Remove the muffins from the pan and serve.

Oreo Muffins

Makes 1 dozen

1 3/4 cups all purpose flour
1/2 cup granulated sugar
1 tbs. baking powder
1/2 tsp. salt
3/4 cup whole milk
1/3 cup sour cream
1 egg
1/4 cup melted unsalted butter
20 Oreo cookies, crushed

Preheat the oven to 400°. Spray a 12 count muffin tin with non stick cooking spray. In a mixing bowl, add the all purpose flour, granulated sugar, baking powder and salt. Whisk until combined.

In a small bowl, add the milk, sour cream, egg and butter. Whisk until combined and add to the dry ingredients. Mix only until the batter is moistened and combined. Gently fold in the Oreo cookies.

Spoon the batter into the muffin cups filling them about 2/3 full. Bake for 20 minutes or until a toothpick inserted in the center of the muffins comes out clean. Remove the muffins from the oven and cool for 10 minutes in the muffin tin. Remove the muffins from the pan and cool at least 10 minutes before serving.

Super Easy German Chocolate Cake Muffins

Makes 1 dozen jumbo muffins

3 tbs. chopped pecans
3 tbs. sweetened flaked coconut
3 tbs. light brown sugar
18 oz. box German chocolate cake mix

Preheat the oven to 400°. Spray a 12 count jumbo muffin tin with non stick cooking spray. In a small bowl, add the pecans, coconut and brown sugar. Whisk until combined.

Prepare the cake batter according to the box directions reducing the water to 1/4 cup. Spoon the cake batter into the prepared pan filling them about 1/2 full. Sprinkle the pecan topping over the top of the batter.

Bake for 20 minutes or until a toothpick inserted in the center of the muffins comes out clean. Remove the muffins from the oven and cool for 10 minutes in the muffin tin. Remove the muffins from the pan and cool completely before serving.

Graham Muffins

Makes 1 dozen

3 cups graham cracker crumbs
1/4 cup granulated sugar
1 tbs. baking powder
2 beaten eggs
1 1/2 cups whole milk
1/3 cup melted unsalted butter

Preheat the oven to 400°. Spray a 12 count muffin tin with non stick cooking spray. In a mixing bowl, add the graham cracker crumbs, granulated sugar and baking powder. Whisk until combined.

In a separate bowl, add the eggs, milk and butter. Whisk until combined and add to the dry ingredients. Stir until the batter is moistened and combined.

Spoon the batter into the muffin cups filling them about 2/3 full. Bake for 18 minutes or until a toothpick inserted in the center of the muffins comes out clean. Remove the muffins from the oven and cool the muffins in the pan for 10 minutes. Remove the muffins from the pan. Serve warm or at room temperature.

Honey Pecan Sticky Bun Muffins

Makes 20 muffins

3 cups all purpose flour
3 tsp. baking powder
1 tsp. salt
1/3 cup granulated sugar
1/2 cup unsalted butter
1 cup evaporated milk
1 beaten egg
1/3 cup light brown sugar
1 1/2 tsp. ground cinnamon
1/2 tsp. grated orange zest
3 tbs. melted unsalted butter
1/3 cup honey
2/3 cup chopped pecans

Preheat the oven to 425°. Spray your muffin tins with non stick cooking spray. In a mixing bowl, add the all purpose flour, baking powder, salt and granulated sugar. Whisk until combined. Add 1/2 cup butter to the dry ingredients. Using a pastry blender, cut the butter into the dry ingredients until you have coarse crumbs. In a small bowl, add the evaporated milk and egg. Whisk until combined and add to the dry ingredients. Mix until combined and a soft dough forms.

Lightly flour your work surface. Place the dough on your surface. Roll the dough into a 15" x 10" rectangle. In a small bowl, add the brown sugar, cinnamon, orange zest, 3 tablespoons melted butter and honey. Whisk until combined. Spread half the mixture over the dough. Sprinkle 1/3 cup pecans over the top of the dough.

Starting with a long side, roll the dough up like a jelly roll. Tuck the ends under and seal any seams. Cut the roll into twelve 1" slices. Place the slices in the muffin cups. Sprinkle the remaining honey mixture and pecans over the slices.

Bake for 20 minutes. Remove the muffins from the oven and immediately remove the muffins from the pans. Cool the muffins for 5 minutes before serving.

Pecan Pie Muffins

Makes 2 dozen

1 cup light brown sugar
1 cup chopped pecans
1/2 cup all purpose flour
1/2 tsp. baking powder
1/4 tsp. salt
1/2 cup melted butter
2 beaten eggs
1 tsp. vanilla extract
1/2 cup finely chopped pecans

In a mixing bowl, add the brown sugar, 1 cup chopped pecans, all purpose flour, baking powder and salt. Stir until combined. In a separate bowl, add the butter, eggs and vanilla extract. Whisk until combined and add to the dry ingredients. Mix only until the batter is moistened and combined.

Spray your muffin pans with non stick cooking spray. Spoon 1/2 cup finely chopped pecans into the bottom of the muffin cups. Spoon the batter into the muffin cups filling them about 2/3 full.

Preheat the oven to 425°. Bake for 12 minutes or until the muffins are lightly browned. Remove the muffins from the oven and cool the muffins in the pans for 2 minutes. Run a knife around the muffins to loosen them from the pans. Serve warm or at room temperature.

Pumpkin Streusel Muffins

Makes 1 dozen

1/4 cup unsalted butter, softened
1/2 cup granulated sugar
1/4 cup plus 3 tbs. light brown sugar
2/3 cup canned pumpkin
1/2 cup whole milk
2 eggs
1 tsp. grated orange zest
2 1/3 cups all purpose flour
2 tsp. baking powder
1 tsp. baking soda
1 tsp. pumpkin pie spice
1/4 tsp. salt
2 tbs. cold unsalted butter

Preheat the oven to 375°. Spray a 12 count muffin tin with non stick cooking spray. In a mixing bowl, add 1/4 cup softened butter, granulated sugar and 1/4 cup brown sugar. Using a mixer on medium speed, beat until light and fluffy. Turn the mixer speed to low. Add the pumpkin, milk, eggs and orange zest. Mix until well combined.

In a separate bowl, add 2 cups all purpose flour, baking powder, baking soda, pumpkin pie spice and salt. Whisk until combined and add to the wet ingredients. Mix only until the batter is moistened and combined. Spoon the batter into the muffin cups filling them about 2/3 full.

In a small bowl, add 1/3 cup all purpose flour, 3 tablespoons brown sugar and 2 tablespoons cold butter. Using a fork, cut the butter into the dry ingredients until you have small crumbs. Sprinkle over the top of the muffin batter.

Bake for 20 minutes or until a toothpick inserted in the center of the muffins comes out clean. Remove the muffins from the oven and cool the muffins for 5 minutes in the pan. Remove the muffins from the pan and serve warm or at room temperature.

Sticky Bun Pumpkin Muffins

Makes 2 dozen

1/2 cup melted unsalted butter
1/2 cup light brown sugar
2 tbs. light corn syrup
2 cups toasted pecans, chopped
3 1/2 cups all purpose flour
3 cups granulated sugar
1 tbs. pumpkin pie spice
1 tsp. baking soda
1 tsp. salt
15 oz. can pumpkin
1 cup vegetable oil
4 eggs

Preheat the oven to 350°. Spray your muffin tins with non stick cooking spray. In a small bowl, add the butter, brown sugar and corn syrup. Stir until combined. Spoon 1 teaspoon of the mixture into each muffin cup. Sprinkle 1 tablespoon pecans over the syrup.

In a mixing bowl, add the all purpose flour, granulated sugar, pumpkin pie spice, baking soda and salt. Whisk until combined. In a separate bowl, add the pumpkin, vegetable oil and eggs. Whisk until smooth and combined. Add the wet ingredients to the dry ingredients. Mix only until the batter is moistened and combined.

Spoon the batter into the muffin cups filling them about 3/4 full. Bake for 25 minutes or until a toothpick inserted in the center of the muffins comes out clean. Remove the muffins from the oven and immediately invert the pans onto a serving platter. Remove the muffins from the pans. Place the muffins, topping side up, on a cooling rack. Spoon any remaining syrup and pecans left in the pan over the muffins. Cool for 5 minutes before serving.

Pumpkin Chocolate Chip Muffins

Makes 2 dozen

4 eggs
2 cups granulated sugar
15 oz. can pumpkin
1 1/2 cups vegetable oil
3 cups all purpose flour
2 tsp. baking soda
1 tsp. baking powder
1 tsp. ground cinnamon
1 tsp. salt
2 cups semisweet chocolate chips

Preheat the oven to 400°. Spray two 12 count muffin tins with non stick cooking spray. In a mixing bowl, add the eggs, granulated sugar, pumpkin and vegetable oil. Whisk until smooth and combined.

Add the all purpose flour, baking soda, baking powder, cinnamon and salt. Mix only until the batter is moistened and combined. Add the chocolate chips and stir until combined.

Spoon the batter into the muffin cups filling them about 2/3 full. Bake for 15 minutes or until a toothpick inserted in the center of the muffins comes out clean. Remove the muffins from the oven and cool the muffins in the pans for 10 minutes. Remove the muffins from the pans. Serve warm or at room temperature.

Maple Pumpkin Muffins

Makes 1 dozen

2 cups all purpose flour
3/4 cup plus 2 tbs. light brown sugar
2 tsp. baking powder
1 tsp. ground cinnamon
1/2 tsp. baking soda
1/2 tsp. pumpkin pie spice
1/4 tsp. salt
2 eggs
1 cup canned pumpkin
3/4 cup evaporated milk
1/4 cup vegetable oil
3 tbs. maple syrup
3/4 cup chopped pecans
3 oz. cream cheese, softened
2 tsp. light brown sugar

Preheat the oven to 400°. Spray a 12 count muffin tin with non stick cooking spray. In a mixing bowl, add the all purpose flour, 3/4 cup brown sugar, baking powder, cinnamon, baking soda, pumpkin pie spice and salt. Whisk until combined.

In a separate bowl, add the eggs, pumpkin, milk, vegetable oil and 1 tablespoon maple syrup. Whisk until combined and add to the dry ingredients. Mix only until the batter is moistened and combined. Stir in 1/2 cup pecans.

In a mixing bowl, add the cream cheese and 2 tablespoons brown sugar. Whisk until smooth and combined. Add to the batter and stir until the batter is marbled. Spoon the batter into the muffin cups filling them about 2/3 full.

In a small bowl, add 1/4 cup pecans and 2 teaspoons brown sugar. Stir until combined and sprinkle over the top of the batter. Bake for 20 minutes or until a toothpick inserted in the center of the muffins comes out clean. Remove the muffins from the oven and cool the muffins for 5 minutes in the pan. Remove the muffins from the pan and serve warm or at room temperature.

Pumpkin Ginger Muffins

Makes 1 dozen

2 cups all purpose flour
1/2 cup plus 2 tsp. granulated sugar
1 tbs. baking powder
1 1/2 tsp. ground ginger
1/2 tsp. ground cinnamon
1/4 tsp. ground cloves
1/4 tsp. salt
1/8 tsp. ground nutmeg
2/3 cup evaporated milk
1/4 cup sweetened flaked coconut
2 eggs
1/2 cup vegetable oil
1 cup canned pumpkin
12 walnut halves

Preheat the oven to 375°. Spray a 12 count muffin tin with non stick cooking spray. In a mixing bowl, add the all purpose flour, 1/2 cup granulated sugar, baking powder, ginger, cinnamon, cloves, salt and nutmeg. Whisk until combined.

In a separate bowl, add the milk, coconut, eggs, vegetable oil and pumpkin. Whisk until well combined and add to the dry ingredients. Mix only until the batter is moistened and combined.

Spoon the batter into the muffin cups filling them about 2/3 full. Place a walnut half in the center of the batter for each muffin. Sprinkle 2 teaspoons granulated sugar over the top of the batter.

Bake for 20 minutes or until a toothpick inserted in the center of the muffins comes out clean. Remove the muffins from the oven and cool the muffins for 5 minutes in the pan. Remove the muffins from the pan and serve warm or at room temperature.

Coffee Cake Muffins With Brown Butter Icing

Makes 1 dozen

2 1/2 cups all purpose flour
1/2 cup light brown sugar
1 tsp. ground cinnamon
1/3 cup unsalted butter, softened
1 cup chopped walnuts
1/2 cup granulated sugar
2 1/2 tsp. baking powder
1/4 tsp. salt
3/4 cup sour cream
1/3 cup melted unsalted butter
1/4 cup plus 2 tbs. whole milk
2 tsp. vanilla extract
1 egg
12 cupcake liners
1/4 cup cold unsalted butter, cut into small pieces
1 1/2 cups powdered sugar

In a small bowl, add 1/2 cup all purpose flour, brown sugar, 1/2 teaspoon cinnamon and 1/3 cup softened butter. Using your fingers, pinch the mixture together until you have crumbles. Refrigerate the mixture for 15 minutes.

Preheat the oven to 400°. In a mixing bowl, add 2 cups all purpose flour, granulated sugar, baking powder, salt and 1/2 teaspoon cinnamon. Stir until combined. In a separate bowl, add the sour cream, 1/3 cup melted butter, 1/4 cup milk, 1 teaspoon vanilla extract and egg. Whisk until combined and add to the dry ingredients. Mix only until the batter is moistened and combined.

Line your muffin tin with the cupcake liners. Spoon the batter into the liners filling them about 1/3 full. Sprinkle 1 tablespoon streusel mixture over the batter in each muffin cup. Spoon the remaining batter over the streusel filling them about 2/3 full. Sprinkle the remaining streusel over the top.

Bake for 18 minutes or until a toothpick inserted in the center of the muffins comes out clean. Remove the muffins from the oven and cool the muffins in the pan for 5 minutes. Remove the muffins from the pan and cool for 20 minutes.

Coffee Cake Muffins With Brown Butter Icing cont'd

In a 4 cup microwavable bowl, add 1/4 cup cold butter. Microwave for 3 minutes or until the butter in the bottom of the bowl begins to turn brown. Remove the butter from the microwave and cool for 5 minutes. Be careful as butter will brown quickly. Do not over cook the butter.

Add the powdered sugar and 1 teaspoon vanilla extract to the butter. Whisk until well combined and a drizzling consistency. Add 2 tablespoons milk, 1 tablespoon at a time, until the proper consistency is reached. Drizzle the icing over the muffins and serve.

Spice Cake Muffins

Makes 2 dozen

18 oz. box spice cake mix
1/2 cup melted unsalted butter
1/2 cup granulated sugar
1 tsp. ground cinnamon

Preheat the oven to 350°. Spray two 12 count muffin tins with non stick cooking spray. Prepare the cake mix according to package directions. Spoon the batter into the muffin cups filling them about 2/3 full.

Bake for 20 minutes or until a toothpick inserted in the muffins comes out clean. Remove the muffins from the oven. Cool the muffins in the pans for 5 minutes. Remove the muffins from the pans and cool for 5 minutes.

Add the melted butter to a small bowl. Add the granulated sugar and cinnamon to a small bowl. Whisk until combined. Dip the top of each muffin in the butter. Roll the top of the muffins in the cinnamon sugar. Serve warm or at room temperature.

Cream Cheese Carrot Muffins

Makes 1 dozen

14 oz. can sliced carrots, drained
1 3/4 cups all purpose flour
1 1/4 cups granulated sugar
1 1/4 tsp. baking soda
1/2 tsp. salt
1/2 tsp. ground cinnamon
1/8 tsp. ground allspice
1/8 tsp. ground cloves
1/8 tsp. ground nutmeg
2 eggs
1/3 cup vegetable oil
8 oz. cream cheese, softened

Add the carrots to a food processor. Process until smooth. In a large mixing bowl, add the all purpose flour, 1 cup granulated sugar, baking soda, salt, cinnamon, allspice, cloves and nutmeg. Stir until combined.

Add the pureed carrots to a small bowl. Add 1 egg and vegetable oil to the bowl. Whisk until combined and add to the dry ingredients. Stir only until the batter is moistened and combined.

Spray a 12 cup muffin tin with non stick cooking spray. Preheat the oven to 350°. Spoon the batter into the muffin cups filing them about 1/3 full. In a small bowl, add the cream cheese, 1 egg and 1/4 cup granulated sugar. Whisk until smooth and combined. Spoon one tablespoon cream cheese in the center of the batter. Spoon the remaining batter over the cream cheese.

Bake for 20 minutes or until a toothpick inserted in the center of the muffins comes out clean. Remove the muffins from the oven and cool the muffins for 5 minutes in the pan. Remove the muffins from the pan and cool for 10 minutes before serving.

Simple & Delicious Lemon Muffins

Makes 1 dozen

3 cups all purpose flour
1 cup granulated sugar
2 1/2 tsp. baking powder
1/2 tsp. salt
2 eggs
1 1/4 cups whole milk
1/2 cup melted unsalted butter
1 tbs. grated lemon zest

Preheat the oven to 350°. Spray a 12 count muffin tin with non stick cooking spray.

In a mixing bowl, add the all purpose flour, granulated sugar, baking powder and salt. Whisk until combined. In a separate bowl, add the eggs, milk, butter and lemon zest. Whisk until smooth and combined. Add the wet ingredients to the dry ingredients. Mix only until the batter is moistened and combined.

Spoon the batter into the muffin cups filling them about 2/3 full. Bake for 25 minutes or until the muffins are golden brown. Remove the muffins from the oven and cool the muffins in the pan for 10 minutes. Remove the muffins from the pan. Serve warm or at room temperature.

Lemon Walnut Muffins

Makes 1 dozen

1 3/4 cups all purpose flour
1/2 cup plus 3 tbs. granulated sugar
3 tsp. baking powder
1 tsp. salt
2/3 cup chopped walnuts
1 egg
2/3 cup whole milk
1 tsp. grated lemon zest
1 tbs. lemon juice
1/3 cup melted vegetable shortening
12 walnut halves

Preheat the oven to 400°. Spray a 12 count muffin tin with non stick cooking spray. In a mixing bowl, add the all purpose flour, 1/2 cup granulated sugar, baking powder, salt and 2/3 cup chopped walnuts. Whisk until combined.

In a separate bowl, add the egg, milk, 1/2 teaspoon lemon zest, lemon juice and vegetable shortening. Whisk until smooth and combined. Add the wet ingredients to the dry ingredients. Mix only until the batter is moistened and combined.

Spoon the batter into the muffin cups filling them about 2/3 full. In a small bowl, add 3 tablespoons granulated sugar and 1/2 teaspoon lemon zest. Whisk until combined and sprinkle over the top of the muffins. Place a walnut half in the center of each muffin.

Bake for 20 minutes or until the muffins are golden brown. Remove the muffins from the oven and cool the muffins in the pan for 5 minutes. Remove the muffins from the pan. Serve warm or at room temperature.

Cherry Rosemary Muffins

Makes 2 dozen

4 cups all purpose flour
1 tsp. salt
1 1/2 cups granulated sugar
1 1/2 tbs. baking powder
2 tbs. grated orange zest
1/2 cup orange juice
2 beaten eggs
1 1/2 cups whole milk
1/2 cup melted unsalted butter
1 1/2 cups dried cherries, chopped
2 tbs. chopped fresh rosemary

Preheat the oven to 375°. Spray your muffin tins with non stick cooking spray.

In a mixing bowl, add the all purpose flour, salt, granulated sugar, baking powder and orange zest. Whisk until combined. In a separate bowl, add the orange juice, eggs, milk and butter. Whisk until smooth and combined and add to the dry ingredients. Mix only until the batter is moistened and combined. Fold in the dried cherries and rosemary.

Spoon the batter into the muffin cups filling them about 3/4 full. Bake for 25 minutes or until a toothpick inserted in the center of the muffins comes out clean. Remove the muffins from the oven and cool the muffins in the pans for 10 minutes. Remove the muffins from the pans and serve.

Poppy Seed Pound Cake Muffins

Makes 1 dozen

2 cups all purpose flour
1 tbs. poppy seeds
1/2 tsp. salt
1/4 tsp. baking soda
1/2 cup unsalted butter, softened
1 cup granulated sugar
2 eggs
1 cup plain yogurt
1 tsp. vanilla extract

Preheat the oven to 400°. Spray a 12 count muffin tin with non stick cooking spray. In a mixing bowl, add the all purpose flour, poppy seeds, salt and baking soda. Stir until combined.

In a mixing bowl, add the butter and granulated sugar. Using a mixer on medium speed, beat until smooth and combined. Add the eggs and mix until combined. Add the yogurt and vanilla extract to the bowl. Mix until well combined. Turn the mixer off and add the dry ingredients. Stir only until the batter is moistened and combined.

Spoon the batter into the muffin cups filling them about 3/4 full. Bake for 15 minutes or until a toothpick inserted in the center of the muffins comes out clean. Remove the muffins from the oven and cool the muffins in the pan for 5 minutes. Remove the muffins from the pan and serve warm or at room temperature.

Marmalade Muffins

Makes 1 dozen

2 cups all purpose flour
2 tsp. baking powder
3/4 tsp. salt
1 1/2 cups granulated sugar
1 cup unsalted butter, softened
2 eggs
1 1/2 tsp. vanilla extract
1 cup orange marmalade
1 cup buttermilk

In a mixing bowl, add the all purpose flour, baking powder, salt and granulated sugar. Stir until combined. Add the butter, eggs and vanilla extract to a small bowl. Whisk until combined. Add half the dry ingredients to the eggs. Whisk until the batter is moistened. Add the marmalade and remaining dry ingredients. Mix only until the batter is moistened. Add the buttermilk and mix only until the batter is moistened and combined.

Spray a 12 count muffin tin with non stick cooking spray. Spoon the batter into the muffin cups filling them about 2/3 full. Preheat the oven to 350°. Bake for 20 minutes or until a toothpick inserted in the center of the muffins comes out clean. Remove the muffins from the oven and cool the muffins in the pan for 5 minutes. Remove the muffins from the pan and serve.

Chocolate Chip Muffins

Makes 1 dozen

2 cups all purpose flour
1/2 cup granulated sugar
1 tbs. baking powder
1/2 tsp. salt
3/4 cup whole milk
1 egg
1/3 cup vegetable oil
3/4 cup miniature semisweet chocolate chips

Preheat the oven to 400°. Spray a 12 count muffin tin with non stick cooking spray. In a mixing bowl, add the all purpose flour, granulated sugar, baking powder and salt. Whisk until combined.

In a small bowl, add the milk, egg and vegetable oil. Whisk until combined and add to the dry ingredients. Mix only until the batter is moistened and combined. Fold in the chocolate chips.

Spoon the batter into the muffin cups filling them about 2/3 full. Bake for 18-20 minutes or until a toothpick inserted in the center of the muffins comes out clean. Remove the muffins from the oven and cool the muffins in the pan for 5 minutes. Remove the muffins from the pan and serve.

Chocolate Chip Oatmeal Muffins

Makes 1 dozen

1/2 cup unsalted butter, softened
3/4 cup light brown sugar
1 egg
1 cup all purpose flour
1 tsp. baking powder
1/4 tsp. baking soda
1/4 tsp. salt
3/4 cup applesauce
1 cup old fashioned oats
1 cup semisweet chocolate chips

Preheat the oven to 350°. Spray a 12 count muffin tin with non stick cooking spray. In a mixing bowl, add the butter and brown sugar. Using a mixer on medium speed, beat until smooth and fluffy. Add the egg and mix until combined.

Add the all purpose flour, baking powder, baking soda, salt and applesauce. Mix only until the batter is moistened and combined. Turn the mixer off and stir in the oats and chocolate chips.

Spoon the batter into the muffin cups filling them about 2/3 full. Bake for 25 minutes or until a toothpick inserted in the center of the muffins comes out clean. Remove the muffins from the oven and cool the muffins in the pan for 5 minutes. Remove the muffins from the pan and serve.

Orange Cream Cheese Muffins

Makes 6 jumbo muffins

3 oz. cream cheese, softened
1/4 cup granulated sugar
1 egg
1/2 cup orange juice
1 3/4 cups Bisquick
1/4 cup chopped pecans
6 tsp. orange marmalade

Preheat the oven to 400°. Spray a 6 count jumbo muffin pan with non stick cooking spray. In a mixing bowl, add the cream cheese and granulated sugar. Using a mixer on medium speed, beat until smooth and combined. Add the egg and orange juice. Mix until combined. Turn the mixer off.

Add the Bisquick and pecans. Stir only until the batter is moistened and combined. Spoon the batter into the muffin cups filling them about 3/4 full. Spoon 1 teaspoon orange marmalade in the center of the muffins.

Bake for 20 minutes or until the muffins are golden brown. Remove the muffins from the oven and cool the muffins in the pan for 5 minutes. Remove the muffins from the pan and cool for 15 minutes before serving.

Cream Cheese Cranberry Muffins

Makes 2 dozen

1 cup unsalted butter, softened
8 oz. cream cheese, softened
1 1/2 cups granulated sugar
1 1/2 tsp. vanilla extract
4 eggs
2 cups all purpose flour
1 1/2 tsp. baking powder
1/2 tsp. salt
2 cups fresh or frozen cranberries
1/2 cup chopped pecans

Preheat the oven to 350°. Spray your muffin tins with non stick cooking spray. In a mixing bowl, add the butter, cream cheese and granulated sugar. Using a mixer on medium speed, beat for 4 minutes. Add the vanilla extract and eggs. Beat for 3 minutes.

Add the all purpose flour, baking powder and salt. Mix only until the batter is moistened and combined. Turn the mixer off and stir in the cranberries and pecans.

Spoon the batter into the muffin cups filling them about 3/4 full. Bake for 20 minutes or until a toothpick inserted in the center of the muffins comes out clean. Remove the muffins from the oven and cool the muffins in the pans for 5 minutes. Remove the muffins from the pans and serve.

Granola Streusel Cranberry Muffins

Makes 1 dozen

2 cups all purpose flour
3/4 cup sweetened dried cranberries
1/2 cup plus 2 tbs. granulated sugar
1/2 cup powdered nonfat dry milk
3 tsp. baking powder
1/2 tsp. pumpkin pie spice
1/2 tsp. salt
3/4 cup water
1/3 cup vegetable oil
1 beaten egg
2 tbs. melted unsalted butter
1/3 cup oats & honey granola

Preheat the oven to 375°. Spray a 12 count muffin tin with non stick cooking spray. In a mixing bowl, add the all purpose flour, cranberries, 1/2 cup granulated sugar, powdered milk, baking powder, pumpkin pie spice and salt. Whisk until combined.

In a small bowl, add the water, vegetable oil and egg. Whisk until combined and add to the dry ingredients. Mix only until the batter is moistened and combined.

Spoon the batter into the muffin cups filling them about 3/4 full. In a small bowl, add the butter, granola and 2 tablespoons granulated sugar. Whisk until combined and sprinkle over the batter.

Bake for 15 minutes or until a toothpick inserted in the center of the muffins comes out clean. Remove the muffins from the oven and cool the muffins in the pan for 5 minutes. Remove the muffins from the pan and serve.

Cranberry Oat Bran Muffins

Makes 1 dozen

2 cups all purpose flour
1 cup oat bran cereal
1/2 cup light brown sugar
2 tsp. baking powder
1/2 tsp. baking soda
1/2 tsp. salt
1/2 cup mayonnaise
3 egg whites, beaten until foamy
1/2 cup whole milk
1/3 cup orange juice
1 tsp. grated orange zest
1 cup chopped fresh cranberries

Preheat the oven to 375°. Spray a 12 count muffin tin with non stick cooking spray. In a mixing bowl, add the all purpose flour, oat bran, brown sugar, baking powder, baking soda and salt. Whisk until combined.

In a mixing bowl, add the mayonnaise, egg whites, milk, orange juice and orange zest. Whisk until combined and add to the dry ingredients. Mix only until the batter is moistened and combined. Gently fold in the cranberries.

Spoon the batter into the muffin cups filling them about 3/4 full. Bake for 15-18 minutes or until a toothpick inserted in the center of the muffins comes out clean and the muffins are golden brown. Remove the muffins from the oven and cool the muffins in the pan for 5 minutes. Remove the muffins from the pan and serve.

Cranberry Raisin Muffins

Makes about 10 muffins

1/2 cup plus 3 tbs. granulated sugar
1/4 cup orange juice
1/2 cup fresh cranberries, chopped
1/3 cup golden raisins
1 1/3 cups all purpose flour
1/2 cup plain white cornmeal
2 tsp. baking powder
3/4 cup buttermilk
3 tbs. melted unsalted butter
1 beaten egg

Preheat the oven to 425°. Spray your muffin tin with non stick cooking spray. In a small bowl, 3 tablespoons granulated sugar and orange juice. Stir until the sugar melts. Add the cranberries and raisins. Stir until combined.

In a mixing bowl, add the all purpose flour, cornmeal, 1/2 cup granulated sugar and baking powder. Whisk until combined. In a small bowl, add the buttermilk, butter and egg. Whisk until combined and add to the dry ingredients. Mix until the batter is moistened and combined. Gently fold in the cranberry mixture.

Spoon the batter into the muffin cups filling them about 3/4 full. Bake for 15-18 minutes or until a toothpick inserted in the center of the muffins comes out clean and the muffins are golden brown. Remove the muffins from the oven and cool the muffins in the pan for 5 minutes. Remove the muffins from the pan and serve.

Crumbcake Muffins

Makes about 16 muffins

2 cups miniature semisweet chocolate chips
2 cups plus 1 tbs. all purpose flour
3 tbs. granulated sugar
1 tbs. baking powder
1/4 tsp. salt
1/2 cup melted unsalted butter
2/3 cup whole milk
2 eggs
1 tsp. vanilla extract
1/3 cup chopped walnuts
1/3 cup light brown sugar
2 tbs. cold unsalted butter, cut into small pieces

In a mixing bowl, add 1 1/2 cups chocolate chips, 2 cups all purpose flour, granulated sugar, baking powder and salt. Whisk until combined. In a small bowl, add 1/2 cup melted butter, milk, eggs and vanilla extract. Whisk until combined and add to the dry ingredients. Mix only until the batter is moistened and combined.

Preheat the oven to 400°. Spray your muffin tins with non stick cooking spray. Spoon the batter into the muffin cups filling them about 3/4 full. In a small bowl, add 1/2 cup chocolate chips, walnuts, brown sugar and 2 tablespoons butter. Using a fork cut the butter into the dry ingredients until you have crumbs. Sprinkle the crumbs over the top of the batter.

Bake for 18-20 minutes or until a toothpick inserted in the center of the muffins comes out clean. Remove the muffins from the oven and cool the muffins in the pans for 5 minutes. Remove the muffins from the pans and cool completely before serving.

Apple Oat Bran Muffins

Makes 1 dozen

3/4 cup all purpose flour
3/4 cup whole wheat flour
1 1/2 tsp. ground cinnamon
1 tsp. baking powder
1/2 tsp. baking soda
1/4 tsp. salt
1 cup whole milk
1/2 cup oat bran
1/4 cup light brown sugar
2 tbs. vegetable oil
1 egg
1 1/2 cups peeled, cored & chopped apple

Preheat the oven to 400°. Spray a 12 count muffin tin with non stick cooking spray. In a mixing bowl, add the all purpose flour, whole wheat flour, cinnamon, baking powder, baking soda and salt. Whisk until combined.

In a mixing bowl, add the milk, oat bran, brown sugar, vegetable oil and egg. Whisk until combined and add to the dry ingredients. Mix only until the batter is moistened and combined. Gently fold in the apple.

Spoon the batter into the muffin cups filling them about 3/4 full. Bake for 15-18 minutes or until a toothpick inserted in the center of the muffins comes out clean and the muffins are golden brown. Remove the muffins from the oven and cool the muffins in the pan for 5 minutes. Remove the muffins from the pan and serve.

Caramel Apple Muffins

Makes 1 dozen

1/2 cup light brown sugar
2 cups plus 1 1/2 tbs. all purpose flour
1/4 tsp. ground cinnamon
1 1/2 tbs. unsalted butter
1 cup sour cream
1 cup granulated sugar
2 eggs
1 tbs. vanilla extract
2 tsp. baking powder
1/2 tsp. baking soda
1/2 tsp. salt
2 cups peeled and diced Granny Smith apples
14 oz. pkg. caramels, unwrapped
3 tbs. whipping cream
1 cup salted roasted pecans, chopped

Preheat the oven to 375°. Spray a 12 count muffin tin with non stick cooking spray. In a small bowl, add the brown sugar, 1 1/2 tablespoons all purpose flour, cinnamon and butter. Using a fork, mix until you have crumbles.

In a mixing bowl, add the sour cream, granulated sugar, eggs and vanilla extract. Using a mixer on low speed, beat until smooth and combined. Add 2 cups all purpose flour, baking powder, baking soda and salt. Mix only until the batter is moistened and combined. Turn the mixer off and stir in the apples.

Spoon the batter into the muffin cups filling them about 3/4 full. Bake for 18 minutes or until a toothpick inserted in the center of the muffins comes out clean. Remove the muffins from the oven and immediately remove the muffins from the pan. Cool the muffins for 30 minutes.

In a microwavable bowl, add the caramels and whipping cream. Stir every 30 seconds. Microwave for 2 minutes or until the caramels are melted and smooth. Let the caramels sit for 5 minutes.

Line two baking sheets with parchment paper. Place the pecans in a shallow bowl. Dip about 3/4 of each muffin into the caramel allowing the excess caramel to drip off back into the bowl. Dip the top of the muffins in the pecans. Place the muffins on the parchment paper. Let the muffins sit until the caramel hardens before serving.

Golden Delicious Sour Cream Muffins

Makes 1 dozen

1 cup sour cream
1 beaten egg
3 tbs. granulated sugar
2 tbs. vegetable oil
1 1/2 cups all purpose flour
1 tsp. baking powder
1/2 tsp. salt
1/4 tsp. baking soda
1/8 tsp. ground allspice
1/2 cup raisins
1 cup chopped & peeled Golden Delicious apple

Preheat the oven to 400°. Spray a 12 count muffin tin with non stick cooking spray. In a mixing bowl, add the sour cream, egg, granulated sugar and vegetable oil. Whisk until well combined. In a small bowl, add the all purpose flour, baking powder, salt, baking soda, allspice, raisins and apple. Whisk until combined and add to the wet ingredients. Mix only until the batter is moistened and combined.

Spoon the batter into the muffin cups filling them almost to the top of the muffin cup. Bake for 20 minutes or until a toothpick inserted in the center of the muffins comes out clean. Remove the muffins from the oven and immediately remove the muffins from the pan. Serve warm.

Apple Butter Spice Muffins

Makes 1 dozen

1/2 cup granulated sugar
1 tsp. ground cinnamon
1/4 tsp. ground nutmeg
1/8 tsp. ground allspice
1/2 cup chopped pecans
2 cups all purpose flour
2 tsp. baking powder
1/4 tsp. salt
1 cup whole milk
1/4 cup vegetable oil
1 egg
1/4 cup apple butter

Preheat the oven to 400°. Spray a 12 count muffin tin with non stick cooking spray. In a small bowl, add the granulated sugar, cinnamon, nutmeg and allspice. Stir until combined. Spoon 2 tablespoons sugar mixture into a separate small bowl. Add the pecans to 2 tablespoons sugar mixture and stir until combined.

In a mixing bowl, add the all purpose flour, baking powder and salt. Whisk until combined. Add the remaining sugar mixture, without pecans, to the bowl. Whisk until combined. In a small bowl, add the milk, vegetable oil and egg. Whisk until combined and add to the dry ingredients. Mix only until the batter is moistened and combined.

Spoon 1 teaspoon batter into each muffin cup. Spoon 1 teaspoon apple butter over the batter. Spoon the remaining batter over the apple butter filling them about 2/3 full. Sprinkle the reserved sugar pecan mixture over the top of the batter.

Bake for 20 minutes or until a toothpick inserted in the center of the muffins comes out clean and the muffins are golden brown. Remove the muffins from the oven and cool the muffins in the pan for 10 minutes. Remove the muffins from the pan and serve.

Apple Pecan Streusel Muffins

Makes about 18 muffins

1 cup unsalted butter, softened
3/4 cup granulated sugar
1 1/4 cups light brown sugar
2 eggs
2 cups plus 2 tbs. all purpose flour
1 tsp. baking powder
1 1/2 tsp. ground cinnamon
1/4 tsp. baking soda
1/4 tsp. salt
1 cup sour cream
2 cups toasted pecans, chopped
1 cup peeled and chopped Granny Smith apple
1 tbs. vanilla extract
2 tbs. melted unsalted butter

In a mixing bowl, add 1 cup softened butter. Using a mixer on medium speed, beat until the butter is light and fluffy. Add the granulated sugar and 3/4 cup brown sugar to the bowl. Mix for 3 minutes. Add the eggs and beat for 2 minutes.

In a separate bowl, add 2 cups all purpose flour, baking powder, 1/2 teaspoon cinnamon, baking soda and salt. Stir until combined. Turn the mixer to low and add the dry ingredients along with the sour cream to the wet ingredients. Mix only until the batter is moistened and combined. Turn the mixer off and stir in 1 cup pecans, apple and the vanilla extract.

In a small bowl, add 1/2 cup brown sugar, 2 tablespoons all purpose flour and 1 teaspoon cinnamon. Stir until combined. Add 1 cup pecans and the melted butter. Stir until combined and crumbs form.

Spray your muffin tins with non stick cooking spray. Preheat the oven to 350°. Spoon the batter into the muffin cups filling them about 3/4 full. Sprinkle 1 tablespoon pecan streusel over the top of the batter.

Bake for 22 minutes or until a toothpick inserted in the center of the muffins comes out clean. Remove the muffins from the oven and cool the muffins in the pans for 5 minutes. Remove the muffins from the pans and cool for 15 minutes before serving.

Apricot Oatmeal Muffins

Makes about 18 muffins

2 1/2 cups all purpose flour
1/2 cup light brown sugar
3 tsp. baking powder
1/2 tsp. salt
1 cup quick cooking oats
1 cup chopped dried apricots
1/2 cup unsalted butter
3/4 cup boiling water
2 beaten eggs
1 cup whole milk
2 tsp. grated orange zest

Spray your muffin tins with non stick cooking spray. Preheat the oven to 400°. In a mixing bowl, add the all purpose flour, brown sugar, baking powder and salt. Whisk until combined.

In a mixing bowl, add the oats, apricots, butter and boiling water. Stir until the butter melts. Cool for 5 minutes. Add the eggs, milk and orange zest. Whisk until combined and add to the dry ingredients. Mix only until the batter is moistened and combined.

Spoon the batter into the muffin cups filling them about 2/3 full. Bake for 20 minutes or until a toothpick inserted in the center of the muffins comes out clean. Remove the muffins from the oven and cool the muffins in the pans for 5 minutes. Remove the muffins from the pans and cool for 15 minutes before serving.

Anjou Pear Cheese Muffins

Makes 1 dozen

2 cups all purpose flour
1/4 cup light brown sugar
3 tsp. baking powder
1/2 tsp. salt
3/4 cup shredded Swiss cheese
1 beaten egg
2 tbs. vegetable oil
1 Anjou pear, cored and finely chopped
1/2 cup chopped walnuts

Spray a 12 count muffin tin with non stick cooking spray. Preheat the oven to 400°. In a mixing bowl, add the all purpose flour, brown sugar, baking powder, salt and Swiss cheese. Whisk until combined.

In a separate bowl, add the egg, vegetable oil, pear and walnuts. Whisk until combined and add to the dry ingredients. Mix only until the batter is moistened and combined.

Spoon the batter into the muffin cups filling them about 2/3 full. Bake for 20 minutes or until a toothpick inserted in the center of the muffins comes out clean. Remove the muffins from the oven and cool the muffins in the pan for 5 minutes. Remove the muffins from the pan and cool for 15 minutes before serving.

Jumbo Oatmeal Muffins

Makes 8 muffins

1 1/2 cups all purpose flour
1 cup quick cooking oats
1 1/2 tsp. baking powder
3/4 tsp. baking soda
1/8 tsp. salt
1 1/2 tsp. ground cinnamon
1/2 cup light brown sugar
1/4 cup softened unsalted butter
1 egg
1 1/4 cups whole milk
3/4 cup raisins
1/2 cup chopped pecans

Preheat the oven to 375°. Spray eight 6 oz. custard cups with non stick cooking spray. In a mixing bowl, add the all purpose flour, oats, baking powder, baking soda, salt and cinnamon. Whisk until combined.

In a separate bowl, add the brown sugar, butter and egg. Whisk until smooth and combined. Add the milk and whisk until combined. Add to the dry ingredients. Mix only until the batter is moistened and combined. Stir in the raisins and pecans.

Place the custard cups on a baking sheet. Spoon the batter into the custard cups filling them about 2/3 full. Bake for 20 minutes or until a toothpick inserted in the center of the muffins comes out clean. Remove the muffins from the oven and cool the muffins for 5 minutes. Remove the muffins from the custard cups and serve.

Basic Muffins

These muffins are not too sweet and are delicious with butter and jelly. Add 1 cup fresh fruit if desired to the muffins.

Makes 1 dozen

2 cups all purpose flour
2 tbs. plus 1 tsp. granulated sugar
4 tsp. baking powder
1 tsp. salt
2 eggs
3/4 cup whole milk
1/4 cup vegetable oil

Preheat the oven to 400°. Spray a 12 count muffin tin with non stick cooking spray. In a mixing bowl, add the all purpose flour, granulated sugar, baking powder and salt. Whisk until combined. In a separate bowl, add the eggs, milk and vegetable oil. Whisk until combined and add to the dry ingredients.

Spoon the batter into the muffin cups filling them about 3/4 full. Bake for 20 minutes or until the muffins are golden brown. Remove the muffins from the oven and cool the muffins in the pan for 5 minutes. Remove the muffins from the pan and serve.

Sweet Refrigerator Muffins With Variations

Makes 2 dozen

4 1/2 cups all purpose flour
1 cup light brown sugar
1/2 cup granulated sugar
4 tsp. baking powder
1 tsp. baking soda
1 tsp. salt
2 cups buttermilk
3/4 cup vegetable oil
1 1/2 tsp. vanilla extract
3 eggs

In a mixing bowl, add the all purpose flour, brown sugar, granulated sugar, baking powder, baking soda and salt. Whisk until combined.

In a separate bowl, add the buttermilk, vegetable oil, vanilla extract and eggs. Whisk until combined and add to the dry ingredients. Mix only until the batter is moistened and combined. You can refrigerate the batter in a covered container up to 5 days at this point.

To bake the muffins, preheat the oven to 375°. Spray your muffin tins with non stick cooking spray. Spoon the batter into the muffin cups filling them about 2/3 full. Bake for 20 minutes or until a toothpick inserted in the center of the muffins comes out clean. Remove the muffins from the oven and cool for 10 minutes in the pans. Remove the muffins from the pans and serve warm or at room temperature.

Raisin Spice Muffins: For each dozen muffins, add 1/4 cup raisins, 1/2 teaspoon ground cinnamon, 1/8 teaspoon ground allspice, 1/8 teaspoon ground nutmeg and 1/8 teaspoon ground cloves to the dry ingredients. Mix and bake as directed above.

Maple Walnut Muffins: For each dozen muffins, add 1/2 cup chopped walnuts and 1/2 teaspoon maple extract to the wet ingredients. Mix and bake as directed above.

Pineapple Coconut Muffins: For each dozen muffins, add 1/2 cup drained crushed pineapple and 1/4 cup sweetened flaked coconut to the wet ingredients. Mix and bake as directed above.

Chocolate Chip Muffins: For each dozen muffins, add 1/2 cup miniature semisweet chocolate chips to the dry ingredients. Mix and bake as directed above.

Sweet Refrigerator Muffins With Variations cont'd

Dried Fruit Muffins: For each dozen muffins, add 1/2 cup chopped dried fruit to the dry ingredients. Mix and bake as directed above.

Cinnamon Topped Muffins: After baking the muffins, dip the top of each muffin in melted butter. Dip the top of muffin in cinnamon sugar to taste.

Honey Raisin Muffins

Makes about 10 muffins

1 1/4 cups all purpose flour
1 tbs. baking powder
1/4 tsp. salt
2 cups Raisin Bran cereal
1 cup whole milk
1/4 cup honey
1 egg
3 tbs. vegetable oil

In a mixing bowl, add the all purpose flour, baking powder and salt. Whisk until combined. In a separate bowl, add the Raisin Bran, milk and honey. Let the cereal sit for 2 minutes. Add the egg and vegetable oil to the cereal. Whisk until well combined and add to the dry ingredients. Mix only until the batter is moistened and combined.

Spray 10 muffin cups with non stick cooking spray. Preheat the oven to 400°. Spoon the batter into the muffin cups filling them about 2/3 full. Bake for 20 minutes or until a toothpick inserted in the center of the muffins comes out clean. Remove the muffins from the oven and cool the muffins in the pan for 5 minutes. Remove the muffins from the pan and serve warm or at room temperature.

Honey Muffins

Makes 1 dozen

2 cups all purpose flour
1/4 cup granulated sugar
2 tsp. baking powder
1 tsp. baking soda
1/2 tsp. salt
1/2 cup honey
1/2 cup orange juice
1/3 cup melted unsalted butter
2 beaten eggs
1 tsp. vanilla extract

In a mixing bowl, add the all purpose flour, granulated sugar, baking powder, baking soda and salt. Whisk until combined. In a separate bowl, add the honey, orange juice, butter, eggs and vanilla extract. Whisk until well combined and add to the dry ingredients. Mix only until the batter is moistened and combined.

Spray a 12 count muffin tin with non stick cooking spray. Preheat the oven to 375°. Spoon the batter into the muffin cups filling them about 2/3 full. Bake for 15-18 minutes or until a toothpick inserted in the center of the muffins comes out clean. Remove the muffins from the oven and cool the muffins in the pan for 5 minutes. Remove the muffins from the pan and serve warm or at room temperature.

Ginger Butternut Squash Muffins

Makes 1 dozen

1 1/2 cups all purpose flour
1/3 cup whole wheat flour
1/3 cup granulated sugar
1/4 cup dark brown sugar
2 1/2 tsp. baking powder
1 tsp. ground cinnamon
1/2 tsp. baking soda
1/2 tsp. salt
1/2 tsp. ground ginger
1 cup cooked butternut squash, pureed
2 beaten eggs
1/3 cup vegetable oil
1/4 cup finely chopped walnuts
2 tbs. finely chopped crystallized ginger

In a mixing bowl, add the all purpose flour, whole wheat flour, granulated sugar, brown sugar, baking powder, cinnamon, baking soda, salt and ground ginger. Stir until combined.

Add the butternut squash, eggs and vegetable oil to a small bowl. Whisk until combined and add to the dry ingredients. Mix only until the batter is moistened and combined. Fold in the walnuts and crystallized ginger.

Spray a 12 count muffin tin with non stick cooking spray. Spoon the batter into the muffin cups filling them about 2/3 full. Preheat the oven to 375°. Bake for 18 minutes or until a toothpick inserted in the center of the muffins comes out clean. Remove the muffins from the oven and cool the muffins in the pan for 5 minutes. Remove the muffins from the pan and cool completely before serving.

Yellow Squash Muffins

Makes 1 dozen

1 cup all purpose flour
1 cup whole wheat flour
1/3 cup light brown sugar
2 tsp. baking powder
1 1/2 tsp. ground cinnamon
1/2 tsp. baking soda
1/2 tsp. salt
1/2 tsp. ground cloves
1/4 tsp. ground nutmeg
6 tbs. unsalted butter
1/2 cup golden raisins
3/4 cup whole milk
1/2 cup cooked & mashed yellow squash, drained
1 egg

In a mixing bowl, add the all purpose flour, whole wheat flour, brown sugar, baking powder, cinnamon, baking soda, salt, cloves and nutmeg. Whisk until combined. Add the butter to the bowl. Using a pastry blender, cut the butter into the dry ingredients until you have small crumbs. Add the raisins and stir until combined.

In a small bowl, add the milk, squash and egg. Whisk until combined and add to the dry ingredients. Mix only until the batter is moistened and combined.

Spray a 12 count muffin tin with non stick cooking spray. Spoon the batter into the muffin cups filling them about 2/3 full. Preheat the oven to 375°. Bake for 25 minutes or until a toothpick inserted in the center of the muffins comes out clean and the muffins are golden brown. Remove the muffins from the oven and cool the muffins in the pan for 5 minutes. Remove the muffins from the pan and cool completely before serving.

You can substitute zucchini, butternut or acorn squash for the yellow squash if desired.

Double Chocolate Zucchini Muffins

Makes 1 dozen large muffins

2 1/3 cups all purpose flour
1 1/4 cups granulated sugar
1/3 cup unsweetened baking cocoa
2 tsp. baking powder
1 1/2 tsp. ground cinnamon
1 tsp. baking soda
1/2 tsp. salt
1 cup sour cream
1/2 cup vegetable oil
2 beaten eggs
1/4 cup whole milk
1 cup milk chocolate chips
1 cup shredded zucchini

Preheat the oven to 400°. Spray a 12 count jumbo muffin tin with non stick cooking spray. In a mixing bowl, add the all purpose flour, granulated sugar, baking cocoa, baking powder, cinnamon, baking soda and salt. Whisk until combined.

In a separate bowl, add the sour cream, vegetable oil, eggs and milk. Whisk until smooth and combined and add to the dry ingredients. Mix only until the batter is moistened and combined. Fold in the milk chocolate chips and zucchini.

Spoon the batter into the muffin cups filling them about 1/2 full. Bake for 25 minutes or until a toothpick inserted in the center of the muffins comes out clean. Remove the muffins from the oven. Invert the muffin tin onto a serving platter. Cool the muffins completely before serving.

You can use a standard muffin tin if desired. The recipe will make about 18 muffins.

Carrot Zucchini Muffins

Makes 1 dozen

2 tbs. vegetable shortening
1/2 cup light brown sugar
2 egg whites, beaten until foamy
2/3 cup whole milk
2 cups dry quick oats
1 cup all purpose flour
1 tbs. baking powder
1/4 tsp. ground nutmeg
1 cup shredded carrot
1/2 cup shredded zucchini
1 tbs. chopped almonds
1 tbs. vegetable oil

Preheat the oven to 400°. Spray a 12 count muffin tin with non stick cooking spray. In a mixing bowl, add the vegetable shortening and brown sugar. Using a mixer on medium speed, beat until smooth and creamy. Add the egg whites and milk. Mix until combined.

Add 1 3/4 cups oats, all purpose flour, baking powder and nutmeg. Mix only until the batter is moistened and combined. Turn the mixer off. Gently fold in the carrots and zucchini.

Spoon the batter into the muffin cups filling them about 3/4 full. In a small bowl, add 1/4 cup oats, almonds and vegetable oil. Stir until combined and sprinkle over the batter. Lightly press the topping into the batter.

Bake for 20 minutes or until a toothpick inserted in the center of the muffins comes out clean and the muffins are golden brown. Remove the muffins from the oven. Cool the muffins for 5 minutes in the pan. Remove the muffins from the pan and serve.

Zucchini Pecan Muffins

Makes 1 dozen

1 1/2 cups all purpose flour
3/4 cup granulated sugar
1 tsp. baking soda
1 tsp. ground cinnamon
1/2 tsp. salt
1/2 cup vegetable oil
1/4 cup whole milk
1 tsp. vanilla extract
1 egg
1 cup shredded zucchini
1/2 cup chopped pecans

Preheat the oven to 350°. Spray a 12 count muffin tin with non stick cooking spray. In a mixing bowl, add the all purpose flour, granulated sugar, baking soda, cinnamon and salt. Whisk until combined.

In a separate bowl, add the vegetable oil, milk, vanilla extract and egg. Whisk until combined. Add the zucchini and pecans. Whisk until combined and add to the dry ingredients. Mix only until the batter is moistened and combined.

Spoon the batter into the muffin cups filling them about 3/4 full. Bake for 25 minutes or until a toothpick inserted in the center of the muffins comes out clean and the muffins are golden brown. Remove the muffins from the oven. Cool the muffins for 5 minutes in the pan. Remove the muffins from the pan and serve.

Lemon Applesauce Muffins

Makes 1 dozen

1 cup all purpose flour
1 cup dry rolled oats
2/3 cup golden raisins
1/2 cup granulated sugar
1/4 cup wheat germ
1 1/2 tsp. baking soda
1 tsp. baking powder
1 cup applesauce
1/2 cup plus 3 tbs. frozen lemonade concentrate, thawed
1/3 cup whole milk
1 egg
1 egg white
2 tbs. vegetable oil
1/2 tsp. lemon extract
1/2 cup powdered sugar

Preheat the oven to 375°. Spray a 12 count muffin tin with non stick cooking spray. In a mixing bowl, add the all purpose flour. oats, raisins, granulated sugar, wheat germ, baking soda and baking powder. Whisk until combined.

In a separate bowl, add the applesauce, 1/2 cup lemonade concentrate, milk, egg, egg white, vegetable oil and lemon extract. Whisk until well combined and add to the dry ingredients. Mix only until the batter is moistened and combined.

Spoon the batter into the muffin cups filling them about 3/4 full. Bake for 15-18 minutes or until a toothpick inserted in the center of the muffins comes out clean. Remove the muffins from the oven and cool the muffins in the pan for 10 minutes.

In a small bowl, add the powdered sugar and 2 tablespoons frozen lemonade concentrate. Whisk until combined and a smooth glaze forms. Add the remaining tablespoon lemonade concentrate if needed to make a smooth glaze. Drizzle the glaze over the warm muffins. Remove the muffins from the pan and serve warm or at room temperature.

Applesauce Muffins With Cinnamon Streusel

Makes 1 dozen

4 cups plus 3 tbs. Bisquick
1/2 cup granulated sugar
2 1/4 tsp. ground cinnamon
2/3 cup chunky applesauce
1/2 cup whole milk
1/4 cup vegetable oil
2 eggs
1/3 cup granulated sugar
1/4 cup light brown sugar
2 tbs. melted unsalted butter

Preheat the oven to 400°. Spray a 12 count muffin tin with non stick cooking spray. In a mixing bowl, add 4 cups Bisquick, 1/2 cup granulated sugar and 2 teaspoons cinnamon. Stir until combined.

In a separate bowl, add the applesauce, milk, vegetable oil and eggs. Whisk until combined and add to the dry ingredients. Mix only until the batter is moistened and combined.

In a small bowl, add 1/3 cup granulated sugar, brown sugar, 1/4 teaspoon cinnamon, 3 tablespoons Bisquick and melted butter. Stir until combined and crumbly.

Spoon the batter into the muffin cups filling them about 3/4 full. Sprinkle the crumbs over the top of the batter. Bake for 20 minutes or until a toothpick inserted in the center of the muffins comes out clean. Remove the muffins from the oven and cool the muffins in the pan for 5 minutes. Remove the muffins from the pan and cool for 15 minutes before serving.

Banana Honey Muffins

Makes 1 dozen

1 1/2 cups oat bran flakes cereal
1 cup mashed ripe banana
3/4 cup whole milk
1/4 cup melted unsalted butter
1 beaten egg
2 tbs. honey
1 1/4 cups all purpose flour
1 tbs. baking powder
1/4 tsp. salt

Preheat the oven to 400°. Spray a 12 count muffin tin with non stick cooking spray. In a mixing bowl, add the oat bran flakes cereal, banana, milk, butter, egg and honey. Stir until combined. Let the cereal sit for 5 minutes.

In a separate bowl, add the all purpose flour, baking powder and salt. Whisk until combined and add to the wet ingredients. Mix only until the batter is moistened and combined.

Spoon the batter into the muffin cups filling them about 3/4 full. Bake for 20 minutes or until a toothpick inserted in the center of the muffins comes out clean. Remove the muffins from the oven and cool the muffins in the pan for 5 minutes. Remove the muffins from the pan and cool for 10 minutes before serving.

Banana Nut Muffins With Cream Cheese Honey Filling

Makes 2 dozen

1 cup unsalted butter, softened
2 cups light brown sugar
3 eggs
1/4 cup sour cream
1 tsp. vanilla extract
3 1/4 cups all purpose flour
1 1/8 tsp. ground cinnamon
3/4 tsp. baking powder
3/4 tsp. baking soda
3/4 tsp. salt
1/4 tsp. ground nutmeg
2 1/2 cups mashed ripe bananas
1 cup toasted pecans, chopped
8 oz. cream cheese, softened
3 tbs. honey

Preheat the oven to 350°. In a mixing bowl, add the butter. Using a mixer on medium speed, beat until smooth and creamy. Add the brown sugar and beat for 3 minutes. Add the eggs and beat for 3 minutes. Add the sour cream and vanilla extract to the bowl. Mix until combined.

In a separate bowl, add the all purpose flour, 1 teaspoon cinnamon, baking powder, baking soda, salt and nutmeg. Stir until combined. Turn the mixer to low and add the dry ingredients. Mix only until the batter is moistened and combined. Turn the mixer off and fold in the bananas and pecans.

Spray your muffin tins with non stick cooking spray. Spoon the batter into the muffin cups filling them about 3/4 full. Bake for 25 minutes or until a toothpick inserted in the center of the muffins comes out clean. Remove the muffins from the oven and cool the muffins in the pans for 10 minutes. Remove the muffins from the pans and cool for 30 minutes before filling.

In a mixing bowl, add the cream cheese, 1/8 teaspoon cinnamon and honey. Using a mixer on medium speed, beat until the cream cheese is light, fluffy and well combined. Spoon the filling into a pastry bag with a large round tip. Place the cake tip in the center of each muffin and squeeze the filling into each muffin. Place a small swirl of filling on the top of each muffin and serve.

Banana Cinnamon Muffins

Makes 18 muffins

2 cups Bisquick
2 1/4 tsp. ground cinnamon
1/3 cup plus 1 tbs. granulated sugar
1 beaten egg
1 cup whole milk
1/4 cup vegetable oil
3 ripe bananas, peeled and mashed

Preheat the oven to 425°. Spray your muffin tins with non stick cooking spray. In a mixing bowl, add the Bisquick, 2 teaspoons cinnamon and 1/3 cup granulated sugar. Whisk until combined.

In a small bowl, add the egg, milk and vegetable oil. Whisk until combined. Add the bananas and mix until combined. Add to the dry ingredients and mix only until the batter is moistened and combined.

Spoon the batter into the muffin cups filling them about 3/4 full. In a small bowl, add 1 tablespoon granulated sugar and 1/4 teaspoon cinnamon. Stir until combined and sprinkle over the batter.

Bake for 20 minutes or until a toothpick inserted in the center of the muffins comes out clean. Remove the muffins from the oven and cool the muffins in the pans for 10 minutes. Remove the muffins from the pans and serve.

Banana Ginger Muffins

Makes 1 dozen

1/3 cup whole milk
1/3 cup vegetable oil
1/2 cup molasses
1 egg
2 ripe bananas, peeled and mashed
1 1/4 cups all purpose flour
1/2 cup whole wheat flour
1/4 cup granulated sugar
1/4 cup wheat germ
2 1/2 tsp. baking powder
1/2 tsp. salt
1/4 tsp. baking soda
1 tsp. ground ginger
1/4 tsp. allspice
1/4 tsp. ground cinnamon

Preheat the oven to 375°. Spray a 12 count muffin tin with non stick cooking spray. In a mixing bowl, add the milk, vegetable oil, molasses and egg. Whisk until well combined. Add the bananas and mix until combined.

In a separate bowl, add the all purpose flour, whole wheat flour, granulated sugar, wheat germ, baking powder, salt, baking soda, ginger, allspice and cinnamon. Whisk until combined and add to the wet ingredients.

Spoon the batter into the muffin cups filling them about 3/4 full. Bake for 15-20 minutes or until a toothpick inserted in the center of the muffins comes out clean. Remove the muffins from the oven and cool the muffins in the pan for 10 minutes. Remove the muffins from the pan and serve.

Banana Mini Muffins With Peach Cream Spread

Makes 48 mini muffins

2 ripe bananas, peeled and mashed
1 cup light brown sugar
2 egg whites
2 tbs. vegetable oil
1 1/4 cups all purpose flour
3/4 cup whole wheat flour
2 tsp. baking powder
1/2 tsp. baking soda
1/2 tsp. ground cinnamon
3 tbs. granulated sugar
1/2 cup frozen peaches, thawed and drained
1/4 cup ricotta cheese
2 tbs. powdered sugar

Preheat the oven to 400°. Spray two 24 count muffin tins with non stick cooking spray. In a mixing bowl, add the bananas, brown sugar, egg whites and vegetable oil. Whisk until well blended.

In a separate mixing bowl, add the all purpose flour, whole wheat flour, baking powder, baking soda, cinnamon and 1 tablespoon granulated sugar. Whisk until combined and add to the wet ingredients. Mix only until the batter is moistened and combined. Let the batter sit for 5 minutes.

Spoon the batter into the muffin cups filling them half full. Sprinkle 2 tablespoons granulated sugar over the top of the batter. Bake for 15 minutes or until the muffins are golden brown and a toothpick inserted in the center of the muffins comes out clean. Remove the muffins from the oven and immediately remove the muffins from the pan. Cool for 10 minutes before serving.

In a food processor, add the peaches, ricotta cheese and powdered sugar. Process until smooth and combined. Spread on the muffins and serve.

Peanut Muffins

Makes 1 dozen

1 1/2 cups all purpose flour
1/4 cup granulated sugar
1 tbs. baking powder
1/4 tsp. salt
2 eggs
1/2 cup melted unsalted butter
1/2 cup whole milk
3/4 cup dry roasted peanuts, chopped

Preheat the oven to 400°. Spray a 12 count muffin tin with non stick cooking spray. In a mixing bowl, add the all purpose flour, granulated sugar, baking powder and salt. Whisk until combined. In a small bowl, add the eggs, butter and milk. Whisk until combined and add to the dry ingredients. Add the peanuts and whisk until combined.

Spoon the batter into the muffin cups filling them about 2/3 full. Bake for 15 minutes or until a toothpick inserted in the center of the muffins comes out clean. Remove the muffins from the oven and cool the muffins in the pan for 10 minutes. Remove the muffins from the pan and serve.

Fig Newton Muffins

Makes 1 dozen

1 3/4 cups all purpose flour
1/4 cup granulated sugar
1 tbs. baking powder
1/3 cup melted unsalted butter
1 beaten egg
3/4 cup apple juice
10 Fig Newton cookies, chopped

Preheat the oven to 400°. Spray a 12 count muffin tin with non stick cooking spray. In a mixing bowl, add the all purpose flour, granulated sugar and baking powder. Whisk until combined.

In a separate bowl, add the butter, egg and apple juice. Whisk until combined and add to the dry ingredients. Mix only until the batter is moistened and combined. Gently fold in the Fig Newtons.

Spoon the batter into the muffin cups filling them about 2/3 full. Bake for 15 minutes or until a toothpick inserted in the center of the muffins comes out clean. Remove the muffins from the oven and cool the muffins in the pan for 10 minutes. Remove the muffins from the pan and serve.

Jelly Filled Muffins

Makes 1 dozen

1 1/2 cups all purpose flour
1/2 cup granulated sugar
2 tsp. baking powder
1/4 tsp. salt
1/4 tsp. ground nutmeg
1 egg
1/2 cup whole milk
1/3 cup plus 3 tbs. melted unsalted butter
1/2 tsp. vanilla extract
1/4 cup strawberry jelly
1/3 cup granulated sugar
1/2 tsp. ground cinnamon

Preheat the oven to 400°. Spray a 12 count muffin tin with non stick cooking spray. In a mixing bowl, add the all purpose flour, 1/2 cup granulated sugar, baking powder, salt and nutmeg. Whisk until combined.

In a small bowl, add the egg, milk, 1/3 cup melted butter and vanilla extract. Whisk until combined and add to the dry ingredients. Mix only until the batter is moistened and combined.

Spoon the batter into the muffin cups filling them about 2/3 full. Spoon 1 teaspoon strawberry jelly in the center of each muffin. Bake for 20 minutes or until a toothpick inserted in the center of the muffins comes out clean. Remove the muffins from the oven and cool the muffins in the pan for 5 minutes. Brush 3 tablespoons melted butter over the top of the muffins.

In a small bowl, add 1/3 cup granulated sugar and cinnamon. Stir until combined and sprinkle over the top of the muffins. Remove the muffins from the pan and serve.

Maple Magic Muffins

Makes 1 dozen

1/2 cup plus 3 tbs. maple syrup
1/4 cup chopped walnuts
2 tbs. melted unsalted butter
2 cups all purpose flour
3/4 cup granulated sugar
2 tsp. baking powder
1/2 tsp. baking soda
1/2 tsp. salt
1/4 tsp. ground cinnamon
3/4 cup plus 1 tbs. whole milk
1/2 cup vegetable oil
1 egg
1/2 tsp. vanilla extract

Preheat the oven to 400°. Spray a 12 count muffin tin with non stick cooking spray. Place the muffin tin on a baking sheet to catch any drips. Spoon 2 teaspoons maple syrup, 1 teaspoon walnuts and 1/2 teaspoon melted butter into each muffin cup.

In a mixing bowl, add the all purpose flour, granulated sugar, baking powder, baking soda, salt and cinnamon. Whisk until combined. In a separate bowl, add the milk, vegetable oil, egg and vanilla extract. Whisk until smooth and combined and add to the dry ingredients. Mix only until the batter is moistened and combined.

Spoon the batter into the muffin cups filling them about 2/3 full. Bake for 20 minutes or until a toothpick inserted in the center of the muffins comes out clean. Remove the muffins from the oven. Invert the muffin tin onto a serving platter. Cool the muffins for 5 minutes before serving.

Rhubarb Blueberry Muffins

Makes 1 dozen

1/4 cup softened unsalted butter
3/4 cup granulated sugar
1 egg
1/4 cup sour cream
1 1/2 cups all purpose flour
2 tsp. baking powder
1 tsp. salt
1/3 cup whole milk
1 cup fresh blueberries
1 cup chopped fresh rhubarb

Preheat the oven to 400°. Spray a 12 count muffin tin with non stick cooking spray. In a mixing bowl, add the butter and granulated sugar. Using a mixer on medium speed, beat until smooth and creamy. Add the egg and sour cream to the bowl. Mix until well combined.

Turn the mixer to low. In a small bowl, add the all purpose flour, baking powder and salt. Whisk until combined and add to the wet ingredients. Add the milk to the bowl. Mix only until the batter is moistened and combined. Turn the mixer off and stir in the blueberries and rhubarb.

Spoon the batter into the muffin cups filling them about 2/3 full. Bake for 20 minutes or until a toothpick inserted in the center of the muffins comes out clean. Remove the muffins from the oven and cool the muffins in the pan for 5 minutes.

Brown Sugar Banana Muffins

Makes 1 dozen

1/2 cup unsalted butter, softened
1 cup light brown sugar
2 eggs
1 cup mashed ripe bananas
1/4 cup buttermilk
1 tsp. vanilla extract
2 1/4 cups all purpose flour
3/4 tsp. baking soda
1/2 tsp. baking powder
1/2 tsp. salt
1/2 cup chopped toasted pecans

Preheat the oven to 350°. Spray a 12 count muffin tin with non stick cooking spray. In a mixing bowl, add the butter and brown sugar. Using a mixer on medium speed, beat until smooth and creamy. Add the eggs and bananas to the bowl. Mix until well combined. Add the buttermilk and vanilla extract to the bowl. Mix until combined.

Turn the mixer to low. In a small bowl, add the all purpose flour, baking soda, baking powder, salt and pecans. Whisk until combined and add to the wet ingredients. Mix only until the batter is moistened and combined.

Spoon the batter into the muffin cups filling them about 2/3 full. Bake for 20 minutes or until a toothpick inserted in the center of the muffins comes out clean. Remove the muffins from the oven and cool the muffins in the pan for 10 minutes. Serve warm or at room temperature.

Banana Blueberry Muffins

Makes 1 dozen

1 cup frozen blueberries
2 1/4 cups plus 2 tbs. all purpose flour
2 tsp. baking powder
1/2 tsp. ground cinnamon
1/4 tsp. salt
1 cup mashed ripe banana
2 eggs
3/4 cup light brown sugar
1/3 cup melted unsalted butter
1/2 tsp. vanilla extract

Preheat the oven to 375°. Spray a 12 count muffin tin with non stick cooking spray. In a small bowl, add the blueberries and 2 tablespoons all purpose flour. Toss until the blueberries are coated in the flour.

In a mixing bowl, add 2 1/4 cups all purpose flour, baking powder, cinnamon and salt. Whisk until combined. In a separate bowl, add the banana, eggs, brown sugar, butter and vanilla extract. Whisk until smooth and combined and add to the dry ingredients. Mix only until the batter is moistened and combined.

Spoon the batter into the muffin cups filling them about 2/3 full. Bake for 20 minutes or until the muffins are golden brown. Remove the muffins from the oven and cool the muffins in the pan for 10 minutes. Remove the muffins from the pan and serve.

Blueberry Cinnamon Muffins

Makes 1 dozen

1 1/4 cups all purpose flour
1/2 cup dry Cream of Wheat Cinnamon Swirl cereal
1/2 cup granulated sugar
1 tbs. baking powder
2 tsp. ground cinnamon
1/2 tsp. salt
1 cup whole milk
1 egg
2 tbs. vegetable oil
1 tsp. vanilla extract
1 cup fresh or frozen blueberries
2 tbs. apple juice

Preheat the oven to 400°. Spray a 12 count muffin tin with non stick cooking spray. In a mixing bowl, add the all purpose flour, Cream of Wheat cereal, granulated sugar, baking powder, cinnamon and salt. Whisk until combined. In a separate bowl, add the milk, egg, vegetable oil and vanilla extract. Whisk until smooth and combined and add to the dry ingredients. Mix only until the batter is moistened and combined. Fold in the blueberries and apple juice.

Spoon the batter into the muffin cups filling them about 2/3 full. Bake for 18 minutes or until a toothpick inserted in the center of the muffins comes out clean. Remove the muffins from the oven and cool the muffins in the pan for 10 minutes. Remove the muffins from the pan and serve.

Wild Rice Blueberry Muffins

Makes 1 dozen

1 1/2 cups all purpose flour
1/2 cup granulated sugar
2 tsp. baking powder
1 tsp. ground coriander
1/2 tsp. salt
1 cup fresh blueberries
1/2 cup whole milk
1/4 cup melted unsalted butter
2 eggs
1/2 cup cooked wild rice

Preheat the oven to 400°. Spray a 12 count muffin tin with non stick cooking spray. In a mixing bowl, add the all purpose flour, granulated sugar, baking powder, coriander and salt. Whisk until combined. Add the blueberries and toss until the blueberries are coated in the dry ingredients.

In a separate bowl, add the milk, butter, eggs and wild rice. Whisk until combined. Add the wet ingredients to the dry ingredients. Mix only until the batter is moistened and combined.

Spoon the batter into the muffin cups filling them about 2/3 full. Bake for 15 minutes or until a toothpick inserted in the center of the muffins comes out clean. Remove the muffins from the oven and cool the muffins in the pan for 10 minutes. Remove the muffins from the pan and serve.

Streusel Blueberry Muffins

Makes 1 dozen

1 1/2 cups plus 1/3 cup all purpose flour
1/2 cup plus 1/3 cup granulated sugar
1 tsp. ground cinnamon
3 tbs. unsalted butter, cut into small pieces
2 tsp. baking powder
1/2 tsp. salt
1 cup whole milk
1/4 cup unsalted butter, melted
1 beaten egg
1 tsp. vanilla extract
1 cup fresh blueberries

Preheat the oven to 375°. Spray a 12 count muffin tin with non stick cooking spray. In a small bowl, add 1/3 cup all purpose flour, 1/3 cup granulated sugar and cinnamon. Whisk until combined. Add 3 tablespoons butter to the bowl. Using a pastry blender, cut the butter into the dry ingredients until you have coarse crumbs. Set the streusel aside.

In a mixing bowl, add 1 1/2 cups all purpose flour, 1/2 cup granulated sugar, baking powder and salt. Whisk until combined. In a small bowl, add the milk, 1/4 cup melted butter, egg and vanilla extract. Whisk until combined and add to the dry ingredients. Mix only until the batter is moistened and combined. Gently fold in the blueberries.

Spoon the batter into the muffin cups filling them about 2/3 full. Sprinkle the streusel over the batter. Bake for 25 minutes or until a toothpick inserted in the center of the muffins comes out clean. Remove the muffins from the oven and cool the muffins in the pan for 10 minutes. Remove the muffins from the pan and serve.

Apricot Muffins

Makes 1 dozen

1 cup dried apricots, chopped
1 cup boiling water
1/2 cup softened unsalted butter
1 1/4 cups granulated sugar
3/4 cup sour cream
2 cups all purpose flour
1 tsp. baking soda
1/2 tsp. salt
1 tbs. grated orange zest
1/2 cup chopped pecans
1/4 cup orange juice

Preheat the oven to 400°. Spray a 12 count muffin tin with non stick cooking spray. In a small bowl, add the apricots and water. Let the apricots sit for 5 minutes. Drain all the water from the apricots.

In a mixing bowl, add the butter and 1 cup granulated sugar. Using a mixer on medium speed, beat until light and fluffy. Add the sour cream and mix until combined. Add the all purpose flour, baking soda, salt and orange zest. Mix only until the batter is moistened and combined. Turn the mixer off and stir in the apricots and pecans.

Spoon the batter into the muffin cups filling them about 3/4 full. Bake for 18 minutes or until a toothpick inserted in the center of the muffins comes out clean. Remove the muffins from the oven and cool the muffins in the pan for 10 minutes. Remove the muffins from the pan.

In a small bowl, add 1/4 cup granulated sugar and orange juice. Whisk until combined. Dip the tops of each muffin in the orange juice glaze and serve.

Poppy Seed Muffins With Orange Glaze

Makes 1 dozen

2 cups all purpose flour
1 cup granulated sugar
1 tbs. grated orange zest
1 1/2 tsp. baking powder
1/2 tsp. baking soda
1 cup whole milk
3 eggs
2 tbs. poppy seeds
2 tsp. vanilla extract
1 cup powdered sugar
2 tbs. orange juice

Preheat the oven to 375°. Spray a 12 count muffin tin with non stick cooking spray. In a mixing bowl, add the all purpose flour, granulated sugar, orange zest, baking powder and baking soda. Stir until combined.

In a small bowl, add the milk, eggs, poppy seeds and 1 teaspoon vanilla extract. Whisk until combined and add to the dry ingredients. Mix only until the batter is moistened and combined.

Spoon the batter into the muffin cups filling them about 3/4 full. Bake for 20 minutes or until a toothpick inserted in the center of the muffins comes out clean. Remove the muffins from the oven and cool the muffins in the pan for 5 minutes. Remove the muffins from the pan.

In a small bowl, add 1 teaspoon vanilla extract, powdered sugar and orange juice. Whisk until combined and drizzle over the warm muffins.

Orange Poppy Seeds Muffins With Orange Spread

Makes 10 muffins

1 1/3 cups all purpose flour
1 cup granulated sugar
1 tbs. poppy seeds
1/2 tsp. baking soda
1/4 tsp. salt
1 egg
1/2 cup sour cream
1/3 cup melted unsalted butter
2 tbs. orange juice
2 tbs. grated orange zest
1/2 cup unsaltcd butter, softened
3 oz. cream cheese, softened
1/4 cup powdered sugar

Preheat the oven to 400°. Spray your muffin tin with non stick cooking spray. In a mixing bowl, add the all purpose flour, granulated sugar, poppy seeds, baking soda and salt. Whisk until combined.

In a small bowl, add the egg, sour cream, 1/3 cup melted butter, orange juice and 1 tablespoon orange zest. Whisk until combined and add to the dry ingredients. Mix only until the batter is moistened and combined.

Spoon the batter into the muffin cups filling them about 2/3 full. Bake for 18-20 minutes or until a toothpick inserted in the center of the muffins comes out clean. Remove the muffins from the oven and cool the muffins in the pan for 5 minutes. Remove the muffins from the pan.

In a mixing bowl, add 1 tablespoon orange zest, 1/2 cup softened butter, cream cheese and powdered sugar. Using a mixer on medium speed, beat until smooth and creamy. Serve the spread with the warm muffins.

Lemon Poppy Seed Muffins

Makes 1 dozen jumbo muffins

3 cups all purpose flour
1 cup granulated sugar
3 tbs. poppy seeds
1 tbs. grated lemon zest
2 tsp. baking powder
1 tsp. baking soda
1/2 tsp. salt
2 cups plain yogurt
1/2 cup fresh lemon juice
1/4 cup vegetable oil
2 beaten eggs
1 1/2 tsp. vanilla extract

Preheat the oven to 400°. Spray a 12 count jumbo muffin tin with non stick cooking spray. In a mixing bowl, add the all purpose flour, granulated sugar, poppy seeds, lemon zest, baking powder, baking soda and salt. Stir until combined.

In a small bowl, add the yogurt, lemon juice, vegetable oil, eggs and vanilla extract. Whisk until combined and add to the dry ingredients. Mix only until the batter is moistened and combined.

Spoon the batter into the muffin cups filling them about 2/3 full. Bake for 25 minutes or until a toothpick inserted in the center of the muffins comes out clean. Remove the muffins from the oven and cool the muffins in the pan for 5 minutes. Remove the muffins from the pan and cool at least 10 minutes before serving.

Chocolate Popovers

Makes 6 popovers

3/4 cup plus 2 tbs. all purpose flour
1/4 cup granulated sugar
2 tbs. unsweetened baking cocoa
1/4 tsp. salt
4 eggs
1 cup whole milk
2 tbs. melted unsalted butter
1/2 tsp. vanilla extract
1/4 cup powdered sugar

Move your oven rack to the lower third of your oven. Preheat the oven to 375°. Spray a 6 count popover pan with non stick cooking spray. In a mixing bowl, add the all purpose flour, granulated sugar, baking cocoa and salt. Whisk until combined.

In a separate mixing bowl, add the eggs. Using a mixer on low speed, beat for 1 minute. Add the milk, butter and vanilla extract. Beat until smooth and combined. Add the dry ingredients and beat until the batter is smooth.

Pour the batter into the prepared pan filling them about 2/3 full. Bake for 50 minutes. Remove the popovers from the oven and immediately remove the popovers from the pan. Sprinkle the powdered sugar over the top and serve.

Strawberry Popovers

Makes 9 popovers

1 cup heavy whipping cream
1/3 cup plus 1 tbs. granulated sugar
1 tsp. vanilla extract
2 cups chopped fresh strawberries
4 1/2 tsp. vegetable shortening
4 eggs
2 cups whole milk
2 cups all purpose flour
1 tsp. salt

In a mixing bowl, add the heavy whipping cream. Using a mixer on medium speed, beat until the cream begins to thicken. Add 1/3 cup granulated sugar and vanilla extract to the bowl. Beat until stiff peaks form. Turn the mixer off and fold in the strawberries. Cover the bowl and refrigerate until ready to serve with the popovers.

Grease a 9 count popover pan with the vegetable shortening. Preheat the oven to 450°. In a small bowl, add the eggs. Whisk until the eggs are smooth. Add the milk and whisk until smooth and combined. Add the all purpose flour, 1 tablespoon granulated sugar and salt. Whisk until the batter is smooth and combined. Do not over beat or the popovers will be tough.

Pour the batter into the prepared pan filling them about half full. Bake for 15 minutes. Reduce the oven temperature to 350°. Bake for 15 minutes or until the popovers are puffed and firm. Remove the popovers from the oven. Using a sharp knife, immediately cut a slit in the top of each popover to allow the steam to escape.

Remove the popovers from the pan and place on a serving platter. Spoon the strawberry cream over the popovers and serve.

Pistachio Cranberry Biscotti

Makes 16 biscotti

2 cups all purpose flour
2 tsp. baking powder
1/2 tsp. ground cinnamon
2/3 cup granulated sugar
3/4 cup pistachios
3/4 cup dried cranberries
1/3 cup unsalted butter, softened
2 eggs

In a mixing bowl, add the all purpose flour, baking powder, cinnamon, granulated sugar, pistachios and cranberries. Stir until combined. In a separate bowl, add the butter and eggs. Using a mixer on medium speed, beat until smooth and combined. Turn the mixer to low and add the dry ingredients. Mix until the batter is smooth and combined.

Cover the bowl and refrigerate the dough for 30 minutes or until the dough is firm. Remove the dough from the refrigerator. Divide the dough into two equal portions. Lightly flour your work surface. Roll each portion into a 10" x 2" rectangle. Place each portion on a separate ungreased baking sheet. Preheat the oven to 350°. Bake for 25 minutes or until the biscotti is firm. Remove the biscotti from the oven and cool for 5 minutes.

Remove the biscotti from the baking sheets. Use a serrated knife and cut each portion into 3/4" slices. The biscotti will be hard so use a sawing motion with the knife. Place the biscotti slices on the baking sheet. Bake at 325° for 5 minutes on each side or until the biscotti are golden brown. Remove the biscotti from the oven and immediately remove the biscotti from the pan. Cool for 20 minutes before serving. Store the cooled biscotti in an airtight container up to 4 days.

Cranberry Cappuccino Biscotti

Makes about 2 1/2 dozen

2 1/3 cups all purpose flour
1 cup granulated sugar
2 tbs. unsweetened baking cocoa
2 tbs. instant coffee granules
1 1/2 tsp. baking powder
1 tsp. ground cinnamon
1/2 tsp. salt
2 eggs
2 egg whites
1 tbs. vanilla extract
1 1/2 cups fresh cranberries, chopped
3/4 cup chopped almonds
2 cups white chocolate chips, melted

Preheat the oven to 325°. In a mixing bowl, add the all purpose flour, granulated sugar, baking cocoa, coffee granules, baking powder, cinnamon and salt. Whisk until combined.

In a separate bowl, add the eggs, egg whites and vanilla extract. Whisk until combined and add to the dry ingredients. Using a mixer on medium speed, mix only until the batter is moistened and combined. Add the cranberries and almonds to the bowl. Mix until combined.

Lightly flour your work surface. Divide the dough into two equal portions. Place the dough on your surface and roll each half into a log about 12" long and 1 1/2" wide. Place the logs on an ungreased baking sheet. Bake for 30 minutes or until the biscotti are firm. Remove the baking sheet from the oven and remove the biscotti from the baking sheet. Cool the biscotti on a wire rack.

Turn the oven temperature to 300°. Cut the biscotti into 1/2" slices. Place the slices, upright, on a baking sheet. Bake for 30 minutes. Remove the biscotti from the oven and remove the biscotti from the baking sheet. Cool the biscotti on a wire rack.

When the biscotti are cool, dip the tops of the biscotti in the white chocolate. Place on waxed paper until the white chocolate dries. Store the biscotti in an airtight container.

Pumpkin Biscotti

Makes about 30 pieces

1 cup raw pumpkin seeds
1 cup granulated sugar
6 tbs. unsalted butter, softened
1 cup canned pumpkin
2 eggs
3 1/2 cups Bisquick
1 tbs. pumpkin pie spice

Preheat the oven to 325°. Place the pumpkin seeds, in a single layer, in a shallow baking dish. Bake for 8 minutes or until the seeds are toasted. Remove the pan from the oven and cool for 10 minutes.

In a mixing bowl, add the granulated sugar and butter. Using a mixer on medium speed, beat for 3 minutes. Add the pumpkin and eggs to the bowl. Mix until the batter is smooth and combined. Add the Bisquick and pumpkin pie spice. Mix only until the batter is well combined. Turn the mixer off and fold in the pumpkin seeds.

Cover the bowl and freeze the dough for 1 hour or until the dough is firm. Remove the dough from the freezer. Lightly spray a baking sheet with non stick cooking spray. Dust your hands with flour.

Divide the dough into two equal portions. Pat each portion into a flat log about 12" x 3" in size. Place the logs on the baking sheet. Bake for 35 minutes or until the biscotti is firm. Remove the baking sheet from the oven and immediately remove the biscotti from the pan. Cool for 1 hour at room temperature.

Use a serrated knife and cut each log into 3/4" slices. The biscotti will be hard so use a sawing motion with the knife. Place the biscotti slices on the baking sheet. Bake at 325° for 20 minutes. Remove the baking sheet from the oven and immediately remove the biscotti from the pan. Cool for 20 minutes before serving. Store the cooled biscotti in an airtight container up to 4 days.

Dessert Spoonbread With Lemon Berries

Makes 4 cups

2 cups whole milk
4 tbs. unsalted butter
2 beaten eggs
1/3 cup plain white cornmeal
3/4 cup plus 2 tbs. granulated sugar
1 tbs. all purpose flour
1 tsp. salt
1 cup cold cooked rice
1 quart strawberries, hulled
2 tbs. cornstarch
1/2 cup water
1 beaten egg yolk
1 tsp. grated lemon zest
3 tbs. fresh lemon juice

Preheat the oven to 375°. In a sauce pan over low heat, add the milk and 2 tablespoons butter. Stir constantly and cook until the butter melts. In a small bowl, add the eggs, cornmeal, 2 tablespoons granulated sugar, all purpose flour and salt. Whisk until combined. Add to the sauce pan and whisk until combined. Add the rice to the pan. Stir constantly and cook for 1 minute or until the mixture thickens. Remove the pan from the heat.

Butter a 2 quart casserole dish with 1 tablespoon butter. Spoon the mixture into the casserole dish. Bake for 35 minutes or until the spoon bread is set and golden brown. Remove the spoon bread from the oven and cool completely,

Slice the strawberries and set aside. In a sauce pan over medium heat, add the cornstarch, 3/4 cup granulated sugar, water, egg yolk, lemon zest and lemon juice. Stir constantly and cook until the sauce thickens and bubbles. Remove the pan from the heat and add 1 tablespoon butter. Stir until the butter melts. Cool the sauce completely. When the sauce is cool, add the strawberries. Stir until combined and spoon over servings of the spoon bread.

5 BISCUITS & SCONES

Biscuits and scones are not hard to make. The key is cold butter or shortening and your oven must be preheated. Handle the dough as little as necessary for the flakiest biscuits and scones.

Cut baked biscuits and scones into small pieces for croutons. Once the biscuits and scones are cut, place the pieces on a baking sheet. Bake at 325° for 10-15 minutes or until the croutons are toasted. Remove the croutons from the oven and cool before serving. Excellent for snacking, salads and soups.

Easy Homemade Biscuits

Makes about 15 biscuits

1/3 cup cold unsalted butter, cut into small pieces
2 1/4 cups self rising flour
1 cup buttermilk
4 tbs. melted unsalted butter

Preheat the oven to 450°. In a mixing bowl, add 1/3 cup cold butter and self rising flour. Using a pastry blender, cut the butter into the dry ingredients until you have coarse crumbs. Add the buttermilk and mix until a soft dough forms.

Generously flour your work surface. Place the dough on your surface. Knead the dough 4 times. Pat the dough to a 1/2" thickness. Using a 2" biscuit cutter, cut out the biscuits. Cut the biscuits as close together as possible to get as many biscuits as possible out of the first rolling. Roll the dough scraps again and cut out the remaining biscuits.

Grease a baking sheet with 1 tablespoon melted butter. Place the biscuits, about 2" apart, on the baking sheet. Brush 1 tablespoon melted butter over the biscuits. Bake for 10-13 minutes or until the biscuits are golden brown. Remove the biscuits from the oven and brush 2 tablespoons melted butter over the top of the biscuits. Serve hot.

Simple Butter Biscuits

Makes 16 biscuits

2 1/4 cups Bisquick
1/3 cup buttermilk
7 tbs. melted unsalted butter

In a mixing bowl, add the Bisquick, buttermilk and 5 tablespoons butter. Stir until combined and a soft dough forms. Preheat the oven to 450°. Grease a baking sheet with 1 tablespoon butter.

Lightly flour your work surface. Place the dough on your surface. Pat the dough to a 1/2" thickness. Using a 2" biscuit cutter, cut out the biscuits. Cut the biscuits as close together as possible to get as many biscuits as possible out of the first rolling. Roll the dough scraps again and cut out the remaining biscuits.

Place the biscuits, about 2" apart, on the baking sheet. Bake for 10 minutes or until the biscuits are golden brown. Remove the biscuits from the oven and brush 1 tablespoon melted butter over the top of the biscuits. Serve hot.

Sour Cream Biscuits

Makes about 1 dozen biscuits

1/4 cup vegetable shortening
2 cups self rising flour
1 cup sour cream
3 tbs. melted unsalted butter

Preheat the oven to 450°. In a mixing bowl, add the vegetable shortening and self rising flour. Using a pastry blender, cut the shortening into the dry ingredients until you have coarse crumbs. Add the sour cream and mix until a soft dough forms.

Generously flour your work surface. Place the dough on your surface. Pat the dough to a 1/2" thickness. Using a 2" biscuit cutter, cut out the biscuits. Cut the biscuits as close together as possible to get as many biscuits as possible out of the first rolling. Roll the dough scraps again and cut out the remaining biscuits.

Grease a baking sheet with 1 tablespoon melted butter. Place the biscuits, about 2" apart, on the baking sheet. Bake for 10-13 minutes or until the biscuits are golden brown. Remove the biscuits from the oven and brush 2 tablespoons melted butter over the top of the biscuits. Serve hot.

Chive & Lemon Biscuits

Makes 9 biscuits

2 cups all purpose flour
3 tsp. baking powder
1 tsp. granulated sugar
1 tsp. salt
1/2 cup cold unsalted butter
3/4 cup half and half
1/2 cup minced fresh chives
1 1/2 tsp. grated lemon zest
1 tsp. vegetable shortening
1 egg
1 tbs. water

Add the all purpose flour, baking powder, granulated sugar and salt to a mixing bowl. Stir until combined. Add the butter to the bowl. Using a pastry blender, cut the butter into the dry ingredients until you have coarse crumbs. Add the half and half, chives and lemon zest to the bowl. Mix until combined and a soft dough forms.

Lightly flour your work surface. Place the dough on your surface. Pat the dough to a 3/4" thickness. Using a 2 1/2" biscuit cutter, cut out the biscuits. Cut the biscuits as close together as possible to get as many biscuits as possible out of the first rolling. Roll the dough scraps again and cut out the remaining biscuits.

Preheat the oven to 400°. Grease a baking sheet with the vegetable shortening. Place the biscuits, about 2" apart, on the baking sheet. In a small bowl, add the egg and water. Whisk until combined and brush over the biscuits. Bake for 15 minutes or until the biscuits are golden brown. Remove the biscuits from the oven and serve.

Ham & Swiss Biscuits

Makes about 15 biscuits

1/4 cup vegetable shortening
2 cups self rising flour
2/3 cup finely chopped ham
2/3 cup shredded Swiss cheese
2/3 cup whole milk
3 tbs. melted unsalted butter

Preheat the oven to 450°. In a mixing bowl, add the vegetable shortening, self rising flour, ham and Swiss cheese. Using a pastry blender, cut the shortening into the dry ingredients until you have coarse crumbs. Add the milk and mix until a soft dough forms.

Generously flour your work surface. Place the dough on your surface. Pat the dough to a 1/2" thickness. Using a 2" biscuit cutter, cut out the biscuits. Cut the biscuits as close together as possible to get as many biscuits as possible out of the first rolling. Roll the dough scraps again and cut out the remaining biscuits.

Grease a baking sheet with 1 tablespoon melted butter. Place the biscuits, about 2" apart, on the baking sheet. Bake for 10-13 minutes or until the biscuits are golden brown. Remove the biscuits from the oven and brush 2 tablespoons melted butter over the top of the biscuits. Serve hot.

Herb Blue Cheese Biscuits

Makes about 40 bite size biscuits

4 oz. blue cheese, crumbled
2 tbs. minced green onion
1 tsp. dried oregano
1 tsp. dried thyme
2 cups all purpose flour
1 tbs. baking powder
1/4 tsp. baking soda
1/2 tsp. salt
1/3 cup plus 2 tbs. cold unsalted butter
3/4 cup buttermilk

Add the blue cheese, green onion, oregano and thyme to a small bowl. Stir until combined. In a mixing bowl, add the all purpose flour, baking powder, baking soda and salt. Stir until combined. Add 1/3 cup butter and blue cheese mixture to the bowl. Using a pastry blender, cut the butter and blue cheese into the dry ingredients until you have coarse crumbs. Add the buttermilk and mix until combined and a soft dough forms.

Lightly flour your work surface. Place the dough on your surface. Knead the dough 4 times or until the dough is smooth. Roll the dough to a 1/2" thickness. Using a 1 1/2" biscuit cutter, cut out the biscuits. Cut the biscuits as close together as possible to get as many biscuits as possible out of the first rolling. Roll the dough scraps again and cut out the remaining biscuits.

Preheat the oven to 450°. Grease your baking sheets with 2 tablespoons butter. Place the biscuits, about 2" apart, on the baking sheet. Bake for 8 minutes or until the biscuits are golden brown. Remove the biscuits from the oven and serve.

Herb Parmesan Biscuits: Substitute 1/3 cup freshly grated Parmesan cheese for the blue cheese. Mix and bake as directed above.

Blue Cheese Biscuits

Makes 1 dozen

2 cups self rising flour
1 cup sour cream
1/2 cup plus 1 tbs. melted unsalted butter
4 oz. pkg. crumbled blue cheese

Preheat the oven to 425°. In a mixing bowl, add the self rising flour, sour cream, 1/2 cup butter and blue cheese. Stir until combined and soft dough forms. Grease a baking sheet with 1 tablespoon butter.

Lightly flour your work surface. Place the dough on your surface. Knead the dough 4 times or until the dough is smooth. Roll the dough to a 3/4" thickness. Using a 2" biscuit cutter, cut out the biscuits. Cut the biscuits as close together as possible to get as many biscuits as possible out of the first rolling. Roll the dough scraps again and cut out the remaining biscuits.

Place the biscuits, about 2" apart, on the baking sheet. Bake for 15-18 minutes or until the biscuits are golden brown. Remove the biscuits from the oven and serve.

Basil Biscuits

Makes 1 dozen

1 1/2 cups self rising flour
6 tbs. cold unsalted butter, cut into small pieces
7 tbs. whole milk
1/4 cup minced fresh basil

Preheat the oven to 350°. Add the self rising flour and butter to a food processor. Pulse until you have coarse crumbs. Sprinkle the milk over the flour. Pulse until combined and a soft dough forms.

Lightly flour your work surface. Place the dough on your surface. Sprinkle the basil over the dough. Knead the dough 4 times or until the basil is incorporated in the dough. Roll the dough to a 1/2" thickness. Using a 1 1/2" biscuit cutter, cut out the biscuits. Cut the biscuits as close together as possible to get as many biscuits as possible out of the first rolling. Roll the dough scraps again and cut out the remaining biscuits.

Place the biscuits, about 2" apart, on an ungreased baking sheet. Bake for 18 minutes or until the biscuits are golden brown. Remove the biscuits from the oven and serve.

Hot Cheese Drop Biscuits

Makes about 2 dozen

2 cups all purpose flour
2 tsp. baking powder
1/2 tsp. salt
1/2 tsp. cayenne pepper
1 cup shredded cheddar cheese
1/4 cup cold vegetable shortening
1 cup buttermilk
2 tbs. unsalted butter

In a mixing bowl, add the all purpose flour, baking powder, salt and cayenne pepper. Stir until combined. Add the cheddar cheese and vegetable shortening to the bowl. Using a pastry blender, cut the cheese and shortening into the dry ingredients until you have coarse crumbs. Add the buttermilk and stir until a soft dough forms and the ingredients are combined.

Preheat the oven to 450°. Grease two large baking sheets with the butter. Drop the biscuits, by tablespoonfuls, onto the baking sheets. Space the biscuits about 2" apart. Bake for 8-10 minutes or until the biscuits are golden brown. Remove the biscuits from the oven and serve.

Cornmeal Drop Biscuits

Makes 10 servings

1 tbs. unsalted butter
1 1/3 cups all purpose flour
1/2 cup plain white cornmeal
2 1/2 tsp. baking powder
1/2 tsp. salt
1/2 tsp. dry mustard
1/2 cup vegetable shortening
1/2 cup shredded cheddar cheese
1 cup whole milk

Preheat the oven to 375°. Grease a baking sheet with the butter. In a mixing bowl, add the all purpose flour, cornmeal, baking powder, salt and dry mustard. Stir until combined. Add the vegetable shortening to the dry ingredients. Using a pastry blender, cut the shortening into the dry ingredients until you have coarse crumbs. Add the cheddar cheese and milk. Mix only until a soft dough forms.

Drop the biscuits, by 1/4 cupfuls, onto the baking sheet. Space the biscuits about 2" apart. Bake for 25 minutes or until the biscuits are golden brown. Remove the biscuits from the oven and serve.

Rolled Cornmeal Biscuits

Makes about 24 biscuits

3/4 cup scalded whole milk
1/2 cup plain white cornmeal
1 1/2 cups all purpose flour
4 tsp. baking powder
1 tsp. salt
1/4 cup vegetable shortening
3 tbs. melted unsalted butter

In a mixing bowl, add the milk and cornmeal. Stir until combined. Add the all purpose flour, baking powder, salt and vegetable shortening to the bowl. Stir until well combined and the shortening softens.

Lightly flour your work surface. Place the dough on your surface and knead about 6 times or until the dough is smooth. Roll the dough to 1/8" thickness. Using a 2" biscuit cutter, cut out the biscuits. Cut the biscuits as close together as possible to get as many biscuits as possible out of the first rolling. Roll the dough scraps again and cut out the remaining biscuits.

Brush the tops of the biscuits with melted butter. Spray a large baking sheet with non stick cooking spray. Place one biscuit on top of another biscuit to form a 2 biscuit stack. Press the edges together.

Preheat the oven to 425°. Place the biscuits on the baking sheet spacing them close together. Bake for 15 minutes or until the biscuits are done and golden brown. Remove the biscuits from the oven and serve.

Paprika Cheese Biscuits

Makes 8 biscuits

2 1/4 cups Bisquick
1/2 cup shredded cheddar cheese
2/3 cup whole milk
1 tbs. melted unsalted butter
1/2 tsp. paprika

In a mixing bowl, add the Bisquick and cheddar cheese. Stir until combined. Add the milk and stir until the batter is moistened and combined.

Lightly flour your work surface. Place the dough on your surface and knead the dough 10 times or until the dough is smooth. Preheat the oven to 450°. Roll the dough to a 1/2" thickness. Using a 2 1/2" biscuit cutter, cut out the biscuits. Cut the biscuits as close together as possible to get as many biscuits as possible out of the first rolling. Roll the dough scraps again and cut out the remaining biscuits.

Place the biscuits, about 2" apart, on a baking sheet. Brush the melted butter over the top of the biscuits. Sprinkle the paprika over the biscuits. Bake for 8-10 minutes or until the biscuits are golden brown. Remove the biscuits from the oven and serve.

You can substitute cayenne pepper or your favorite seasonings for the paprika if desired. Unbaked biscuits can be frozen up to 1 month. Remove the biscuits from the freezer and bake as directed above. Add about 5 minutes cooking time to the frozen biscuits.

Rolled Ham Biscuits

Makes about 20 biscuits

2 cups self rising flour
1/2 cup cold unsalted butter, cut into small pieces
1/2 cup whole milk
1 egg
1/2 cup chopped ham
1/2 cup condensed cream of chicken soup
1 tbs. chopped fresh cilantro

Preheat the oven to 450°. Lightly spray a 9 x 13 baking pan with non stick cooking spray. In a food processor, add the self rising flour and butter. Pulse until you have coarse crumbs. Add the milk and egg to the food processor. Pulse until combined and a soft dough forms.

Lightly flour your work surface. Place the dough on your surface. Roll the dough to a 20" x 10" rectangle. In a clean food processor, add the ham, cream of chicken soup and cilantro. Process until smooth and combined. Spread over the dough.

Starting with a long side, roll the dough up like a jelly roll. Cut into 1" slices with a sharp knife. Place the biscuits in the baking pan. Bake for 20 minutes or until the biscuits are golden brown. Remove the biscuits from the oven and serve.

Cheddar Cheese Biscuits

These biscuits are good for breakfast sandwiches and to serve with just about any meal, soup or salad.

Makes about 25-30 biscuits

2 1/2 cups all purpose flour
1 1/2 tbs. baking powder
1 tsp. salt
1 cup vegetable shortening
1 cup freshly shredded cheddar cheese
1 cup buttermilk

In a mixing bowl, add the all purpose flour, baking powder and salt. Stir until combined. Add the vegetable shortening to the bowl. Using a pastry blender, cut the shortening into the dry ingredients until you have small crumbs. Add the cheddar cheese and stir until combined. Add the buttermilk and stir until a soft dough forms.

Lightly flour your work surface. Place the dough on your surface and knead the dough 4 times. Place the dough in a mixing bowl. Cover the bowl and refrigerate the dough for 1 hour.

Preheat the oven to 350°. Lightly flour your work surface. Place the dough on your surface. Roll the dough to a 1" thickness. Using a 1 1/2" biscuit cutter, cut out the biscuits. Cut the biscuits as close together as possible to get as many biscuits as possible out of the first rolling. Roll the dough scraps again and cut out the remaining biscuits.

Line your baking sheets with parchment paper. Place the biscuits, about 2" apart, on the baking sheets. Bake for 20 minutes or until the biscuits are golden brown. Remove the biscuits from the oven and serve.

Unbaked biscuits can be frozen up to 1 month. Remove the biscuits from the freezer and bake as directed above. Add about 5 minutes cooking time to the frozen biscuits.

Cheese Biscuit Barbecue Bites

Makes about 40 biscuits

2 cups self rising flour
2/3 cup dry quick cooking grits
1/4 tsp. black pepper
1/2 cup cold unsalted butter, cubed
1 cup shredded cheddar cheese
2 tbs. finely chopped green onion
3/4 cup buttermilk
3 tbs. melted unsalted butter
4 cups shredded cooked pork butt
1/2 cup barbecue sauce

Preheat the oven to 425°. In a mixing bowl, add the self rising flour, grits and black pepper. Stir until combined. Add the butter to the bowl. Using a pastry blender, cut the butter into the dry ingredients until you have small crumbs. Add the cheddar cheese and green onion to the bowl. Stir until combined. Add the buttermilk and stir until a soft dough forms.

Lightly flour your work surface. Place the dough on your surface. Knead the dough 4 times. Roll the dough to a 1/2" thickness. Using a 1 1/2" biscuit cutter, cut out the biscuits. Cut the biscuits as close together as possible to get as many biscuits as possible out of the first rolling. Roll the dough scraps again and cut out the remaining biscuits.

Preheat the oven to 450°. Grease your baking sheets with 1 tablespoon melted butter. Place the biscuits, about 2" apart, on the baking sheet. Brush the tops of the biscuits with 2 tablespoons melted butter. Bake for 10 minutes or until the biscuits are golden brown. Remove the biscuits from the oven.

In a sauce pan over medium heat, add the pork butt and barbecue sauce. Stir constantly and cook until the pork is hot. Remove the pan from the heat.

Split the biscuits open and fill the biscuits with the pork before serving.

Biscuit Breadsticks

Makes 8 servings

1 1/2 cups all purpose flour
2 tsp. granulated sugar
2 tsp. baking powder
1 tsp. salt
3/4 cup whole milk
3 tbs. melted unsalted butter
1 cup shredded mozzarella cheese

Preheat the oven to 450°. In a mixing bowl, add the all purpose flour, granulated sugar, baking powder and salt. Whisk until combined. Add the milk and mix until a soft dough forms.

Lightly flour your work surface. Knead the dough 6 times. Roll the dough into an 8" x 4" rectangle. Cut the dough, lengthwise, into 8 strips. Lightly spray a baking sheet with non stick cooking spray. Place the strips on the baking sheet.

Brush the melted butter over the breadsticks. Bake for 10 minutes or until the breadsticks are golden brown. Remove the breadsticks from the oven and sprinkle the mozzarella cheese over the top of the breadsticks. Bake for 2 minutes or until the cheese melts. Remove the breadsticks from the oven and serve.

Daisy Biscuits

Makes about 20 biscuits

3 oz. cream cheese
1/3 cup cold unsalted butter
2 1/2 cups self rising flour
1 cup whole milk
2 tbs. orange marmalade
2 tbs. raspberry jam

Add the cream cheese, butter and self rising flour to a mixing bowl. Using a pastry blender, cut the cream cheese and butter into the flour until you have coarse crumbs. Add the milk and stir until combined and a soft dough forms.

Lightly flour your work surface. Place the dough on your surface. Knead the dough 4 times. Roll the dough to a 1/2" thickness. Using a 2" biscuit cutter, cut out the biscuits. Cut the biscuits as close together as possible to get as many biscuits as possible out of the first rolling. Roll the dough scraps again and cut out the remaining biscuits.

Preheat the oven to 450°. Place the biscuits, about 2" apart, on an ungreased baking sheet. With a sharp knife, make 6 slits on each biscuit to form petals. Do not cut the dough all the way through. Make a thumbprint in the center of the biscuits. Spoon the orange marmalade in the indentation on half the biscuits.
Spoon the raspberry jam in the indentation on the remaining biscuits.

Bake for 10 minutes or until the biscuits are golden brown. Remove the biscuits from the oven and serve.

Whipping Cream Biscuits

Makes 12 biscuits

2 cups all purpose flour
1 1/3 tbs. baking powder
1/4 tsp. salt
1 tbs. granulated sugar
1/4 cup plus 1 tbs. unsalted butter
1 cup plus 1 tbs. heavy whipping cream

Preheat the oven to 425°. In a mixing bowl, add the all purpose flour, baking powder, salt and granulated sugar. Stir until combined. Add 1/4 cup butter to the bowl. Using a pastry blender, cut the butter into the dry ingredients until you have coarse crumbs. Add the heavy whipping cream and mix until combined and a soft dough forms.

Lightly flour your work surface. Place the dough on your surface. Knead the dough 4 times. Roll the dough to a 1/2" thickness. Using a 2" biscuit cutter, cut out the biscuits. Cut the biscuits as close together as possible to get as many biscuits as possible out of the first rolling. Roll the dough scraps again and cut out the remaining biscuits.

Grease a baking sheet with 1 tablespoon butter. Place the biscuits on the baking sheet. Bake for 10 minutes or until the biscuits are golden brown. Remove the biscuits from the oven and serve.

Poppy Seed Biscuits

Makes 1 dozen

1/4 cup whole milk
2 tbs. honey
1/2 cup cottage cheese
2 1/4 cups Bisquick
1 tbs. poppy seeds

In a blender, add the milk, honey and cottage cheese. Process until smooth and combined. Add the Bisquick and poppy seeds to a bowl. Add the milk mixture and stir until combined and a soft dough forms.

Lightly flour your work surface. Place the dough on your surface. Knead the dough 4 times. Roll the dough to a 1/2" thickness. Using a 2 1/2" biscuit cutter, cut out the biscuits. Cut the biscuits as close together as possible to get as many biscuits as possible out of the first rolling. Roll the dough scraps again and cut out the remaining biscuits.

Preheat the oven to 425°. Place the biscuits, about 2" apart, on a baking sheet. Bake for 10 minutes or until the biscuits are golden brown. Remove the biscuits from the oven and serve.

Praline Biscuits

Makes 1 dozen

1/2 cup melted unsalted butter
1/2 cup dark brown sugar
36 pecan halves
Ground cinnamon to taste
2 cups Bisquick
1/3 cup unsweetened applesauce
1/3 cup whole milk

Preheat the oven to 450°. Spray a 12 count muffin tin with non stick cooking spray. Spoon 2 teaspoons melted butter and 2 teaspoons brown sugar in the bottom of the muffin cups. Place 3 pecan halves in each muffin cup. Sprinkle ground cinnamon to taste over the butter and brown sugar.

In a mixing bowl, add the Bisquick, applesauce and milk. Whisk until combined and spoon into the muffin cups. Bake for 10 minutes or until the biscuits are golden brown. Remove the biscuits from the oven and immediately invert the muffin tin onto a serving platter. Serve warm.

Apple Pie Biscuits

Makes 20 biscuits

1/2 cup plus 1 tbs. granulated sugar
1/2 tsp. ground cinnamon
1/2 cup apple pie filling, finely chopped
1 tsp. light brown sugar
1/8 tsp. ground cinnamon
2 cups Bisquick
1/3 cup half and half
3 1/2 tbs. softened cream cheese
2 tbs. melted unsalted butter

In a small bowl, add 1 tablespoon granulated sugar and 1/2 teaspoon cinnamon. Stir until combined. In a small bowl, add the apple pie filling, brown sugar and 1/8 teaspoon cinnamon. Stir until combined.

In a mixing bowl, add the Bisquick, 1/2 cup granulated sugar and half and half. Stir only until combined and the dough is moistened. Lightly flour your work surface. Place the dough on your surface. Roll the dough to a 1/4" thickness. Using a 1 1/2" biscuit cutter, cut out 20 biscuits. Cut the biscuits as close together as possible to get as many biscuits as possible out of the first rolling.

Place the biscuits on an ungreased baking sheet. Place the biscuits, about 2" apart, on the baking sheet. Spoon 1/2 teaspoon cream cheese in the center of each biscuit. Spoon 1/2 teaspoon apple pie filling on top of the cream cheese on each biscuit. Roll the dough scraps to cut out 20 biscuits. Place the biscuits over the filling. Press the edges together to seal the filling inside the biscuits. Brush the butter over the top of the biscuits. Sprinkle the cinnamon sugar over the top of the biscuits.

Preheat the oven to 425°. Bake for 10 minutes or until the biscuits are golden brown. Remove the biscuits from the oven and serve. The filling will be hot so be careful when eating hot biscuits.

Cranberry Tea Biscuits

Makes about 12 biscuits

2 cups all purpose flour
3 tsp. baking powder
1/4 tsp. baking soda
1 tsp. salt
3 tbs. vegetable shortening
1 cup jellied cranberry sauce
1 beaten egg
1/4 cup sour cream
1/2 cup grated cheddar cheese

Add the all purpose flour, baking powder, baking soda and salt to a mixing bowl. Whisk until combined. Add the vegetable shortening to the bowl. Using a pastry blender, cut the shortening into the flour until you have coarse crumbs.

In a small bowl, add the cranberry sauce, egg and sour cream. Whisk until well combined and add to the dry ingredients. Mix until the dough is combined and a soft dough forms.

Lightly flour your work surface. Place the dough on your surface. Knead the dough 4 times. Roll the dough into a rectangle about 1/2" thick. Cut the dough into 12 squares. Sprinkle the cheddar cheese over the top of the biscuits.

Preheat the oven to 450°. Place the biscuits, about 2" apart, on an ungreased baking sheet. Bake for 15 minutes or until the biscuits are golden brown. Remove the biscuits from the oven and serve.

Cranberry Orange Glazed Butter Biscuits

Makes 16 biscuits

2 cups plus 2 tbs. Bisquick
1/3 cup buttermilk
1/2 cup chopped dried cranberries
6 tbs. melted unsalted butter
6 tbs. powdered sugar
1 tbs. orange juice
1/4 tsp. grated orange zest

In a mixing bowl, add the Bisquick, buttermilk, cranberries and 5 tablespoons butter. Stir until combined and soft dough forms. Preheat the oven to 450°. Grease a baking sheet with 1 tablespoon butter.

Lightly flour your work surface. Place the dough on your surface. Pat the dough to a 1/2" thickness. Using a 2" biscuit cutter, cut out the biscuits. Cut the biscuits as close together as possible to get as many biscuits as possible out of the first rolling. Roll the dough scraps again and cut out the remaining biscuits.

Place the biscuits, about 2" apart, on the baking sheet. Bake for 10 minutes or until the biscuits are golden brown. Remove the biscuits from the oven.

In a small bowl, add the powdered sugar, orange juice and orange zest. Whisk until combined and drizzle over the hot biscuits. Serve the biscuits hot.

Blueberry Biscuits

Makes about 16 biscuits

2 cups all purpose flour
3 tsp. baking powder
1 tsp. salt
4 tbs. granulated sugar
1/3 cup unsalted butter
1 egg, separated
1/3 cup buttermilk
1 cup fresh blueberries
1 tsp. water

Preheat the oven to 425°. In a mixing bowl, add the all purpose flour, baking powder, salt and 2 tablespoons granulated sugar. Whisk until combined. Add the butter to the bowl. Using a pastry blender, cut the butter into the flour until you have coarse crumbs.

In a small bowl, add the egg yolk and buttermilk. Reserve 1 tablespoon egg white in a small bowl and set aside. Add the remaining egg white to the bowl. Whisk until well combined and add to the dry ingredients. Mix until the dough is combined and a soft dough forms. Gently fold in the blueberries.

Lightly flour your work surface. Place the dough on your surface. Do not use a rolling pin for this recipe. Pat the dough into a rectangle about 1/4" to 1/2" thick. Cut the dough into 16 squares. Add the water to the reserved 1 tablespoon egg white. Whisk until combined and brush over the top of the biscuits. Sprinkle 2 tablespoons granulated sugar over the top of the biscuits.

Place the biscuits, about 2" apart, on an ungreased baking sheet. Bake for 10-15 minutes or until the biscuits are golden brown. Remove the biscuits from the oven and serve.

Ginger Biscuits

Makes about 15 biscuits

3 cups Bisquick
3 tbs. granulated sugar
1/2 tsp. ground ginger
2 tbs. cold unsalted butter
6 oz. carton orange yogurt
1 egg
1 egg white, beaten until foamy

Preheat the oven to 425°. In a mixing bowl, add the Bisquick, granulated sugar and ginger. Stir until combined. Add the cold butter to the bowl. Using a pastry blender, cut the butter into the dry ingredients until you have coarse crumbs. Add the orange yogurt and egg. Stir until the dough is moistened and combined.

Lightly flour your work surface. Place the dough on your surface. Knead the dough 4 times. Roll the dough to a 1/2" thickness. Using a 2 1/2" biscuit cutter, cut out the biscuits. Cut the biscuits as close together as possible to get as many biscuits as possible out of the first rolling. Roll the dough scraps again and cut out the remaining biscuits.

Place the biscuits on a baking sheet spacing them about 2" apart. Brush the egg white over the top of the biscuits. Bake for 13-15 minutes or until the biscuits are golden brown. Remove the biscuits from the oven and serve.

Honey Glazed Drop Biscuits

Makes about 10-12 biscuits

3 1/4 cups self rising flour
1 cup whole milk
1/2 cup mayonnaise
1/2 cup honey
1/2 cup melted unsalted butter

Preheat the oven to 425°. Spray a baking sheet with non stick cooking spray. In a mixing bowl, add the self rising flour, milk and mayonnaise. Stir until combined and a soft dough forms.

Lightly flour your work surface. Place the dough on your surface. Knead the dough 8 times. Drop the biscuits, by 1/4 cupfuls, onto the baking sheet. Space the biscuits about 2" apart. Bake for 13-15 minutes or until the biscuits are golden brown. Remove the biscuits from the oven.

In a small bowl, add the honey and butter. Whisk until combined. Brush half the honey butter over the hot biscuits. Serve the remaining honey butter with the biscuits.

Skillet Drop Biscuits

Makes 1 dozen

1 1/3 cups whole milk
1 cup mayonnaise
4 cups self rising flour
1 tbs. unsalted butter

Preheat the oven to 425°. In a mixing bowl, add the milk and mayonnaise. Whisk until combined. Add the self rising flour and stir until a soft dough forms and the dough is well combined.

Add the butter to a 10" cast iron skillet. Place the skillet in the oven until the butter melts and the skillet is hot. Drop the dough, by 1/4 cupfuls, into the hot skillet. Space the biscuits close together in the skillet.

Bake for 25 minutes or until the biscuits are tender and golden brown. Remove the biscuits from the oven and serve.

Southern Buttermilk Drop Biscuits

Makes about 25 small biscuits

2 cups all purpose flour
1 tbs. baking powder
3/4 tsp. salt
1/2 tsp. baking soda
1/2 tsp. cream of tartar
1/4 cup vegetable shortening
1 cup buttermilk
1/2 cup unsalted butter, cut into thin slices

Preheat the oven to 450°. In a mixing bowl, add the all purpose flour, baking powder, salt, baking soda and cream of tartar. Stir until combined. Add the vegetable shortening to the bowl. Using a pastry blender, cut the shortening into the dry ingredients until you have coarse crumbs. Add the buttermilk to the bowl. Stir until the dough is combined and a soft dough forms.

Spray your baking sheets with non stick cooking spray. Drop the biscuits, by tablespoonfuls, onto the baking sheets. Space the biscuits about 1" apart. Place a slice of butter over the top of each biscuit. Bake for 10 minutes or until the biscuits are golden brown. Remove the biscuits from the oven and serve.

Whole Wheat Honey Biscuits

Makes about 10 biscuits

1 cup whole wheat flour
1 cup all purpose flour
4 tsp. baking powder
1/2 tsp. salt
1/4 cup vegetable shortening
1 tbs. honey
2/3 cup water

Preheat the oven to 400°. In a mixing bowl, add the whole wheat flour, all purpose flour, baking powder and salt. Stir until combined. Add the vegetable shortening to the bowl. Using a pastry blender, cut the shortening into the dry ingredients until you have coarse crumbs. Add the honey and 1/2 cup water to the dry ingredients. Stir until the dough is combined and a soft dough forms. Add the remaining water if needed to make a soft dough.

Lightly flour your work surface. Place the dough on your surface. Knead the dough 4 times. Roll the dough to a 1/2" thickness. Using a 2 1/2" biscuit cutter, cut out the biscuits. Cut the biscuits as close together as possible to get as many biscuits as possible out of the first rolling. Roll the dough scraps again and cut out the remaining biscuits.

Place the biscuits on a baking sheet. Bake for 13-15 minutes or until the biscuits are golden brown. Remove the biscuits from the oven and serve.

Biscuit Skillet Bread

Makes 8 servings

10.75 oz. can cream of mushroom soup
2 beaten eggs
2 tbs. vegetable oil
1 tsp. dried minced onion
2 cups Bisquick
1/4 cup unsalted butter
1/4 cup grated Parmesan cheese

Preheat the oven to 400°. In a mixing bowl, add the cream of mushroom soup, eggs and vegetable oil. Whisk until combined. Add the minced onion and Bisquick. Whisk only until the batter is moistened and combined.

Place the butter in an 8" cast iron skillet. Place the skillet in the oven until the butter melts and the skillet is hot. Swirl the skillet so the bottom of the skillet is coated in the butter. Spoon the batter into the skillet. Sprinkle the Parmesan cheese over the top.

Bake for 25 minutes or until a toothpick inserted in the center of the bread comes out clean and the bread is golden brown. Remove the bread from the oven and cut into wedges to serve.

Drop Biscuits With Sausage Gravy

Makes 4 servings

1 cup plus 3 tbs. all purpose flour
1 1/2 tsp. baking powder
1/8 tsp. salt
2 1/4 cups whole milk
3 tsp. melted unsalted butter
8 oz. ground pork sausage
1 tbs. cold unsalted butter
1/8 tsp. salt
1/2 tsp. black pepper

Preheat the oven to 450°. In a mixing bowl, add 1 cup all purpose flour, baking powder, salt, 1/2 cup milk and 1 teaspoon melted butter. Whisk until combined and a soft dough forms. Brush a small baking pan with 2 teaspoons melted butter. Drop the biscuits, by rounded tablespoonfuls, onto the baking sheet. Space the biscuits about 1" apart. Bake for 10-12 minutes or until the biscuits are golden brown. Remove the biscuits from the oven.

While the biscuits are cooking, make the gravy. In a skillet over medium heat, add the pork sausage. Stir frequently to break the sausage into crumbles as it cooks. Cook for 8 minutes or until the sausage is well browned and no longer pink.

Add 1 tablespoon cold butter to the skillet. Stir until the butter melts. Sprinkle 3 tablespoons all purpose flour over the sausage. stir constantly and cook for 1 minute. Add 1 3/4 cups milk, salt and black pepper to the skillet. Stir constantly and cook until the gravy thickens and bubbles. Remove the skillet from the heat and spoon over the hot biscuits.

Fried Egg Biscuits

I make these often for the family for breakfast or a quick dinner. Add cinnamon, pumpkin pie spice, apple pie spice or your favorite savory or sweet seasoning to alter the biscuits to your taste instead of salt and black pepper.

Makes 8 biscuits

8 cold cooked biscuits
3 beaten eggs
2 tbs. whole milk
Salt and black pepper to taste
4 tbs. unsalted butter

Cut the biscuits in half. In a mixing bowl, add the eggs and milk. Whisk until combined. Season to taste with salt and black pepper. You can cook the biscuits on a large griddle or in a skillet. You will need to cook the biscuits in batches using a skillet.

In a skillet over medium heat, add 2 tablespoons butter. Do not dip the biscuits ahead of time in the egg. Dip the biscuits when you are ready to cook them. When the butter melts and is hot, dip the biscuits in the egg mixture. Allow the excess egg to drip off back into the bowl.

Place the biscuits in the skillet. Cook for 3 minutes on each side or until the biscuits are golden brown. Remove the biscuits from the skillet and serve. Add the remaining butter as needed to cook all the biscuits.

If you are using a large griddle, you may not need all the butter. Start with 2 tablespoons butter. Place the dipped biscuits on the griddle. The temperature of the griddle should be about 375°. Cook about 3 minutes on each side or until the biscuits are golden brown. Add the remaining butter as needed to cook all the biscuits.

Tennessee Butter Biscuit Bread

Makes 8 servings

3 tbs. unsalted butter
1 cup self rising flour
1/2 cup buttermilk
All purpose flour as needed

Add the butter to a 12" cast iron skillet. Preheat the oven to 450°. Place the skillet in the oven until the butter melts and the skillet is sizzling hot. In a mixing bowl, add the self rising flour and buttermilk. Whisk until the dough is moistened.

Lightly flour your work surface with all purpose flour. Place the dough on your surface. Knead 5 times or until the dough is smooth. Pat the dough to a 1/4" thickness. Using a 2 1/2" biscuit cutter, cut out the bread. Roll the dough scraps to cut out all the bread if needed.

Place the bread rounds in the hot skillet. Bake for 12 minutes or until golden brown. Remove the skillet from the oven and serve.

Biscuit Cinnamon Rolls

Makes 1 dozen

1/4 cup vegetable shortening
1/4 cup cold unsalted butter, cut into small cubes
2 1/2 cups self rising flour
1 cup buttermilk
6 tbs. unsalted butter, softened
1/4 cup granulated sugar
1/4 cup light brown sugar
1/2 tsp. ground cinnamon
1 cup powdered sugar
1/2 tsp. vanilla extract
3 tbs. heavy whipping cream

Place the vegetable shortening in the freezer until frozen. Cut the vegetable shortening into small cubes. Add the vegetable shortening, 1/4 cup cold butter and self rising flour to a mixing bowl. Using a pastry blender, cut the vegetable shortening and butter into the flour until you have coarse crumbs. Add the buttermilk and stir until combined and a soft dough forms. The dough will be shaggy at this point.

Heavily flour your work surface. Place the dough on your surface and knead 8 times or until the dough is smooth. Roll the dough into a rectangle about 14" x 10" in size. The dough is tender so be careful when spreading the butter. Spread 6 tablespoons softened butter over the top of the dough. Sprinkle the granulated sugar, brown sugar and cinnamon over the dough.

Starting with a long side, roll the dough up like a jelly roll. Tuck the ends under and pinch any seams closed with your fingers. Cut the dough into 1" slices. Spray a 9" round cake pan with non stick cooking spray. Place the slices in the cake pan.

Preheat the oven to 450°. Bake for 12-15 minutes or until the rolls are golden brown. Remove the rolls from the oven and cool for 5 minutes before glazing. To make the glaze, add the powdered sugar, vanilla extract and 1 tablespoon heavy whipping cream to a small bowl. Whisk until combined. Add the remaining heavy whipping cream, 1 teaspoon at a time, until a creamy glaze forms. Drizzle the glaze over the hot rolls and serve.

Orange Pan Biscuit Rolls

Makes 4 rolls

1/2 cup all purpose flour
3/4 tsp. baking powder
1/8 tsp. cream of tartar
1/8 tsp. salt
1/2 tsp. grated orange zest
2 tbs. vegetable shortening
3 tbs. whole milk
1 tbs. melted unsalted butter
1 tbs. granulated sugar
1/8 tsp. ground nutmeg

In a mixing bowl, add the all purpose flour, baking powder, cream of tartar, salt and orange zest. Stir until combined. Add the vegetable shortening to the bowl. Using a pastry blender, cut the shortening into the dry ingredients until you have coarse crumbs. Add the milk and stir just until the dough is moistened.

Flour your hands. Divide the dough into 4 equal portions. Using your hands, roll each piece of dough into a ball. Add the butter to a small bowl. In a small bowl, add the granulated sugar and nutmeg. Stir until combined. Dip each ball in the butter and roll each ball in the granulated sugar.

Preheat the oven to 450°. Spray a 9" round cake pan with non stick cooking spray. Place the rolls in the pan spacing them equally apart. Bake for 12 minutes or until the rolls are golden brown. Remove the rolls from the oven and serve.

Pecan Sweet Potato Biscuits

Makes about 18-20 biscuits

2 3/4 cups all purpose flour
4 tsp. baking powder
1 1/4 tsp. salt
1/2 tsp. ground cinnamon
1/2 tsp. ground nutmeg
3/4 cup chopped pecans
2 cups cooked mashed sweet potatoes
3/4 cup granulated sugar
1/2 cup melted unsalted butter
1 tsp. vanilla extract

In a mixing bowl, add the all purpose flour, baking powder, salt, cinnamon, nutmeg and pecans. Whisk until combined. Add the sweet potatoes, granulated sugar, butter and vanilla extract to a small bowl. Whisk until combined and add to the dry ingredients. Mix until the dough pulls away from the sides of the bowl and all the ingredients are combined.

Preheat the oven to 450°. Lightly flour your work surface. Place the dough on your surface. Knead the dough 4 times. Roll the dough to a 1/2" thickness. Using a 2 1/2" biscuit cutter, cut out the biscuits. Cut the biscuits as close together as possible to get as many biscuits as possible out of the first rolling. Roll the dough scraps again and cut out the remaining biscuits.

Lightly spray two baking sheets with non stick cooking spray. Place the biscuits on the baking sheets. Bake for 12-14 minutes or until the biscuits are golden brown. Remove the biscuits from the oven and serve.

Strawberry PB & J Biscuit Rolls

Makes 1 dozen

2 3/4 cups Bisquick
2/3 cup whole milk
2 tbs. granulated sugar
2 tbs. melted unsalted butter
10 oz. jar Polaner all fruit strawberry spread
8 oz. cream cheese, softened
2 tbs. creamy peanut butter
1 cup powdered sugar
1 tsp. vanilla extract

In a mixing bowl, add the Bisquick, milk and granulated sugar. Stir until the dough is moistened and combined. Lightly flour your work surface. Place the dough on your surface.

Roll the dough into a 15" x 9" rectangle. Brush the melted butter over the dough. Spread the strawberry spread over the dough. Starting with a long side, roll the dough up like a jelly roll. Using a sharp knife, cut the dough into twelve slices a little large than 1".

Preheat the oven to 375°. Lightly spray a 12 count muffin tin with non stick cooking spray. Place the slices in the muffin tin. Bake for 20-23 minutes or until the rolls are golden brown. Remove the pan from the oven.

In a mixing bowl, add the cream cheese, peanut butter, powdered sugar and vanilla extract. Using a mixer on medium speed, beat until smooth and creamy. Remove the rolls from the pan and frost with the frosting. Serve warm.

Gingerbread Spiced Sweet Potato Biscuits

Makes about 15 biscuits

2 medium sweet potatoes
2/3 cup whole milk
3 cups all purpose flour
3/4 cup granulated sugar
4 tsp. baking powder
1/2 tsp. salt
1 tsp. ground cinnamon
1/4 tsp. ground nutmeg
1/4 tsp. ground ginger
1/2 cup butter flavored shortening

Preheat the oven to 450°. Prick the sweet potatoes with a fork. Place the potatoes on a baking sheet. Bake for 1 hour or until the potatoes are tender. Remove the potatoes from the oven and cool the potatoes completely.

Peed and mash the sweet potatoes. You need 2 cups mashed sweet potatoes for this recipe. Add 2 cups mashed sweet potato and milk to a small bowl. Stir until combined. In a mixing bowl, add the all purpose flour, granulated sugar, baking powder, salt, cinnamon, nutmeg and ginger. Whisk until combined.

Add the butter flavored shortening to the dry ingredients. Using a pastry blender, cut the shortening into the dry ingredients until you have coarse crumbs. Add the sweet potato to the bowl. Stir until combined and a soft dough forms.

Lightly flour your work surface. Place the dough on your surface. Knead the dough 4 times. Roll the dough to a 1/2" thickness. Using a 2 1/2" biscuit cutter, cut out the biscuits. Cut the biscuits as close together as possible to get as many biscuits as possible out of the first rolling. Roll the dough scraps again and cut out the remaining biscuits.

Lightly spray a baking sheet with non stick cooking spray. Place the biscuits on the baking sheet spacing them about 1" apart. Bake for 15 minutes or until the biscuits are golden brown. Remove the biscuits from the oven and serve.

Sour Cream Biscuits With Ham Butter

Makes 10 biscuits

1 tbs. vegetable shortening
1 1/2 cups all purpose flour
2 tsp. baking powder
1/2 tsp. salt
3/4 cup sour cream
1 egg
1 cup cubed cooked ham
1/2 cup unsalted butter, softened

Preheat the oven to 425°. Grease a baking sheet with the vegetable shortening. In a mixing bowl, add the all purpose flour, baking powder and salt. Stir until combined. In a small bowl, add the sour cream and egg. Whisk until combined and add to the dry ingredients. Mix only until the batter is moistened and combined.

Lightly flour your work surface. Place the dough on your surface. Knead the dough 4 times. Roll the dough to a 1/2" thickness. Using a 2 1/2" biscuit cutter, cut out the biscuits. Cut the biscuits as close together as possible to get as many biscuits as possible out of the first rolling. Roll the dough scraps again and cut out the remaining biscuits.

Place the biscuits on the baking sheet. Bake for 12-14 minutes or until the biscuits are golden brown. Remove the biscuits from the oven and serve.

While the biscuits are baking, make the butter. Add the ham to a food processor. Process until the ham is minced. Add the butter and process until combined. Spoon the butter into a bowl. Serve with the hot biscuits.

Southern Biscuit Muffins

Makes 1 dozen

2 tbs. vegetable shortening
2 1/2 cups all purpose flour
1/4 cup granulated sugar
1 1/2 tbs. baking powder
3/4 cup cold unsalted butter, cut into small pieces
1 cup whole milk

Preheat the oven to 400°. Grease a 12 count muffin tin with the vegetable shortening. In a mixing bowl, add the all purpose flour, granulated sugar and baking powder. Stir until combined. Add the butter to the bowl. Using a pastry blender, cut the butter into the dry ingredients until you have coarse crumbs. Add the milk and stir until the batter is moistened and combined.

Spoon the batter into the muffin cups filling them about 3/4 full. Bake for 20 minutes or until the muffins are golden brown. Remove the pan from the oven and cool the muffins in the pan for 2 minutes. Remove the muffins from the pan and serve.

Spinach Feta Scones

Makes 8 scones

2 1/2 cups self rising flour
1 tbs. granulated sugar
1/2 cup cold unsalted butter, cut into small pieces
1 cup chopped fresh spinach
1 cup crumbled feta cheese
1 1/4 cups plus 2 tbs. heavy whipping cream

Preheat the oven to 450°. In a mixing bowl, add the self rising flour and granulated sugar. Stir until combined. Add the butter to the bowl. Using a pastry blender, cut the butter into the dry ingredients until you have small crumbs. Place the bowl in the freezer for 5 minutes.

Remove the bowl from the freezer. Add the spinach and feta cheese to the bowl. Stir until combined. Add 1 cup heavy whipping cream to the bowl. Stir only until the dough is moistened and combined. Add 1/4 cup heavy whipping cream, 1 tablespoon at a time, until the dough is moistened if needed.

Lightly flour your work surface. Place the dough on your surface. Pat the dough into an 8" circle. The dough will be crumbly. Cut the circle into 8 wedges. Line a baking sheet with parchment paper. Place the scones on the parchment paper.

Brush 2 tablespoons heavy whipping cream over the scones. Bake for 15 minutes or until the scones are golden brown. Remove the scones from the oven and serve.

Dill & Caraway Scones

Makes 1 dozen

2 cups all purpose flour
4 1/2 tsp. granulated sugar
1 tbs. onion powder
1 tsp. dried dill
2 tsp. caraway seeds
1 tsp. baking powder
3/4 tsp. salt
1/2 tsp. baking soda
1/2 tsp. black pepper
6 tbs. cold unsalted butter
1 egg yolk
3/4 cup sour cream
1/2 cup ricotta cheese
4 tsp. heavy whipping cream

Preheat the oven to 400°. In a mixing bowl, add the all purpose flour, granulated sugar, onion powder, dill, caraway seeds, baking powder, salt, baking soda and black pepper. Stir until combined. Add the butter to the bowl. Using a pastry blender, cut the butter into the dry ingredients until you have coarse crumbs.

In a separate bowl, add the egg yolk, sour cream and ricotta cheese. Whisk until combined and add to the dry ingredients. Stir until the batter is moistened and combined.

Lightly flour your work surface. Place the dough on your surface. Knead the dough 10 times. Divide the dough into two equal portions. Pat each portion into a 6" circle. Cut each circle into 6 wedges.

Spray a baking sheet with non stick cooking spray. Place the scones on the baking sheet. Brush the heavy whipping cream over the scones. Bake for 15 minutes or until the scones are golden brown. Remove the scones from the oven and serve.

Dill Sour Cream Scones

Makes 1 dozen

2 cups all purpose flour
2 tsp. baking powder
1/2 tsp. baking soda
1/2 tsp. salt
4 tbs. unsalted butter
2 eggs
1/2 cup sour cream
1 tbs. chopped fresh dill

Preheat the oven to 425°. In a mixing bowl, add the all purpose flour, baking powder, baking soda and salt. Whisk until combined. Add the butter to the bowl. Using a pastry blender, cut the butter into the dry ingredients until you have coarse crumbs.

In a small bowl, add the eggs, sour cream and dill. Whisk until combined and add to the dry ingredients. Mix only until a soft dough forms and the dough pulls away from the sides of the bowl.

Lightly flour your work surface. Place the dough on your surface and knead the dough 10 times. Roll the dough into a 9" x 6" rectangle. Cut the dough into six 3" squares. Cut each square diagonally in half. Place the scones, about 2" apart, on an ungreased baking sheet.

Bake for 10-12 minutes or until the scones are golden brown and a toothpick inserted in the center of the scones comes out clean. Remove the scones from the oven and immediately remove the scones from the baking sheet. Cool the scones for 10 minutes before serving.

Confetti Scones

Makes 24 scones

2 tsp. olive oil
1/3 cup minced green bell pepper
1/3 cup minced red bell pepper
1/2 tsp. dried thyme
1 cup all purpose flour
1/4 cup whole wheat flour
1 1/2 tsp. baking powder
1/2 tsp. baking soda
1/2 tsp. granulated sugar
1/4 tsp. cayenne pepper
1/8 tsp. salt
1/3 cup sour cream
1/3 cup whole milk
1/4 cup grated Parmesan cheese
2 tbs. minced green onion

Preheat the oven to 375°. Line two large baking sheets with parchment paper. In a small skillet over medium heat, add the olive oil. When the oil is hot, add the green bell pepper, red bell pepper and thyme. Stir constantly and cook for 5 minutes. Remove the skillet from the heat.

In a mixing bowl, add the all purpose flour, whole wheat flour, baking powder, baking soda, granulated sugar, cayenne pepper and salt. Stir until combined. Add the sour cream, milk, Parmesan cheese, green onion and bell peppers from the skillet. Stir until the dough is moistened and combined. The dough will be sticky.

Drop the dough, by tablespoonfuls, onto the baking sheets. Space the scones about 2" apart. Bake for 13 minutes or until the scones are golden brown. Remove the scones from the oven and serve.

Cornmeal Cheddar Scones

Makes 15 scones

2 cups all purpose flour
3/4 cup stone ground cornmeal
1 tbs. granulated sugar
1 tbs. baking powder
1/2 tsp. baking soda
1/2 tsp. salt
1/8 tsp. black pepper
3/4 cup cold unsalted butter, cubed
1 cup shredded sharp cheddar cheese
1 egg
3/4 cup buttermilk
1/4 cup melted unsalted butter
Salt to taste

Preheat the oven to 425°. Add the all purpose flour, cornmeal, granulated sugar, baking powder, baking soda, salt, black pepper and 3/4 cup butter to a food processor. Pulse 4 times or until the mixture resembles cornmeal. Spoon the mixture into a mixing bowl. Add the cheddar cheese and stir until combined.

In a small bowl, add the egg and buttermilk. Whisk until combined and add to the dry ingredients. Mix only until the dough is moistened and combined. Lightly flour your work surface.

Place the dough on your surface and knead the dough 4 times. Pat the dough into a 10 x 7 rectangle. Cut the rectangle into 15 squares. Line a baking sheet with parchment paper. Place the scones on the parchment paper.

Brush 1/4 cup melted butter over the top of the scones. Sprinkle salt to taste over the scones. Bake for 20 minutes or until the scones are golden brown. Remove the scones from the oven and serve.

Potato Scones

Makes 8 scones

1 1/4 cups all purpose flour
1/2 cup dry mashed potato flakes
1 tbs. granulated sugar
2 1/2 tsp. baking powder
1/2 tsp. baking soda
1/2 tsp. onion salt
1/4 cup unsalted butter
1/2 cup plus 1 tbs. whole milk
1 beaten egg

Preheat the oven to 375°. In a mixing bowl, add the all purpose flour, potato flakes, granulated sugar, baking powder, baking soda and onion salt. Whisk until combined. Add the butter to the bowl. Using a pastry blender, cut the butter into the dry ingredients until you have coarse crumbs. Add 1/2 cup milk and the egg. Mix until the dough is moistened and combined.

Lightly flour your work surface. Place the dough on your surface and knead the dough 5 times. Pat the dough into a 7" circle about 1" thick. Cut the circle into 8 wedges. Brush 1 tablespoon milk over the scones. Place the scones on an ungreased baking sheet.

Bake for 15-20 minutes or until the scones are golden brown. Remove the scones from the oven and serve.

Basic Scones

You can add up to 1 cup fruit, nuts, chocolate chips or your favorite add in's to the recipe for different varieties. Add up to 1 cup finely chopped vegetables or meats for a savory version.

Makes about 20 scones

2 cups all purpose flour
1 tbs. baking powder
1 tbs. granulated sugar
1/2 tsp. salt
1/4 cup butter flavored vegetable shortening
2 eggs
1/2 cup heavy cream

Preheat the oven to 400°. In a mixing bowl, add the all purpose flour, baking powder, granulated sugar and salt. Whisk until combined. Add the butter flavored vegetable shortening to the bowl. Using a pastry blender, cut the butter into the dry ingredients until you have coarse crumbs.

In a small bowl, add 1 egg and 1 egg yolk. Whisk until combined. Add the heavy cream and whisk until combined. Add to the dry ingredients. Stir until the dough is moistened and combined. Add your favorite add in's to the dough. Use your hands to combine the dough. Do not stir until combined when you add additional ingredients as this will make the scones tough.

Lightly flour your work surface. Place the dough on your surface. Pat the dough to 1/2" thickness. Using a 2" biscuit cutter, cut out the scones. Cut the scones as close together as possible to get as many scones as possible out of the first rolling. Roll the dough scraps again and cut out the remaining scones.

Place the scones on an ungreased baking sheet. Add the remaining egg white to a small bowl. Whisk until foamy and brush over the top of the scones. Bake for 10 minutes or until the scones are lightly golden brown. Remove the scones from the oven and serve.

Wheat Germ Scones

Makes 12 scones

1/2 cup wheat germ
1 1/2 cups all purpose flour
2 tbs. light brown sugar
1 tbs. baking powder
1/2 tsp. salt
6 tbs. unsalted butter
1/3 cup chopped golden raisins
2 eggs
1/4 cup whole milk

Preheat the oven to 425°. Reserve 1 tablespoon wheat germ and set aside. Add the remaining wheat germ, all purpose flour, brown sugar, baking powder and salt to a mixing bowl. Whisk until combined. Add the butter to the bowl. Using a pastry blender, cut the butter into the dry ingredients until you have coarse crumbs. Add the raisins and stir until combined.

In a small bowl, add the eggs and milk. Whisk until combined. Reserve 2 tablespoons mixture and set aside. Add the remaining milk mixture to the dry ingredients and mix only until a soft dough forms and the dough pulls away from the sides of the bowl.

Lightly flour your work surface. Place the dough on your surface and knead the dough 10 times. Roll the dough into a 9" x 6" rectangle. Cut the dough into six 3" squares. Cut each square diagonally in half. Place the scones on an ungreased baking sheet.

Brush 2 tablespoons reserved milk mixture over the top of the scones. Sprinkle the reserved 1 tablespoon wheat germ over the scones. Bake for 12 minutes or until the scones are golden brown. Remove the scones from the oven and immediately remove the scones from the baking sheet. Cool the scones for 10 minutes before serving.

Tea Scones

Makes 1 dozen

3 1/2 cups all purpose flour
2 1/4 tsp. baking powder
1/4 cup plus 2 tsp. granulated sugar
1 cup cold unsalted butter
1/2 cup golden raisins
2/3 cup plus 1 tbs. whole milk
1 egg
Raspberry preserves, optional

In a mixing bowl, add the all purpose flour, baking powder and granulated sugar. Stir until combined. Add the butter to the bowl. Using a pastry blender, cut the butter into the dry ingredients until you have coarse crumbs. Add the raisins and stir until combined.

In a small bowl, add 2/3 cup milk and the egg. Whisk until combined and add to the dry ingredients. Mix only until the dough is moistened and combined. Lightly flour your work surface. Place the dough on your surface and knead the dough 4 times.

Pat the dough to a 1" thickness. Using a 2" biscuit cutter, cut out the scones. Cut the scones as close together as possible to get as many scones as possible out of the first rolling. Roll the dough scraps again and cut out the remaining scones.

Preheat the oven to 400°. Lightly spray a baking sheet with non stick cooking spray. Place the scones on the baking sheet. Brush 1 tablespoon milk over the scones. Sprinkle 2 teaspoons granulated sugar over the scones. Bake for 15 minutes or until the scones are lightly golden brown. Remove the scones from the oven and serve with the raspberry preserves.

Apple Cheddar Scones

Makes 6 scones

1 1/2 cups all purpose flour
1/2 cup toasted wheat germ
3 tbs. granulated sugar
2 tsp. baking powder
1/2 tsp. salt
2 tbs. unsalted butter
1 small apple, peeled, cored and chopped
1/4 cup shredded cheddar cheese
1 egg white
1/2 cup whole milk

Preheat the oven to 400°. Spray an 8" round cake pan with non stick cooking spray. In a mixing bowl, add the all purpose flour, wheat germ, granulated sugar, baking powder and salt. Whisk until combined. Add the butter to the bowl. Using a pastry blender, cut the butter into the dry ingredients until you have coarse crumbs. Add the apple and cheddar cheese to the bowl. Stir until combined.

In a small bowl, add the egg white and milk. Whisk until combined and add to the dry ingredients. Mix only until the dough is moistened and combined. Lightly flour your work surface. Place the dough on your surface and knead the dough 6 times.

Pat the dough into the prepared pan. Score the dough into 6 wedges. Bake for 25 minutes or until the top of the scones springs back lightly when touched. Remove the pan from the oven and cool for 5 minutes. Remove the scones from the pan and serve.

Dried Apple & Raisin Scones

Makes 8 scones

1 1/2 cups crunchy honey wheat germ
1/2 cup whole wheat flour
1/4 cup granulated sugar
1 tbs. baking powder
1/3 cup unsalted butter
1/2 cup chopped dried apples
1/2 cup raisins
1/3 cup whole milk
2 egg whites, beaten until foamy

In a mixing bowl, add the wheat germ, whole wheat flour, granulated sugar and baking powder. Stir until combined. Add the butter to the bowl. Using a pastry blender, cut the butter into the dry ingredients until you have coarse crumbs. Add the apples and raisins to the bowl. Stir until combined.

In a small bowl, add the milk and egg whites. Whisk until combined and add to the dry ingredients. Mix only until the dough is moistened and combined. You should have a soft dough that pulls away from the sides of the bowl.

Pat the dough into a 9" circle on an ungreased baking sheet. Cut the circle into 8 wedges. Do not separate the wedges. Preheat the oven to 400°. Bake for 12-15 minutes or until the scones are light golden brown. Remove the scones from the oven. Break apart the scones and serve.

Oatmeal Apple Cranberry Scones

Makes 1 dozen

2 cups all purpose flour
1 cup dry rolled oats
1/3 cup granulated sugar
2 tsp. baking powder
1/2 tsp. salt
1/2 tsp. baking soda
1/2 tsp. ground cinnamon
3/4 cup applesauce
2 tbs. unsalted butter
1/2 cup chopped fresh cranberries
1/2 cup peeled apple, chopped
1/4 cup whole milk
1/4 cup plus 2 tbs. honey

Preheat the oven to 425°. Spray a large baking sheet with non stick cooking spray. In a mixing bowl, add the all purpose flour, oats, granulated sugar, baking powder, salt, baking soda and cinnamon. Whisk until combined. Add 1/2 cup applesauce and butter to the bowl. Using a pastry blender, cut the butter into the dry ingredients until you have coarse crumbs. Add the cranberries and apple to the bowl. Stir until combined.

In a small bowl, add the milk and 1/4 cup honey. Whisk until combined and add to the dry ingredients. Mix only until combined and a soft dough forms. The dough should pull away from the sides of the bowl and form a ball when ready.

Lightly flour your work surface. Place the dough on your surface and knead the dough 10 times. Pat the dough into an 8" circle. Place the dough on the baking sheet. With a sharp knife, score the circle into 12 wedges. Do not cut the scones all the way through. In a small bowl, add 1/4 cup applesauce and 2 tablespoons honey. Whisk until combined and brush over the top of the scones.

Bake for 12-15 minutes or until the scones are lightly browned. Remove the scones from the oven and immediately remove from the baking sheet. Place the scones on a wire rack to cool for 10 minutes. Cut into 12 wedges along the score lines and serve.

Peach Scones

Makes 9 scones

1 cup diced fresh peaches, peeled
1 1/2 tbs. lemon juice
2 tbs. plus 1 tsp. granulated sugar
2 cups Bisquick
1/4 tsp. ground cinnamon
2/3 cup whole milk

Preheat the oven to 350°. In a small bowl, add the peaches, lemon juice and 1 tablespoon granulated sugar. Toss until the peaches are coated in the lemon juice and granulated sugar. In a mixing bowl, add 1 tablespoon granulated sugar, Bisquick and cinnamon. Whisk until combined. Add the milk and stir until a soft dough forms.

Add the peaches and stir only until combined. Lightly spray a baking sheet with non stick cooking spray. Drop the dough on the baking sheet. Use a little less than 1/4 cup for each scone. Space the scones about 2" apart. Sprinkle 1 teaspoon granulated sugar over the scones.

Bake for 25 minutes or until the scones are tender and golden brown. Remove the scones from the oven and cool before serving.

Cranberry Lemon Oat Scones

Makes 1 dozen

1/3 cup plus 1 tbs. granulated sugar
1 1/2 cups all purpose flour
1 1/4 cups oat bran
2 tsp. baking powder
1 tsp. baking soda
3/4 tsp. salt
1/4 cup unsalted butter
3/4 cup lemon yogurt
1 egg
6 oz. pkg. sweet dried cranberries

Preheat the oven to 425°. Spray a baking sheet with non stick cooking spray. In a mixing bowl, add 1/3 cup granulated sugar, all purpose flour, oat bran, baking powder, baking soda and salt. Whisk until combined. Add the butter to the bowl. Using a pastry blender, cut the butter into the dry ingredients until you have coarse crumbs.

In a small bowl, add the lemon yogurt and egg. Whisk until combined and add to the dry ingredients. Mix only until the batter is moistened and combined. Add the cranberries and stir until combined.

Lightly flour your work surface. Place the dough on your surface and divide the dough in half. Pat each half into a 6" circle. With a sharp knife, cut each circle into 6 wedges. Place the scones on the baking sheet. Sprinkle 1 tablespoon granulated sugar over the scones.

Bake for 15-18 minutes or until the scones are golden brown. Remove the scones from the oven and immediately remove from the baking sheet. Serve warm.

Cherry Vanilla Scones

Makes 8 scones

3 cups all purpose flour
1/2 cup granulated sugar
2 1/2 tsp. baking powder
1/2 tsp. baking soda
6 tbs. cold unsalted butter
1 cup vanilla yogurt
1/4 cup plus 2 tbs. whole milk
1 1/3 cups dried cherries
2/3 cup vanilla baking chips

In a mixing bowl, add the all purpose flour, granulated sugar, baking powder and baking soda. Stir until combined. Add the butter to the bowl. Using a pastry blender, cut the butter into the dry ingredients until you have coarse crumbs. Add the yogurt and 1/4 cup milk. Stir only until the batter is moistened and combined.

Lightly flour your work surface. Place the dough on your surface. Sprinkle the dried cherries and vanilla chips over the dough. Knead the dough until the cherries and vanilla chips are combined in the dough. Pat the dough into a 9" circle. Cut the circle into 8 wedges. Spray a baking sheet with non stick cooking spray. Place the wedges on the baking sheet. Brush 2 tablespoons milk over the scones.

Preheat the oven to 400°. Bake for 20 minutes or until the scones are golden brown. Remove the scones from the oven and serve.

Orange Ginger Scones

Makes 1 dozen

2 cups all purpose flour
4 tbs. granulated sugar
2 tsp. baking powder
2 tsp. ground ginger
1/2 tsp. salt
1/4 tsp. baking soda
1/2 cup cold unsalted butter, cubed
3/4 cup sour cream
1 egg
1 1/2 tsp. grated orange zest

Preheat the oven to 400°. In a mixing bowl, add the all purpose flour, 2 tablespoons granulated sugar, baking powder, ginger, salt and baking soda. Stir until combined. Add the butter to the bowl. Using a pastry blender, cut the butter into the dry ingredients until you have coarse crumbs.

In a small bowl, add the sour cream, egg and orange zest. Whisk until combined and add to the dry ingredients. Stir only until the batter is moistened and combined.

Lightly flour your work surface. Place the dough on your surface. Knead the dough until combined. Divide the dough in half. Pat each portion of dough into a 6" circle. Cut each circle into 6 wedges. Place the wedges on the baking sheet. Sprinkle 2 tablespoons granulated sugar over the scones.

Bake for 12-15 minutes or until the scones are golden brown. Remove the scones from the oven and serve.

Pumpkin Ginger Scones

Makes 1 dozen

1/2 cup granulated sugar
2 cups all purpose flour
2 tsp. baking powder
1 tsp. ground cinnamon
1/2 tsp. baking soda
1/2 tsp. salt
4 tbs. unsalted butter
1 egg
1/2 cup canned pumpkin
1/4 cup sour cream
1/2 tsp. grated fresh ginger
1 tablespoon melted unsalted butter

Preheat the oven to 425°. Reserve 1 tablespoon granulated sugar and set aside. In a mixing bowl, add the remaining granulated sugar, all purpose flour, baking powder, cinnamon, baking soda and salt. Stir until combined. Add 4 tablespoons butter to the bowl. Using a pastry blender, cut the butter into the dry ingredients until you have coarse crumbs.

In a small bowl, add the egg, pumpkin, sour cream and ginger. Whisk until combined and add to the dry ingredients. Mix only until combined and a soft dough forms.

Lightly flour your work surface. Place the dough on your surface and knead the dough 10 times. Roll the dough into a 9" x 6" rectangle. Cut the dough into six 3" squares. Cut each square diagonally in half. Place the scones, about 2" apart, on an ungreased baking sheet.

Brush 1 tablespoon melted butter over the top of the scones. Sprinkle 1 tablespoon reserved granulated sugar over the top of the scones. Bake for 12 minutes or until the scones are golden brown. Remove the scones from the oven and immediately remove the scones from the baking sheet. Cool the scones for 10 minutes before serving.

Brown Butter Scones

Makes 28 scones

3/4 cup unsalted butter
3 cups all purpose flour
2/3 cup plus 1 tbs. granulated sugar
1 tbs. baking powder
1/2 tsp. salt
1 cup plus 2 tbs. whipping cream
1 tsp. vanilla extract
1/2 tsp. almond extract
1 egg

In a small sauce pan over medium heat, add the butter. Stir constantly and cook about 5 minutes or until the butter turns golden brown. Remove the pan from the heat and immediately pour the butter into a small bowl. Cover the bowl and freeze the butter for 1 1/2 hours.

Preheat the oven to 425°. In a mixing bowl, add the all purpose flour, 2/3 cup granulated sugar, baking powder and salt. Stir until combined. Remove the butter from the freezer and add to the bowl. Using a pastry blender, cut the butter into the dry ingredients until you have coarse crumbs.

In a small bowl, add 1 cup whipping cream, vanilla extract, almond extract and the egg. Whisk until combined and add to the dry ingredients. Mix only until the dough is moistened and combined. The dough will be shaggy looking.

Line two large baking sheets with parchment paper. Using an 1/8 cup scoop, scoop the batter onto the baking sheets. Space the scones about 2" apart. Brush 2 tablespoons whipping cream over the scones. Sprinkle 1 tablespoon granulated sugar over the top.

Bake for 12 minutes or until the scones are golden brown. Remove the scones from the oven and serve warm.

Irish Sweet Scones

Makes 3 loaves

6 cups all purpose flour
2 cups granulated sugar
2 tbs. baking powder
2 1/2 cups whole milk
2 eggs
2 tsp. vanilla extract
2 cups raisins
3 tbs. melted unsalted butter

Preheat the oven to 350°. Spray three 9 x 5 loaf pans with non stick cooking spray. In a mixing bowl, add the all purpose flour, granulated sugar and baking powder. Whisk until combined.

In a separate bowl, add the milk, eggs and vanilla extract. Whisk until combined and add to the dry ingredients. Mix until the batter is moistened and combined. Stir in the raisins.

Spoon the batter into the prepared pans. Bake for 1 hour or until a toothpick inserted in the center of the loaves comes out clean. Remove the loaves from the oven and remove the loaves from the pans. Brush the melted butter over the loaves. Cool at least 5 minutes before serving.

Chocolate Chip Oatmeal Scones

Makes 8 scones

1 cup Bisquick
3 tbs. light brown sugar
1/2 tsp. ground cinnamon
1 cup dry quick cooking oats
1/2 cup semisweet chocolate chips
1 beaten egg
1/4 cup whole milk

Preheat the oven to 400°. Spray a baking sheet with non stick cooking spray. In a mixing bowl, add the Bisquick, brown sugar, cinnamon, oats and chocolate chips. Whisk until combined.

In a small bowl, add the egg and milk. Whisk until combined and add to the dry ingredients. Mix only until the batter is moistened and combined. The dough will be sticky.

Flour your hands and pat the dough into a 7" circle on the baking sheet. With a sharp knife, cut the dough into 8 wedges. Do not separate the scones. Bake for 10-12 minutes or until the scones are done and lightly browned. Remove the scones from the oven and cool for 5 minutes before serving.

Pumpkin Scones With Cranberry Butter

Makes 8 scones

2 tbs. dried cranberries
1/2 cup boiling water
1/2 cup unsalted butter, softened
3 tbs. powdered sugar
2 1/4 cups all purpose flour
1/4 cup light brown sugar
2 tsp. baking powder
1 1/2 tsp. pumpkin pie spice
1/4 tsp. salt
1/4 tsp. baking soda
1/2 cup cold unsalted butter
1 egg
1/2 cup canned pumpkin
1/3 cup whole milk
2 tbs. chopped pecans

In a small bowl, add the cranberries and boiling water. Let the cranberries sit for 5 minutes. Drain any remaining water from the cranberries. Chop the cranberries. Add 1/2 cup softened butter and powdered sugar to the bowl. Whisk until the butter is combined and fluffy. Cover the bowl and refrigerate for 1 hour before serving.

Preheat the oven to 400°. In a mixing bowl, add the all purpose flour, brown sugar, baking powder, pumpkin pie spice, salt and baking soda. Stir until combined. Add 1/2 cup cold butter to the bowl. Using a pastry blender, cut the butter into the dry ingredients until you have coarse crumbs.

In a small bowl, add the egg, pumpkin and milk. Whisk until combined and add to the dry ingredients. Mix only until a soft dough forms. Add the pecans and stir until combined.

Lightly flour your work surface. Place the dough on your surface. Knead the dough 10 times. Pat the dough into an 8" circle. Cut the circle into 8 wedges. Spray a baking sheet with non stick cooking spray. Place the wedges on the baking sheet.

Bake for 13-15 minutes or until the scones are golden brown. Remove the scones from the oven and serve with the cranberry butter.

Pear Scones

Makes about 30 scones

1 pear, cored
2 1/2 cups all purpose flour
1 cup plus 1 tbs. granulated sugar
1/2 cup whole wheat flour
1 tbs. baking powder
1/2 tsp. baking soda
1/2 tsp. ground ginger
4 tbs. cold unsalted butter
1/2 cup whole milk

Add the pear to a food processor. Process until the pear is shredded. Remove the pear from the food processor and place in a mixing bowl. Add the all purpose flour, 1 cup granulated sugar, whole wheat flour, baking powder, baking soda and ginger to the food processor. Process until combined. Add the butter to the food processor. Pulse until the mixture resembles coarse crumbs. Spoon the dry ingredients into the bowl with the pear. Add the milk to the bowl. Stir only until the batter is moistened and combined.

Lightly flour your work surface. Place the dough on the surface. Knead the dough 10 times. Roll the dough into a rectangle about 1/2" thick. Using a 1 1/2" round biscuit cutter, cut out the scones. Cut the scones as close together as possible on the first rolling. Roll the dough scraps to cut out the remaining scones.

Place the scones on the baking sheets. Sprinkle 1 tablespoon granulated sugar over the top of the scones. Bake for 12-15 minutes or until the scones are golden brown and a toothpick inserted in the scones comes out clean. Remove the scones from the oven and immediately remove the scones from the baking sheets. Serve warm.

Cranberry Orange Scones

Makes 10 scones

2 cups all purpose flour
10 tsp. granulated sugar
1 tbs. grated orange zest
2 tsp. baking powder
1/2 tsp. salt
1/4 tsp. baking soda
1/3 cup cold unsalted butter
1 cup dried cranberries
1/4 cup plus 1 tbs. orange juice
1/4 cup half and half cream
1 egg
1 tbs. whole milk
1/2 cup powdered sugar
1/2 cup unsalted butter, softened
3 tbs. orange marmalade

Preheat the oven to 400°. In a mixing bowl, add the all purpose flour, 7 teaspoons granulated sugar, orange zest, baking powder, salt and baking soda. Whisk until combined. Add 1/3 cup cold butter to the bowl. Using a pastry blender, cut the butter into the dry ingredients until you have coarse crumbs. Add the cranberries and stir until combined.

In a small bowl, add 1/4 cup orange juice, half and half and egg. Whisk until combined and add to the dry ingredients. Mix only until a soft dough forms.

Lightly flour your work surface. Place the dough on your surface. Knead the dough 6 times. Pat the dough into an 8" circle. Cut the circle into 10 wedges. Place the wedges on an ungreased baking sheet.

Brush the scones with the milk. Sprinkle 3 teaspoons granulated sugar over the scones. Bake for 13-15 minutes or until the scones are golden brown. Remove the scones from the oven and let the scones cool while you prepare the glaze.

In a small bowl, add the powdered sugar and 1 tablespoon orange juice. Whisk until combined and drizzle over the hot scones. In a small bowl, add 1/2 cup softened butter and orange marmalade. Stir until combined and serve with the scones.

Honey Currant Scones

Makes 8 scones

2 1/2 cups all purpose flour
2 tsp. grated orange zest
1 tsp. baking powder
1/2 tsp. baking soda
1/2 tsp. salt
1/2 cup unsalted butter
1/2 cup currants
1/2 cup sour cream
1/3 cup honey
1 beaten egg

Preheat the oven to 375°. Spray a baking sheet with non stick cooking spray. In a mixing bowl, add the all purpose flour, orange zest, baking powder, baking soda and salt. Stir until combined. Add the butter to the bowl. Using a pastry blender, cut the butter into the dry ingredients until you have coarse crumbs. Add the currants and stir until combined.

In a small bowl, add the sour cream, honey and egg. Whisk until combined and add to the dry ingredients. Mix only until a soft dough forms and the dough pulls away from the sides of the bowl.

Lightly flour your work surface. Place the dough on your surface. Pat the dough into an 8" square. Cut the dough into 4 squares. Cut each square in half diagonally to form 8 triangles. Place the scones, 1" apart, on the baking sheet.

Bake for 15 minutes or until the scones are golden brown and a toothpick inserted in the scones comes out clean. Remove the scones from the oven and immediately remove the scones from the baking sheet. Cool the scones for 10 minutes before serving.

Apricot Scones

Makes 1 dozen

1 1/2 cups all purpose flour
1 cup oat bran
2 tbs. granulated sugar
1 tbs. baking powder
1/2 tsp. salt
1/2 cup unsalted butter, cut into small pieces
1 beaten egg
3 tbs. whole milk
16 oz. can apricot halves, drained and chopped

Preheat the oven to 400°. In a mixing bowl, add the all purpose flour, oat bran, granulated sugar, baking powder and salt. Stir until combined. Add the butter to the bowl. Using a pastry blender, cut the butter into the dry ingredients until you have coarse crumbs. Add the egg, milk and apricots. Mix only until a soft dough forms and the dough pulls away from the sides of the bowl.

Lightly flour your work surface. Place the dough on your surface. Divide the dough into two equal portions. Pat each portion into a 6" circle about 1" thick. Cut each circle into 6 wedges. Place the wedges on an ungreased baking sheet.

Bake for 12 minutes or until the scones are golden brown and a toothpick inserted in the scones comes out clean. Remove the scones from the oven and immediately remove the scones from the baking sheet. Cool the scones for 10 minutes before serving.

Fruit Cocktail Granola Scones

Makes 6 scones

2 cups all purpose flour
1/3 cup granulated sugar
1 tbs. baking powder
1/2 tsp. salt
1/4 cup unsalted butter
1 cup granola
16 oz. can fruit cocktail, drained
2 beaten eggs

Preheat the oven to 375°. Spray a baking sheet with non stick cooking spray. In a mixing bowl, add the all purpose flour, 1/4 cup granulated sugar, baking powder and salt. Whisk until combined. Add the butter to the bowl. Using a pastry blender, cut the butter into the dry ingredients until you have coarse crumbs. Add the granola and stir until combined. Add the fruit cocktail and eggs. Mix only until combined and a soft dough forms. The dough will pull away from the sides of the bowl when ready.

Lightly flour your work surface. Place the dough on your surface. Roll the dough into a 7" circle. Cut into 6 wedges. Place the wedges on the baking sheet. Sprinkle the remaining granulated sugar over the top of the scones.

Bake for 45 minutes or until a toothpick inserted in the scones comes out clean. Remove the scones from the oven and immediately remove the scones from the baking sheet. Cool the scones for 10 minutes before serving.

Cinnamon Date Scones

Makes 1 dozen

1/4 cup granulated sugar
1/4 tsp. ground cinnamon
2 cups all purpose flour
2 1/2 tsp. baking powder
1/2 tsp. salt
5 tbs. cold unsalted butter
1/2 cup chopped pitted dates
2 eggs
1/3 cup half and half

Preheat the oven to 425°. In a small bowl, add the granulated sugar and cinnamon. Stir until combined. In a mixing bowl, add the all purpose flour, baking powder, salt and 2 tablespoons cinnamon sugar mixture. Whisk until combined. Add the butter to the bowl. Using a pastry blender, cut the butter into the dry ingredients until you have coarse crumbs. Add the dates and stir until combined.

Add the eggs and half and half to a small bowl. Whisk until combined. Reserve 1 tablespoon mixture and set aside. Add the remaining milk mixture to the dry ingredients. Mix only until a soft dough forms and the dough pulls away from the sides of the bowl.

Lightly flour your work surface. Place the dough on your surface and knead the dough 10 times. Roll the dough into a 9" x 6" rectangle. Cut the dough into six 3" squares. Cut each square diagonally in half. Place the scones on an ungreased baking sheet.

Brush 1 tablespoon reserved milk mixture over the top of the scones. Sprinkle the remaining cinnamon sugar over the scones. Bake for 12 minutes or until the scones are golden brown. Remove the scones from the oven and immediately remove the scones from the baking sheet. Cool the scones for 10 minutes before serving.

Buttermilk Oatmeal Scones

Makes about 30 scones

8 tbs. cold unsalted butter, cut into small pieces
2 cups all purpose flour
1 cup dry rolled oats
1/3 cup plus 2 tbs. granulated sugar
1 tbs. baking powder
1/2 tsp. baking soda
1/8 tsp. salt
1 cup plus 2 tbs. buttermilk

Preheat the oven to 375°. Grease two large baking sheets with 2 tablespoons butter. In a mixing bowl, add the all purpose flour, oats, 1/3 cup granulated sugar, baking powder, baking soda and salt. Whisk until combined. Add 6 tablespoons butter to the bowl. Using a pastry blender, cut the butter into the dry ingredients until you have coarse crumbs. Add 1 cup buttermilk and mix only until a soft dough forms.

Lightly flour your work surface. Place the dough on the surface. Knead the dough 10 times. Roll the dough into a rectangle about 1/2" thick. Using a 1 1/2" round biscuit cutter, cut out the scones. Cut the scones as close together as possible on the first rolling. Roll the dough scraps to cut out the remaining scones.

Place the scones on the baking sheets. Brush 2 tablespoons buttermilk over the top of the scones. Sprinkle 2 tablespoons granulated sugar over the top of the scones. Bake for 18 minutes or until the scones are golden brown and a toothpick inserted in the scones comes out clean. Remove the scones from the oven and immediately remove the scones from the baking sheets. Let the scones cool for 10 minutes before serving.

Cheese Straws

In the South, we consider cheese straws to be a quick bread. They are similar to a biscuit and we eat them by the dozens at parties.

Makes about 5 dozen

2 1/2 cups freshly shredded cheddar cheese
1/2 cup unsalted butter, softened
1 tbs. half and half
1 tsp. salt
1 1/2 cups all purpose flour

Do not use the shredded cheese available at the store for this recipe. The caking agent in them will produce tough cheese straws.

In a mixing bowl, add the cheddar cheese, butter, half and half and salt. Using a mixer on medium speed, beat until well blended. Slowly add the all purpose flour and mix until blended and a dough forms. Form the dough into a flat disk. Wrap the dough in plastic wrap and chill for 15 minutes.

Remove the dough from the refrigerator. Lightly flour your work surface. Place the dough on your surface and roll the dough to 1/8" thickness. Using a 2" cutter, cut out the straws. Cut the straws as close together as possible to get as many as possible on the first rolling. Roll the dough scraps to cut out the remaining straws. Do not roll the dough scraps more than once.

Line your baking sheets with parchment paper. Preheat the oven to 350°. Place the straws on the baking sheets spacing them about 1" apart. Bake for 12-15 minutes or until the straws are golden brown. Remove the baking sheets from the oven. Cool the straws on the baking sheets for 20 minutes. Remove the straws from the baking sheets and cool completely.

Pecan Rosemary Cheddar Straws

Makes 6 dozen

2 1/2 cups freshly shredded cheddar cheese
1/2 cup unsalted butter, softened
2 tbs. half and half
1 tsp. salt
1 1/2 cups all purpose flour
2 cups chopped toasted pecans
1 tbs. finely chopped fresh rosemary

Do not use the shredded cheese available at the store for this recipe. The caking agent in them will produce tough cheese straws.

In a mixing bowl, add the cheddar cheese, butter, half and half and salt. Using a mixer on medium speed, beat until well blended. Slowly add the all purpose flour, pecans and rosemary. Mix until blended and a dough forms. Form the dough into a flat disk. Wrap the dough in plastic wrap and chill for 15 minutes.

Remove the dough from the refrigerator. Lightly flour your work surface. Place the dough on your surface and roll the dough to 1/8" thickness. Using a 2" cutter, cut out the straws. Cut the straws as close together as possible to get as many as possible on the first rolling. Roll the dough scraps to cut out the remaining straws. Do not roll the dough scraps more than once.

Line your baking sheets with parchment paper. Preheat the oven to 350°. Place the straws on the baking sheets spacing them about 1" apart. Bake for 15-18 minutes or until the straws are golden brown. Remove the baking sheets from the oven. Cool the straws on the baking sheets for 20 minutes. Remove the straws from the baking sheets and cool completely.

Olive Blue Cheese Cheddar Straws

Makes about 7 dozen

2 1/2 cups freshly shredded cheddar cheese
1/2 cup unsalted butter, softened
1 tbs. half and half
1 tsp. salt
1 1/2 cups all purpose flour
6 oz. can Spanish olives, drained and finely chopped
2 oz. crumbled blue cheese

Do not use the shredded cheese available at the store for this recipe. The caking agent in them will produce tough cheese straws.

In a mixing bowl, add the cheddar cheese, butter, half and half and salt. Using a mixer on medium speed, beat until well blended. Slowly add the all purpose flour, olives and blue cheese. Mix until blended and a dough forms. Form the dough into a flat disk. Wrap the dough in plastic wrap and chill for 15 minutes.

Remove the dough from the refrigerator. Lightly flour your work surface. Place the dough on your surface and roll the dough to 1/8" thickness. Using a 2" cutter, cut out the straws. Cut the straws as close together as possible to get as many as possible on the first rolling. Roll the dough scraps to cut out the remaining straws. Do not roll the dough scraps more than once.

Line your baking sheets with parchment paper. Preheat the oven to 350°. Place the straws on the baking sheets spacing them about 1" apart. Bake for 12-15 minutes or until the straws are golden brown. Remove the baking sheets from the oven. Cool the straws on the baking sheets for 20 minutes. Remove the straws from the baking sheets and cool completely.

Bacon Cheddar Paprika Cheese Straws

Makes about 6 dozen

2 1/2 cups freshly shredded cheddar cheese
1/2 cup unsalted butter, softened
1 tbs. half and half
1 tsp. salt
1 1/2 cups all purpose flour
4 bacon slices, cooked and crumbled
1 tsp. smoked paprika
1/2 tsp. cayenne pepper

Do not use the shredded cheese available at the store for this recipe. The caking agent in them will produce tough cheese straws.

In a mixing bowl, add the cheddar cheese, butter, half and half and salt. Using a mixer on medium speed, beat until well blended. Slowly add the all purpose flour, bacon, smoked paprika and cayenne pepper. Mix until blended and a dough forms. Form the dough into a flat disk. Wrap the dough in plastic wrap and chill for 15 minutes.

Remove the dough from the refrigerator. Lightly flour your work surface. Place the dough on your surface and roll the dough to 1/8" thickness. Using a 2" cutter, cut out the straws. Cut the straws as close together as possible to get as many as possible on the first rolling. Roll the dough scraps to cut out the remaining straws. Do not roll the dough scraps more than once.

Line your baking sheets with parchment paper. Preheat the oven to 350°. Place the straws on the baking sheets spacing them about 1" apart. Bake for 12-15 minutes or until the straws are golden brown. Remove the baking sheets from the oven. Cool the straws on the baking sheets for 20 minutes. Remove the straws from the baking sheets and cool completely.

Pimento Cheese Straws

Makes about 5 dozen

2 1/2 cups freshly shredded cheddar cheese
1/2 cup unsalted butter, softened
1 tbs. half and half
1 tsp. salt
1 1/2 cups all purpose flour
4 oz. jar diced red pimentos, drained and patted dry
1 tsp. dry mustard
1/4 tsp. cayenne pepper

Do not use the shredded cheese available at the store for this recipe. The caking agent in them will produce tough cheese straws.

In a mixing bowl, add the cheddar cheese, butter, half and half and salt. Using a mixer on medium speed, beat until well blended. Slowly add the all purpose flour, red pimentos, dry mustard and cayenne pepper. Mix until blended and a dough forms. Form the dough into a flat disk. Wrap the dough in plastic wrap and chill for 15 minutes.

Remove the dough from the refrigerator. Lightly flour your work surface. Place the dough on your surface and roll the dough to 1/8" thickness. Using a 2" cutter, cut out the straws. Cut the straws as close together as possible to get as many as possible on the first rolling. Roll the dough scraps to cut out the remaining straws. Do not roll the dough scraps more than once.

Line your baking sheets with parchment paper. Preheat the oven to 350°. Place the straws on the baking sheets spacing them about 1" apart. Bake for 12-15 minutes or until the straws are golden brown. Remove the baking sheets from the oven. Cool the straws on the baking sheets for 20 minutes. Remove the straws from the baking sheets and cool completely.

Parmesan Cheddar Basil Straws

Makes about 12 dozen

2 1/2 cups freshly shredded cheddar cheese
1/2 cup unsalted butter, softened
3 tbs. half and half
1 tsp. salt
1 1/2 cups all purpose flour
1 1/2 cups freshly grated Parmigiano Reggiano cheese
3 tbs. finely chopped fresh basil

Do not use the shredded cheese available at the store for this recipe. The caking agent in them will produce tough cheese straws.

In a mixing bowl, add the cheddar cheese, butter, half and half and salt. Using a mixer on medium speed, beat until well blended. Slowly add the all purpose flour, Parmigiano Reggiano cheese and basil. Mix until blended and a dough forms. Form the dough into a flat disk. Wrap the dough in plastic wrap and chill for 15 minutes.

Remove the dough from the refrigerator. Lightly flour your work surface. Place the dough on your surface and roll the dough to 1/8" thickness. Using a 2" cutter, cut out the straws. Cut the straws as close together as possible to get as many as possible on the first rolling. Roll the dough scraps to cut out the remaining straws. Do not roll the dough scraps more than once.

Line your baking sheets with parchment paper. Preheat the oven to 350°. Place the straws on the baking sheets spacing them about 1" apart. Bake for 12-15 minutes or until the straws are golden brown. Remove the baking sheets from the oven. Cool the straws on the baking sheets for 20 minutes. Remove the straws from the baking sheets and cool completely.

6 SWEET & SAVORY FRITTERS & DOUGHNUTS

Fritters are famous in the south. We love fried foods of all kinds. Doughnuts are always a favorite anywhere you go. I love that fritters and doughnuts can be made quickly without the rising time.

Okra Shrimp Fritters

Makes about 30 fritters

2 cups sliced fresh okra
1/2 cup diced green bell pepper
1/2 cup diced onion
1 egg
1/2 cup all purpose flour
1/4 cup heavy cream
1 jalapeno pepper, finely chopped
3/4 tsp. salt
1/4 tsp. black pepper
4 oz. fresh shrimp, peeled, deveined and chopped
Peanut oil for frying

In a mixing bowl, add the okra, green bell pepper, onion, egg, all purpose flour, heavy cream, jalapeno pepper, salt and black pepper. Mix only until the batter is moistened and combined. Fold the shrimp into the batter.

In a deep fryer or deep sauce pan, add the peanut oil to a depth of 3". The temperature of the oil needs to be 350°. You will need to fry the fritters in batches. If you add too many fritters at one time to the oil, the temperature of the oil will drop and the fritters will be greasy.

Drop the fritters, by tablespoonfuls, into the hot oil. Fry for 1 minute on each side or until the fritters are golden brown. Remove the fritters from the hot oil and drain on paper towels. Serve hot. Delicious with salsa.

Eggplant Fritters

Makes 2 dozen

1 eggplant, peeled
2 green onions, chopped
1/3 cup minced green bell pepper
2 tsp. vegetable oil
2 bread slices, toasted and cubed
1/2 tsp. salt
1/4 tsp. garlic powder
1/4 tsp. black pepper
2 beaten eggs
Vegetable oil for frying

Chop the eggplant into bite size pieces. Add the eggplant to a dutch oven. Cover the eggplant with water and place the pan over medium heat. Bring the eggplant to a boil and cook for 10 minutes or until the eggplant is tender. Remove the pan from the heat and drain all the water from the eggplant. Cool completely before using.

In a small skillet over medium heat, add the green onions, green bell pepper and 2 teaspoons vegetable oil. Saute the vegetables for 5 minutes. In a food processor, add the bread. Pulse until the bread resembles fine crumbs. Remove the breadcrumbs and set aside.

Add the eggplant, salt, garlic powder and black pepper to the food processor. Process until pureed. Add the eggplant puree to a mixing bowl. Add the eggs, vegetables from the skillet and breadcrumbs to the bowl. Stir until combined. Cover the bowl and refrigerate until well chilled.

In a deep fryer or deep sauce pan, add the vegetable oil to a depth of 3". The temperature of the oil needs to be 350°. You will need to fry the fritters in batches. If you add too many fritters at one time to the oil, the temperature of the oil will drop and the fritters will be greasy.

Drop the fritters, by tablespoonfuls, into the hot oil. Fry for 1 minute on each side or until the fritters are golden brown. Remove the fritters from the hot oil and drain on paper towels. Serve hot.

Double Corn Fritters

Makes 30 fritters

12 ct. package taco shells, crushed
3/4 cup all purpose flour
2 tsp. baking powder
1/2 tsp. baking soda
2 eggs
1 cup whole milk
1 cup frozen whole kernel corn, thawed
2 cups vegetable oil

Add the crushed taco shells, all purpose flour, baking powder and baking soda to a mixing bowl. Stir until combined. Add the eggs, milk and corn to the dry ingredients. Mix only until the batter is moistened and combined. Let the batter sit for 10 minutes.

In a sauce pan over medium high heat, add the vegetable oil. Heat the oil to 375°. You will need to fry the fritters in batches. If you add too many fritters at one time to the oil, the temperature of the oil will drop and the fritters will be greasy.

Drop the fritters, by tablespoonfuls, into the hot oil. Fry for 2 minutes on each side or until the fritters are golden brown. Remove the fritters from the hot oil and drain on paper towels. Serve hot. Delicious with salsa.

Corn Fritters

Makes 4 servings

1/3 cup all purpose flour
1/8 tsp. salt
1/4 tsp. baking powder
1/4 tsp. paprika
1 egg, separated and at room temperature
3/4 cup frozen whole kernel corn, thawed
Vegetable oil for frying

In a mixing bowl, add the all purpose flour, salt, baking powder and paprika. Stir until combined. Add the egg yolk and corn. Mix until combined. In a small bowl, add the egg white. Using a whisk, beat until soft peaks form. Fold the egg white into the batter.

In a sauce pan over medium high heat, add vegetable oil to a depth of 3" in the pan. Heat the oil to 375°. You will need to fry the fritters in batches. If you add too many fritters at one time to the oil, the temperature of the oil will drop and the fritters will be greasy.

Drop the fritters, by tablespoonfuls, into the hot oil. Fry for 2 minutes on each side or until the fritters are golden brown. Remove the fritters from the hot oil and drain on paper towels. Serve hot.

Squash Fritters

Makes about 1 dozen

10 oz. pkg. frozen sliced yellow squash
2 beaten eggs
1/2 cup saltine cracker crumbs
1/4 tsp. salt
1/4 tsp. black pepper
1/2 cup finely chopped onion
Vegetable oil for frying

In a sauce pan over medium heat, add the squash. Cover the squash with water and cook for 10 minutes or until the squash are tender. Remove the pan from the heat and drain all the water from the squash. Mash the squash with a potato masher.

Add the eggs, saltine crumbs, salt, black pepper and onion to the squash. Stir until combined. In a deep fryer or deep sauce pan, add vegetable oil to a depth of 2". The temperature of the oil needs to be 375°. You will need to fry the fritters in batches. If you add too many fritters at one time to the oil, the temperature of the oil will drop and the fritters will be greasy.

Drop the fritters, by tablespoonfuls, into the hot oil. Fry for 1 minute on each side or until the fritters are golden brown. Remove the fritters from the hot oil and drain on paper towels. Serve hot.

Leek and Potato Fritters

Makes 18 fritters

1 large baking potato, peeled
2 tsp. salt
2 lbs. leeks, washed and thinly sliced
4 eggs, beaten
1/2 cup fine dry breadcrumbs
1/3 cup grated Parmesan cheese
3/4 tsp. black pepper
1/2 cup vegetable oil

Cut the potatoes into 2" cubes. Add the potatoes and 1 teaspoon salt to a sauce pan over medium heat. Add water to cover the potatoes and cook about 20 minutes or until the potatoes are tender. Remove the pan from the heat and drain all the water from the potatoes. Mash the potatoes with a potato masher until smooth.

Add the leeks to a large sauce pan over medium heat. Cover the leeks with water and bring to a boil. Boil the leeks for 3 minutes. Remove the pan from the heat and drain all the water from the leeks.

In a mixing bowl, add the potatoes, leeks, eggs, breadcrumbs, Parmesan cheese, 1 teaspoon salt and black pepper. Stir until well combined. Cover the bowl and chill the fritter dough for 1 hour.

When the dough is chilled, form the dough into 18 patties. You will need to cook the fritters in batches. In a skillet over medium heat, add 1/4 cup vegetable oil. When the oil is hot and begins to shimmer, add the patties.

Cook about 2 minutes per side or until both sides are golden brown. Remove the fritters from the skillet and drain on paper towels. Cook the remaining fritters and add the remaining vegetable oil as needed to cook the fritters.

Cheesy Broccoli Fritters With Cheese Sauce

Makes 1 1/2 dozen

1 egg
2 cups whole milk
2 cups plus 2 tbs. all purpose flour
2 tsp. baking powder
3/4 tsp. salt
1 1/2 cups chopped fresh broccoli
Vegetable oil for frying
3 oz. American cheese, cubed
2 oz. Swiss cheese, cubed
2 tbs. unsalted butter

In a blender, add the egg, 1 cup milk, 2 cups all purpose flour, baking powder, salt and broccoli. Process until the broccoli is finely chopped and the batter combined.

In a deep fryer or large sauce pan over medium high heat, add the vegetable oil. The oil needs to be about 3" deep in the pan. The temperature of the oil needs to be about 360°. You will need to cook the fritters in batches. Add a few fritters at a time to the oil. If you add too many fritters to the oil, the temperature will drop and the fritters will be partially cooked and greasy.

Drop the fritters, by tablespoonfuls, into the hot oil. Fry about 2-3 minutes on each side or until the fritters are golden brown. Remove the fritters from the oil and drain on paper towels. Serve the fritters hot.

Keep the fritters warm while you make a cheese dipping sauce for the fritters. In a blender, add the American cheese, Swiss cheese, butter, 2 tablespoons all purpose flour and 1 cup milk. Process until the sauce is smooth.

Add the cheese sauce to a sauce pan over low heat. Stir constantly and cook until the sauce thickens and bubbles. Remove the pan from the heat and serve with the hot fritters. You can make the cheese sauce before you cook the fritters. Keep the sauce warm.

Beet Fritters

Makes 8 fritters

2 cups peeled and shredded beets
1/4 cup finely chopped onion
1/2 cup soft breadcrumbs
1 egg, beaten
1/4 tsp. ground ginger
1/4 tsp. salt
1/8 tsp. black pepper
Vegetable oil for frying
Sour cream, optional

In a mixing bowl, add the beets, onion, breadcrumbs, egg, ginger, salt and black pepper. Stir until well combined.

In a large skillet over medium heat, add vegetable oil to a depth of 1/4" in the skillet. The oil should be hot and begin to shimmer when ready. Use 1/4 cup batter for each fritter. Drop the fritters into the hot oil. Fry for 4 minutes.

Using a spatula, flip the fritters over. Flatten the fritters with the spatula and fry about 4 minutes on the other side. Remove the fritters from the skillet and drain on paper towels. Serve with sour cream if desired.

Cheese Stuffed Potato Fritters

Makes 10 fritters

2 lbs. baking potatoes, peeled
8 oz. block mozzarella cheese
1/3 cup unsalted butter
5 egg yolks
2 tbs. finely chopped parsley
1 tsp. salt
1/2 tsp. black pepper
1/8 tsp. ground nutmeg
1 cup all purpose flour
2 eggs, beaten
1 1/2 cups Italian seasoned breadcrumbs
Vegetable oil for frying

Cut each potato into eighths. Cut the mozzarella cheese into 10 slices. In a large sauce pan over medium heat, add the potatoes. Cover the potatoes with water and cook about 10 minutes or until the potatoes are tender. Cook until the potatoes are fork tender and can be easily mashed. Remove the pan from the heat and drain all the water from the potatoes.

Add the potatoes and butter to a mixing bowl. Using a mixer on medium speed, beat until the potatoes are smooth. Cool the potatoes for 15 minutes. Stir in the egg yolks, parsley, salt, black pepper and nutmeg. Stir until well blended.

Form the potato batter into 10 round logs. Wrap a slice of mozzarella cheese around each log. Place the all purpose flour in a shallow dish. Add the beaten eggs to a shallow dish. Add the Italian breadcrumbs to a shallow dish. Dredge each fritter in the all purpose flour. Dip each fritter into the beaten egg and then roll each fritter in the breadcrumbs.

In a deep sauce pan over medium high heat, add the vegetable oil. The oil needs to be about 4" deep in the pan. The temperature of the oil needs to be about 360°. You will need to cook the fritters in batches. Add a few fritters at a time to the hot oil. If you add too many fritters to the oil, the temperature will drop and the fritters will be partially cooked and greasy.

Drop the fritters into the hot oil. Fry about 3 minutes on each side or until the fritters are golden brown. Remove the fritters from the oil and drain on paper towels. Serve the fritters hot.

Corn Jalapeno Fritters

Makes about 22 fritters

2 cups whole milk
1 cup quick cooking yellow grits
3 tbs. unsalted butter, softened
1 tsp. baking powder
1 tsp. salt
2 eggs, beaten
1/4 cup chopped red bell pepper
1/2 cup finely chopped green onions
2 tsp. minced jalapeno pepper, seeded
2 tbs. finely chopped basil
1 cup fresh corn, cut from the cob
1/4 cup all purpose flour
2 tbs. olive oil

In a small bowl, add 1/2 cup milk and the grits. Let the grits sit for 3 minutes. In a large sauce pan over medium heat, add 1 1/2 cups milk. Bring the milk to a boil. Stir constantly and slowly add the grits mixture. Whisk until smooth and combined. Cook for 2 minutes or until the grits are thickened.

Remove the pan from the heat. Stir in the butter, baking powder, salt, eggs, red bell pepper, green onions, jalapeno pepper, basil, corn and all purpose flour. Stir until well combined.

You will need to cook the fritters in batches. In a large skillet, add 1 tablespoon olive oil over medium heat. When the oil is hot, drop the fritters, by tablespoonfuls, into the hot oil. Cook the fritters until the tops are covered with bubbles and the edges cooked. Flip the fritters over and cook about 2 minutes on the other side. Remove the fritters from the skillet and drain on paper towels if desired.

Repeat with the remaining tablespoon olive oil until all the fritters are cooked.

Oyster Fritters

Makes about 20 fritters

1 cup pancake mix
1 tsp. baking powder
1 pint oysters, undrained
1 egg
2 tbs. finely chopped onion
Salt and black pepper to taste
1/2 cup vegetable oil

In a mixing bowl, add the pancake mix, baking powder, oysters with liquid, egg and onion. Stir only until the batter is combined. Season the batter to taste with salt and black pepper. I use 1/4 teaspoon salt and 1/4 teaspoon black pepper. You can omit the salt and black pepper if desired. You may prefer to season the fritters after cooking.

In a deep sauce pan over medium high heat, add the vegetable oil. The oil needs to be about 3" deep in the pan. The temperature of the oil needs to be about 360°. You will need to cook the fritters in batches. If you add too many fritters to the oil, the temperature will drop and the fritters will be partially cooked and greasy.

Drop the fritters, by tablespoonfuls, into the hot oil. Fry about 2 minutes on each side or until the fritters are golden brown. Remove the fritters from the oil and drain on paper towels. Serve the fritters hot.

Clam Fritters

Makes 6 servings

1 pint shucked clams, drained
1 onion, finely chopped
2 eggs, beaten
2 tbs. all purpose flour
1/2 to 1 tsp. salt
1/8 tsp. black pepper
2 tbs. whole milk, optional
Vegetable oil for frying

Finely mince the clams with a knife or a food processor. In a mixing bowl, add the clams, onion, eggs, all purpose flour, 1/2 teaspoon salt and black pepper. Stir only until combined. If the batter is too dry and will not hold together, add the milk.

Add the milk, in one teaspoon increments, until the batter will hold together. Add an additional 1/2 teaspoon salt if you like to the batter. Clams will vary in saltiness so you need to err on the side of the caution or the fritters will be too salty. The fritters will be more clam and onion than batter. This is a normal batter for these fritters.

In a deep fryer or large sauce pan over medium high heat, add the vegetable oil. The oil needs to be about 3" deep in the pan. The temperature of the oil needs to be about 360°. You will need to cook the fritters in batches. If you add too many fritters to the oil, the temperature will drop and the fritters will be partially cooked and greasy.

Drop the fritters, by tablespoonfuls, into the hot oil. Fry about 1-2 minutes per side or until the fritters are done and golden brown. Remove the fritters from the oil and drain on paper towels. Serve the fritters hot.

Shrimp Fritters

Makes 5 dozen

1 1/2 lbs. fresh shrimp
1 cup all purpose flour
1 1/2 tsp. baking powder
1 tbs. Creole seasoning
1/2 tsp. garlic powder
2 eggs, separated
3/4 cup whole milk
1 tbs. vegetable oil
2 cups cooked rice
1 onion, chopped
1/2 cup chopped green onions
Vegetable oil for frying

Peel and devein the shrimp. Finely chop the shrimp. In a mixing bowl, add the all purpose flour, baking powder, Creole seasoning and garlic powder. Stir until well blended. In a separate bowl, add the egg yolks, milk and 1 tablespoon vegetable oil. Whisk until well combined and add to the dry ingredients. Stir only until combined.

Stir the rice, shrimp, onion and green onions into the batter. In a mixing bowl, add the egg whites. Using a mixer on medium speed, beat until stiff peaks form. Gently fold the egg whites into the batter.

In a deep fryer or large sauce pan over medium high heat, add the vegetable oil. The oil needs to be about 3" deep in the pan. The temperature of the oil needs to be about 375°. You will need to cook the fritters in batches. If you add too many fritters to the oil, the temperature will drop and the fritters will be partially cooked and greasy.

Drop the fritters, by tablespoonfuls, into the hot oil. Fry about 3 minutes or until the fritters are done and golden brown. Remove the fritters from the oil and drain on paper towels. Serve the fritters hot.

Crab Fritters

Makes 3 dozen

1 lb. fresh crabmeat, flaked
1/4 cup mayonnaise
1 egg, beaten
2 tbs. lemon juice
2 tbs. finely chopped onion
2 tbs. finely chopped red bell pepper
2 tbs. finely chopped celery
1/2 tsp. paprika
1/2 tsp. dry mustard
1/2 tsp. minced garlic
1/4 tsp. salt
1/3 cup fine dry breadcrumbs
1 cup finely crushed saltine crackers
Vegetable oil for frying

In a mixing bowl, add the crabmeat, mayonnaise, egg, lemon juice, onion, red bell pepper, celery, paprika, dry mustard, garlic and salt. Stir until well combined. Add the breadcrumbs and mix until the batter holds together. Add another tablespoon or two of breadcrumbs if the batter is too loose.

Use 1 tablespoon crab mixture and form the fritters into balls. Place the saltine crackers in a shallow dish. Roll the fritters in the crackers.

In a deep fryer or large sauce pan over medium high heat, add the vegetable oil. The oil needs to be about 3" deep in the pan. The temperature of the oil needs to be about 375°. You will need to fry the fritters in batches. If you add too many fritters to the oil, the temperature will drop and the fritters will be partially cooked and greasy.

Add the fritters to the hot oil. Fry about 2 minutes or until the fritters are done and golden brown. Remove the fritters from the oil and drain on paper towels. Serve the fritters hot.

Ham Pineapple Fritters

Makes 8 servings

2/3 cup all purpose flour
1 tsp. baking powder
2 eggs, beaten
1/3 cup whole milk
2 cups ground cooked ham
8 oz. can crushed pineapple, drained
Vegetable oil

In a mixing bowl, add the all purpose flour, baking powder, eggs and milk. Whisk until well combined. Add the ham and pineapple to the bowl. Whisk until well combined.

In a deep fryer or large sauce pan over medium high heat, add the vegetable oil. The oil needs to be about 3" deep in the pan. The temperature of the oil needs to be about 360°. You will need to fry the fritters in batches. If you add too many fritters to the oil, the temperature will drop and the fritters will be partially cooked and greasy.

Drop the batter, by 1/4 cupfuls, into the hot oil. Fry about 3-4 minutes on each side or until the fritters are golden brown. Remove the fritters from the oil and drain on paper towels. Serve the fritters hot.

Ham Fritters with Cream Sauce

Makes 2 dozen

1 1/4 cups all purpose flour
2 tsp. salt
1 tsp. baking powder
2 eggs, beaten
2 1/4 cups whole milk
1 tbs. vegetable oil
1 cup chopped cooked ham
Vegetable oil for frying
1/4 cup vegetable shortening
1 cup shredded cheddar cheese

In a mixing bowl, add 1 cup all purpose flour, 1 teaspoon salt, baking powder, eggs, 1/4 cup milk and 1 tablespoon vegetable oil. Stir until well combined. Stir in the ham and mix only until blended.

In a deep fryer or large sauce pan over medium high heat, add the vegetable oil. The oil needs to be about 3" deep in the pan. The temperature of the oil needs to be about 360°. You will need to fry the fritters in batches. If you add too many fritters to the oil, the temperature will drop and the fritters will be partially cooked and greasy.

Drop the fritters, by tablespoonfuls, into the hot oil. Fry about 2-3 minutes on each side or until the fritters are golden brown. Remove the fritters from the oil and drain on paper towels. Keep the fritters hot while you make the sauce.

In a sauce pan over medium low heat, add 1/4 cup vegetable shortening. When the shortening melts, stir in 1/4 cup all purpose flour. Stir constantly and cook for 1 minute. Continue stirring and slowly add 2 cups milk and 1 teaspoon salt. Stir constantly and cook until the sauce thickens and bubbles. Stir in the cheddar cheese. Remove the pan from the heat. Stir until the cheese melts and the sauce is smooth. Serve the sauce with the hot fritters.

Yellow Squash Fritters

Makes 6 servings

2 cups finely chopped yellow squash
1 cup finely chopped onion
1 egg, beaten
1 tsp. salt
1 tsp. black pepper
1/2 cup plus 1 tbs. all purpose flour
Vegetable oil for frying

Add the yellow squash, onion, egg, salt, black pepper and all purpose flour to a mixing bowl. Stir until well combined.

In a deep fryer or large sauce pan over medium high heat, add the vegetable oil. The oil needs to be about 3" deep in the pan. The temperature of the oil needs to be about 360°. You will need to fry the fritters in batches. If you add too many fritters to the oil, the temperature will drop and the fritters will be partially cooked and greasy.

Drop the fritters, by tablespoonfuls, into the hot oil. Fry about 2 minutes on each side or until the fritters are golden brown. Remove the fritters from the oil and drain on paper towels. Serve the fritters hot.

Zucchini Fritters

Makes 1 dozen

3 zucchini, peeled and grated
1 tbs. minced fresh parsley
1 tsp. minced fresh chives
1 cup pancake mix
1 egg, beaten
1/4 tsp. salt
1/4 tsp. black pepper
1/2 cup vegetable oil

In a mixing bowl, add the zucchini, parsley, chives, pancake mix, egg, salt and black pepper. Whisk until well combined.

In a deep sauce pan over medium heat, add the vegetable oil. The oil needs to be about 3" deep in the pan. The temperature of the oil needs to be about 360°. You will need to fry the fritters in batches. If you add too many fritters to the oil, the temperature will drop and the fritters will be partially cooked and greasy.

Drop the fritters, by tablespoonfuls, into the hot oil. Fry about 2 minutes on each side or until the fritters are golden brown. Remove the fritters from the oil and drain on paper towels. Serve the fritters hot.

Cheesy Zucchini Fritters

Makes 2 dozen

1 1/2 cups all purpose flour
2 tsp. baking powder
1/2 tsp. salt
1 cup chopped zucchini
1/2 cup shredded cheddar cheese
1/4 cup finely chopped onion
1 beaten egg
1 cup whole milk
Vegetable oil for frying

In a mixing bowl, add the all purpose flour, baking powder and salt. Stir until blended. Add the zucchini, cheddar cheese and onion. Stir until combined. Add the egg and whole milk. Mix only until the batter is combined. Do not over mix the batter or the fritters will be tough.

In a deep sauce pan over medium heat, add the vegetable oil. The oil needs to be about 2" deep in the pan. The temperature of the oil needs to be about 360°. You will need to cook the fritters in batches. If you add too many fritters to the oil, the temperature will drop and the fritters will be partially cooked and greasy.

Drop the fritters, by tablespoonfuls, into the hot oil. Fry about 2-3 minutes on each side or until the fritters are golden brown. Remove the fritters from the oil and drain on paper towels. Serve the fritters hot.

Okra Fritters

Makes 6 servings

1 cup thinly sliced okra
1/2 cup chopped onion
1/2 cup chopped tomato
1/4 cup all purpose flour
1/4 cup plain white or yellow cornmeal
1/2 tsp. salt
1/2 tsp. curry powder
1/4 tsp. black pepper
1 egg, beaten
Vegetable oil for frying

In a mixing bowl, add the okra, onion, tomato, all purpose flour, cornmeal, salt, curry powder, black pepper and egg. Whisk until well combined.

In a deep fryer or large sauce pan over medium high heat, add the vegetable oil. The oil needs to be about 3" deep in the pan. The temperature of the oil needs to be about 360°. You will need to cook the fritters in batches. If you add too many fritters to the oil, the temperature will drop and the fritters will be partially cooked and greasy.

Drop the fritters, by tablespoonfuls, into the hot oil. Fry about 2-3 minutes on each side or until the fritters are golden brown. Remove the fritters from the oil and drain on paper towels. Serve the fritters hot.

Rice Fritters

Makes 8-10 fritters

2 cups cold cooked rice
2 eggs, beaten
1/3 cups seedless raisins
1/4 cup finely chopped almonds
2 tbs. all purpose flour
1 tbs. grated lemon zest
1/4 cup melted unsalted butter

In a mixing bowl, add the rice, eggs, raisins and almonds. Whisk until well combined. Add the all purpose flour and lemon zest. Mix until well combined.

You will need to fry the fritters in batches. In a large skillet over medium heat, add the butter. When the butter is hot, drop the fritters by 1/4 cupfuls into the hot skillet. Cook for 2-3 minutes or until the bottom of the fritters are golden brown. Flip the fritters over and cook about 2 minutes on the other side or until both sides are golden brown. Remove the fritters from the skillet and serve hot.

Golden Sweet Potato Fritters

Makes 8 servings

1 1/3 cups beer
6 medium sweet potatoes, washed
3 eggs, separated
1 tbs. vegetable oil
1 tsp. salt
2 2/3 cups all purpose flour
Vegetable oil for frying

Open the beer and let the beer sit at room temperature for several hours or until the beer is flat. In a sauce pan over medium heat, add the sweet potatoes. Cover the sweet potatoes with water. Cook about 30 minutes or until the sweet potatoes are fork tender. Remove the pan from the heat. Drain all the water from the sweet potatoes. Let the sweet potatoes cool completely. When the sweet potatoes are cool, peel the potatoes and cut them into 1/4" slices.

In a separate mixing bowl, add the beer, 3 egg yolks, 1 tablespoon vegetable oil and salt. Using a mixer on medium speed, beat the batter until foamy. Turn the mixer to low and slowly add the all purpose flour. Mix only until the flour is blended into the batter. The batter will be thick. Let the batter sit at room temperature for 30 minutes.

In a mixing bowl, add 3 egg whites. Using a mixer on medium speed, beat the egg whites until stiff peaks form. Fold the egg whites into the batter.

In a deep fryer or large sauce pan over medium high heat, add the vegetable oil. The oil needs to be about 3" deep in the pan. The temperature of the oil needs to be about 360°.

You will need to cook the fritters in batches. If you add too many fritters to the oil, the temperature will drop and the fritters will be partially cooked and greasy. Dip each sweet potato slice into the batter. Immediately drop the fritters into the hot oil. Fry about 2 minutes on each side or until the fritters are golden brown. Remove the fritters from the oil and drain on paper towels. Serve with a sweet or savory sauce, powdered sugar or salt.

Bacon Sweet Potato Fritters

Makes 3 dozen

1 cup plus 2 tbs. all purpose flour
1 tsp. baking powder
2/3 cup whole milk
2 eggs, beaten
2 tbs. melted unsalted butter
4 slices cooked bacon, crumbled
2 cups shredded uncooked sweet potatoes
Vegetable oil for frying

In a mixing bowl, add the all purpose flour and baking powder. Stir until blended. Add the milk, eggs and butter to the bowl. Whisk until well blended. Stir in the bacon and sweet potatoes. Mix only until combined.

In a deep fryer or large sauce pan over medium high heat, add the vegetable oil. The oil needs to be about 3" deep in the pan. The temperature of the oil needs to be about 360°.

You will need to cook the fritters in batches. If you add too many fritters to the oil, the temperature will drop and the fritters will be partially cooked and greasy. Drop the batter, by tablespoonfuls, into the hot oil. Fry about 1-2 minutes on each side or until the fritters are golden brown. Remove the fritters from the oil and drain on paper towels. Serve with maple syrup if desired.

Sweet Potato Fritters with Goat Cheese

Makes 6 servings

2 tbs. unsalted butter
1 apple, sliced
3 tbs. light brown sugar
3 tbs. apple juice
3 sweet potatoes, peeled and grated
1/2 cup grated onion
1 egg
3 tbs. matzo meal
1/2 tsp. salt
1/2 tsp. black pepper
1/2 cup peanut oil
3 oz. goat cheese, thinly sliced

In a skillet over medium heat, add the butter, apple and brown sugar. Stir constantly and cook until the apple is tender. Stir in the apple juice and cook only until the juice is warm. Remove the skillet from the heat.

In a mixing bowl, add the sweet potatoes, onion, egg, matzo meal, salt and black pepper. Stir until well combined. Stir in the apple mixture from the skillet.

In a deep fryer or large sauce pan over medium high heat, add the peanut oil. The temperature of the oil needs to be about 360°.

You will need to cook the fritters in batches. If you add too many fritters to the oil, the temperature will drop and the fritters will be partially cooked and greasy. Drop the batter, by tablespoonfuls, into the hot oil. Fry about 2 minutes on each side or until the fritters are crisp and golden brown. Remove the fritters from the oil and drain on paper towels.

Preheat the oven to 350°. Place the fritters in a shallow baking dish. Place the goat cheese slices over the fritters. Bake for 5 minutes or until the goat cheese softens. Remove the dish from the oven and serve. Serve with cooked apples and syrup if desired.

Beer Battered Hushpuppies

Makes about 3 dozen

1 1/2 cups self rising yellow cornmeal
1/4 cup self rising flour
1 cup finely chopped onion
1 cup finely chopped green bell pepper
1 tomato, finely chopped
1 beaten egg
1 1/2 tsp. Worcestershire sauce
1/8 tsp. Tabasco sauce
1/2 cup beer
Vegetable oil for frying

In a mixing bowl, add the cornmeal and self rising flour. Stir until combined. Add the onion, green bell pepper, tomato, egg, Worcestershire sauce, Tabasco sauce and beer. Mix only until the batter is moistened and combined.

In a deep fryer or deep sauce pan, add vegetable oil to a depth of 2" in the pan. The temperature of the oil needs to be 375°. You will need to fry the hushpuppies in batches. If you add too many hushpuppies at one time to the oil, the temperature of the oil will drop and the hushpuppies will be greasy.

Drop the hushpuppies, by tablespoonfuls, into the hot oil. Fry for 2 minutes on each side or until the hushpuppies are golden brown. Remove the hushpuppies from the hot oil and drain on paper towels. Serve hot.

Southern Hushpuppies

Makes 8 servings

1 1/2 cups self rising white cornmeal
3/4 cup self rising flour
3/4 cup diced onion
1 1/2 tbs. granulated sugar
1 beaten egg
1 1/4 cups buttermilk
Vegetable oil for frying

In a mixing bowl, add the cornmeal, self rising flour, onion and granulated sugar. Stir until combined. Add the egg and buttermilk to the bowl. Stir until the batter is moistened and combined.

In a deep fryer or deep sauce pan, add vegetable oil to a depth of 3" in the pan. The temperature of the oil needs to be 375°. You will need to fry the hushpuppies in batches. If you add too many hushpuppies at one time to the oil, the temperature of the oil will drop and the hushpuppies will be greasy.

Drop the hushpuppies, by tablespoonfuls, into the hot oil. Fry for 2 minutes on each side or until the hushpuppies are golden brown. Remove the hushpuppies from the hot oil and drain on paper towels. Serve hot.

Andouille Hushpuppies

Makes 8 servings

1 1/2 cups white self rising cornmeal
1 cup diced andouille sausage
3/4 cup self rising flour
3/4 cup chopped onion
1 beaten egg
2/3 cup lager beer
1/3 cup buttermilk
Vegetable oil for frying

In a mixing bowl, add the cornmeal, andouille sausage, self rising flour and onion. Stir until combined. Add the egg, beer and buttermilk. Mix only until the batter is moistened and combined. Let the batter sit for 10 minutes.

In a deep fryer or deep sauce pan, add vegetable oil to a depth of 3" in the pan. The temperature of the oil needs to be 375°. You will need to fry the hushpuppies in batches. If you add too many hushpuppies at one time to the oil, the temperature of the oil will drop and the hushpuppies will be greasy.

Drop the hushpuppies, by tablespoonfuls, into the hot oil. Fry for 2 minutes on each side or until the hushpuppies are golden brown. Remove the hushpuppies from the hot oil and drain on paper towels. Serve hot.

Squash Puppies With Dill Sauce

Makes 6 servings

1/2 cup sour cream
1/2 cup mayonnaise
2 tbs. minced fresh dill
2 tsp. grated lemon zest
2 tbs. fresh lemon juice
2 medium zucchini, shredded
1/2 cup chopped onion
1/2 cup plain yellow cornmeal
1/4 cup cornstarch
1/4 cup Bisquick
1/2 tsp. salt
1/2 tsp. lemon pepper seasoning
1 beaten egg
Vegetable oil for frying

In a small bowl, add the sour cream, mayonnaise, dill, lemon zest and lemon juice. Stir until combined. Cover the bowl and refrigerate for 1 hour before serving.

Drain the squash and onion of any liquid. Pat the vegetables dry with paper towels if needed. In a mixing bowl, add the zucchini, onion, cornmeal, cornstarch, Bisquick, salt, lemon pepper seasoning and egg. Whisk until the batter is moistened and combined.

In a deep fryer or deep sauce pan, add vegetable oil to a depth of 3" in the pan. The temperature of the oil needs to be 375°. You will need to fry the hushpuppies in batches. If you add too many hushpuppies at one time to the oil, the temperature of the oil will drop and the hushpuppies will be greasy.

Drop the hushpuppies, by tablespoonfuls, into the hot oil. Fry for 2 minutes on each side or until the hushpuppies are golden brown. Remove the hushpuppies from the hot oil and drain on paper towels. Serve hot with the dill sauce.

Bacon & Caramelized Onion Hushpuppies

Makes 8 servings

5 bacon slices, cooked and crumbled
1 1/2 cups diced onion
1 1/2 cups self rising white cornmeal
3/4 cup self rising flour
1 1/2 tbs. granulated sugar
1 beaten egg
1 1/4 cups buttermilk
Vegetable oil for frying

In a skillet over medium heat, add the bacon. Cook about 8 minutes or until the bacon is crispy. Remove the bacon from the skillet and drain on paper towels. Crumble the bacon.

Add the onions to the skillet. Reduce the heat to low. Saute the onions for 12 minutes or until the onions are golden brown. Remove the skillet from the heat.

In a mixing bowl, add the cornmeal, self rising flour, bacon, onions and granulated sugar. Stir until combined. Add the egg and buttermilk to the bowl. Stir until the batter is moistened and combined.

In a deep fryer or deep sauce pan, add vegetable oil to a depth of 3" in the pan. The temperature of the oil needs to be 375°. You will need to fry the hushpuppies in batches. If you add too many hushpuppies at one time to the oil, the temperature of the oil will drop and the hushpuppies will be greasy.

Drop the hushpuppies, by tablespoonfuls, into the hot oil. Fry for 2 minutes on each side or until the hushpuppies are golden brown. Remove the hushpuppies from the hot oil and drain on paper towels. Serve hot.

Jalapeno Pineapple Hushpuppies

Makes 8 servings

1 1/2 cups self rising white cornmeal
3/4 cup self rising flour
3/4 cup diced onion
1 1/2 tbs. granulated sugar
1/2 cup canned pineapple tidbits, drained
2 tbs. diced jalapeno pepper
1 beaten egg
1 1/4 cups buttermilk
Vegetable oil for frying

In a mixing bowl, add the cornmeal, self rising flour, onion, granulated sugar, pineapple and jalapeno pepper. Stir until combined. Add the egg and buttermilk to the bowl. Stir until the batter is moistened and combined.

In a deep fryer or deep sauce pan, add vegetable oil to a depth of 3" in the pan. The temperature of the oil needs to be 375°. You will need to fry the hushpuppies in batches. If you add too many hushpuppies at one time to the oil, the temperature of the oil will drop and the hushpuppies will be greasy.

Drop the hushpuppies, by tablespoonfuls, into the hot oil. Fry for 2 minutes on each side or until the hushpuppies are golden brown. Remove the hushpuppies from the hot oil and drain on paper towels. Serve hot.

Shrimp & Corn Hushpuppies

Makes 8 servings

1 1/2 cups self rising white cornmeal
3/4 cup self rising flour
3/4 cup diced onion
1 1/2 tbs. granulated sugar
1 1/2 cups chopped cooked shrimp
8 oz. can cream style corn
1 beaten egg
3/4 cup buttermilk
Vegetable oil for frying

In a mixing bowl, add the cornmeal, self rising flour, onion, granulated sugar, shrimp and corn. Stir until combined. Add the egg and buttermilk to the bowl. Stir until the batter is moistened and combined.

In a deep fryer or deep sauce pan, add vegetable oil to a depth of 3" in the pan. The temperature of the oil needs to be 375°. You will need to fry the hushpuppies in batches. If you add too many hushpuppies at one time to the oil, the temperature of the oil will drop and the hushpuppies will be greasy.

Drop the hushpuppies, by tablespoonfuls, into the hot oil. Fry for 2 minutes on each side or until the hushpuppies are golden brown. Remove the hushpuppies from the hot oil and drain on paper towels. Serve hot.

Mexican Hushpuppies

Makes about 3 dozen

2 cups self rising cornmeal
1 cup self rising flour
3 tbs. granulated sugar
3 beaten eggs
1/2 cup whole milk
14 oz. can cream style corn
1 1/2 cups shredded sharp cheddar cheese
2 cups chopped onion
2 jalapeno peppers, seeded and chopped
2 tsp. chili powder
Vegetable oil for frying

In a mixing bowl, add the cornmeal, self rising flour and granulated sugar. Stir until combined. Add the eggs, milk, corn, cheddar cheese, onion, jalapeno peppers and chili powder. Mix only until the batter is moistened and combined.

In a deep fryer or deep sauce pan, add vegetable oil to a depth of 2" in the pan. The temperature of the oil needs to be 375°. You will need to fry the hushpuppies in batches. If you add too many hushpuppies at one time to the oil, the temperature of the oil will drop and the hushpuppies will be greasy.

Drop the hushpuppies, by tablespoonfuls, into the hot oil. Fry for 2 minutes on each side or until the hushpuppies are golden brown. Remove the hushpuppies from the hot oil and drain on paper towels. Serve hot.

Hopping John Hushpuppies

Makes 2 dozen

15 oz. can field peas, drained
1 cup yellow self rising cornmeal
3/4 cup buttermilk
1/2 cup all purpose flour
1/2 cup chopped country ham
1/2 cup cooked rice
1 cup sliced green onions
1 jalapeno pepper, seeded and diced
2 garlic cloves, minced
1 tsp. baking powder
1 tsp. black pepper
2 eggs, beaten
Peanut oil for frying

Add the peas, cornmeal, buttermilk, all purpose flour, ham, rice, green onions, jalapeno pepper, garlic, baking powder, black pepper and eggs to a mixing bowl. Stir until the batter is moistened and combined.

In a deep fryer or deep sauce pan, add the peanut oil to a depth of 3" in the pan. The temperature of the oil needs to be 350°. You will need to fry the hushpuppies in batches. If you add too many hushpuppies at one time to the oil, the temperature of the oil will drop and the hushpuppies will be greasy.

Drop the hushpuppies, by tablespoonfuls, into the hot oil. Fry for 2 minutes on each side or until the hushpuppies are golden brown. Remove the hushpuppies from the hot oil and drain on paper towels. Serve hot.

Cajun Hushpuppies

Makes 6 servings

2 1/4 cups self rising white cornmeal
1/2 cup chopped green bell pepper
1/2 cup chopped onion
1 tsp. salt
1/2 tsp. black pepper
1/4 tsp. cayenne pepper
1 cup buttermilk
2 eggs
Vegetable oil for frying

In a mixing bowl, add the cornmeal, green bell pepper, onion, salt, black pepper and cayenne pepper. Stir until combined. Add the buttermilk and eggs to the bowl. Mix until well combined. Let the batter sit at room temperature for 30 minutes.

In a deep fryer or deep sauce pan, add the peanut oil to a depth of 2" in the pan. The temperature of the oil needs to be 375°. You will need to fry the hushpuppies in batches. If you add too many hushpuppies at one time to the oil, the temperature of the oil will drop and the hushpuppies will be greasy.

Drop the hushpuppies, by teaspoonfuls, into the hot oil. Fry for 2 minutes on each side or until the hushpuppies are golden brown. Remove the hushpuppies from the hot oil and drain on paper towels. Serve hot.

Sliced Apple Fritters

Makes 6 servings

1 cup sour cream
1/2 cup whole milk
1 egg
2 tsp. granulated sugar
1 tsp. ground cinnamon
1 cup self rising flour
1/4 cup vegetable oil
3 apples, cored, peeled and sliced 1/8" thick
Powdered sugar to taste

In a mixing bowl, add the sour cream, milk, egg, granulated sugar, cinnamon and self rising flour. Whisk until the batter is smooth and combined.

In a large skillet over medium high heat, add the vegetable oil. You will need to fry the fritters in batches. If you add too many fritters at one time to the oil, the temperature of the oil will drop and the fritters will be greasy. Dip the apple slices in the batter allowing the excess batter to drip off back into the bowl.

When the oil is hot, add the fritters. Fry about 3 minutes on each side or until the fritters are golden brown. Remove the fritters from the hot oil and drain on paper towels. Sprinkle powdered sugar to taste over the fritters and serve.

Apple Fritters

Makes about 3 dozen

2 1/2 cups all purpose flour
1/2 cup instant nonfat dry milk powder
1/3 cup granulated sugar
2 tsp. baking powder
1 tsp. salt
2 eggs
1 cup water
2 cups peeled apples, chopped
Vegetable oil for frying
Powdered sugar to taste

In a mixing bowl, add the all purpose flour, dry milk powder, granulated sugar, baking powder and salt. Whisk until combined. In a small bowl, add the eggs and water. Whisk until combined and add to the dry ingredients. Mix only until the batter is moistened and combined. Add the apples and stir until combined.

In a deep fryer or deep sauce pan, add vegetable oil to a depth of 2". The temperature of the oil needs to be 375°. You will need to fry the fritters in batches. If you add too many fritters at one time to the oil, the temperature of the oil will drop and the fritters will be greasy.

Drop the fritters, by teaspoonfuls, into the hot oil. Fry for 1 minute on each side or until the fritters are golden brown. Remove the fritters from the hot oil and drain on paper towels. Serve hot.

Banana Fritters

Makes about 5 dozen

1 3/4 cups Bisquick
1/2 cup whole milk
2 eggs
4 bananas, peeled and sliced
Vegetable oil for frying
Powdered sugar to taste

In a mixing bowl, add the Bisquick, milk and eggs. Using a mixer on medium speed, beat the batter until well blended. Add the banana slices and gently stir to coat the slices.

In a deep fryer or large sauce pan over medium high heat, add the vegetable oil. The oil needs to be about 3" deep in the pan. The temperature of the oil needs to be about 360°. You will need to cook the fritters in batches. If you add too many fritters to the oil, the temperature will drop and the fritters will be partially cooked and greasy.

Remove each banana slice from the batter and let the excess batter drop off back into the bowl. Drop the fritters into the hot oil. Fry until the fritters are golden brown. Remove the fritters from the oil and drain on paper towels. Sprinkle the powdered sugar to taste over the hot fritters. Serve the fritters hot.

Apple Fritters with Lemon Sauce

Makes 20 fritters

1 1/2 cups plus 2 tbs. all purpose flour
1/8 tsp. salt
1 1/4 tsp. baking powder
2 eggs
3 tbs. melted unsalted butter
3 apples, peeled and diced
Vegetable oil for frying
Powdered sugar to taste
1 cup granulated sugar
3 tbs. lemon juice

In a food processor, add 1 1/2 cups all purpose flour, salt, baking powder, 1 egg and 2 tablespoons melted butter. Process until combined. Spoon the mixture into a mixing bowl. Add the apples and stir until combined. Shape the fritters into 1 1/2" balls.

In a deep fryer or large sauce pan over medium high heat, add the vegetable oil. The oil needs to be about 3" deep in the pan. The temperature of the oil needs to be about 350°. You will need to cook the fritters in batches. If you add too many fritters to the oil, the temperature will drop and the fritters will be partially cooked and greasy.

Add the fritters to the oil and fry about 2-3 minutes or until the fritters are golden brown. Remove the fritters from the oil and drain on paper towels. Sprinkle the powdered sugar to taste over the hot fritters. Keep the fritters hot while you make the sauce.

In a sauce pan over medium heat, add the granulated sugar, 2 tablespoons all purpose flour, 1 egg, 1 tablespoon butter and the lemon juice. Stir constantly and cook until the sauce thickens and bubbles. Remove the pan from the heat and serve the sauce with the hot fritters.

Puffy Orange Fritters

Makes 3 dozen

2 eggs
1/2 cup granulated sugar
2 tbs. melted unsalted butter
1/2 cup orange juice
1 tbs. grated orange zest
2 cups all purpose flour
2 tsp. baking powder
1/2 tsp. salt
Vegetable oil for frying
Powdered sugar to taste

In a mixing bowl, add the eggs and granulated sugar. Whisk until the eggs and granulated sugar are well blended. Add the melted butter, orange juice and orange zest. Whisk until combined.

Add the all purpose flour, baking powder and salt. Whisk only until the batter is combined. Do not over mix the batter or the fritters will be tough. Let the batter sit at room temperature for 15 minutes.

In a deep fryer or large sauce pan over medium high heat, add the vegetable oil. The oil needs to be about 3" deep in the pan. The temperature of the oil needs to be about 360°. You will need to cook the fritters in batches. If you add too many fritters to the oil, the temperature will drop and the fritters will be partially cooked and greasy.

Drop the fritters, by tablespoonfuls, into the hot oil. Fry about 2-3 minutes on each side or until the fritters are golden brown. Remove the fritters from the oil and drain on paper towels. Sprinkle powdered sugar to taste over the hot fritters before serving.

Southern Pear Fritters

Makes 2 dozen

4 large pears, peeled and cored
2 tbs. powdered sugar
1 tbs. lemon juice
1 cup all purpose flour
1 tsp. baking powder
1/4 tsp. salt
1 egg, beaten
2/3 cup whole milk
Vegetable oil for frying
Additional powdered sugar, optional

Slice the pears a little more than 1/4" thick. In a small bowl, stir together 2 tablespoons powdered sugar and the lemon juice. Dip each pear slice in the lemon juice mixture.

In a mixing bowl, add the all purpose flour, baking powder and salt. Whisk until combined. Add the egg and milk. Whisk until the batter is combined and smooth.

In a deep fryer or large sauce pan over medium high heat, add the vegetable oil. The oil needs to be about 3" deep in the pan. The temperature of the oil needs to be about 360°. You will need to cook the fritters in batches. If you add too many fritters to the oil, the temperature will drop and the fritters will be partially cooked and greasy.

Dip each pear slice in the batter allowing the excess batter to drip off back into the bowl. Drop the fritters into the hot oil. Fry about 2 minutes per side or until the fritters are golden brown. Remove the fritters from the oil and drain on paper towels. Sprinkle powdered sugar to taste over the hot fritters before serving if desired.

Matzoh Honey Fritters

Makes 16 fritters

10 oz. pkg. plain matzoh
2 1/4 cups water
5 beaten eggs
1/2 cup chopped dried plums
1/2 cup granulated sugar
1 tsp. vanilla extract
1/2 tsp. ground cinnamon
Vegetable oil for frying
1/2 cup honey
1 cup toasted chopped walnuts

Break the matzoh into pieces and place in a large mixing bowl. Add the water to the bowl. Let the matzoh stand at least 5 minutes or until the matzoh soften. Add the eggs, plums, granulated sugar, vanilla extract and cinnamon. Whisk until well combined.

In a deep fryer or deep sauce pan, add vegetable oil to a depth of 2". The temperature of the oil needs to be 375°. You will need to fry the fritters in batches. If you add too many fritters at one time to the oil, the temperature of the oil will drop and the fritters will be greasy.

Drop the fritters, by 1/4 cupfuls, into the hot oil. Fry for 1 minute on each side or until the fritters are golden brown. Remove the fritters from the hot oil and drain on paper towels. Place the fritters on a serving platter. Drizzle the honey over the fritters. Sprinkle the walnuts over the top and serve.

Mama's Beignets

Makes 3 dozen

3 tbs. unsalted butter, softened
1 cup granulated sugar
2 eggs
1 tsp. vanilla extract
3 cups all purpose flour
4 tsp. baking powder
1/2 tsp. salt
1/4 tsp. ground nutmeg
2/3 cup half and half
Vegetable oil for frying
Powdered sugar to taste

In a mixing bowl, add the butter and granulated sugar. Using a mixer on medium speed, beat until smooth and combined. Add the eggs and vanilla extract to the bowl. Mix until smooth and combined.

Add the all purpose flour, baking powder, salt, nutmeg and half and half to the bowl. Mix until the dough is well combined. Cover the bowl and refrigerate for 2 hours.

Lightly flour your work surface. Place the dough on your surface. Divide the dough in half. Work with one piece of dough at a time. Roll each piece of dough into a square about 1/4" thick. Cut the beignets into 2" squares.

The beignets contain a lot of sugar and will burn quickly. Watch them carefully while frying.

In a deep fryer or deep sauce pan, add vegetable oil to a depth of 2". The temperature of the oil needs to be 375°. You will need to fry the beignets in batches. If you add too many beignets at one time to the oil, the temperature of the oil will drop and the beignets will be greasy.

Add the beignets to the hot oil. Fry for 1-2 minutes on each side or until the beignets are puffed and golden brown. Remove the beignets from the hot oil and drain on paper towels. Sprinkle powdered sugar to taste over the beignets.

Jam Cake Beignets With Blackberry Dipping Sauce

Makes 32 beignets

2 1/4 cups all purpose flour
1 3/4 tsp. pumpkin pie spice
2 tsp. baking powder
3/4 tsp. baking soda
1/4 tsp. salt
2/3 cup toasted chopped pecans
1/2 cup currants
2/3 cup buttermilk
1/3 cup light brown sugar
1 beaten egg
1 tbs. melted unsalted butter
1 1/2 tsp. vanilla extract
1 1/2 cups butterscotch chips
10 caramels, unwrapped
3/4 cup evaporated milk
1 1/4 cups fresh blackberries
1/3 cup seedless blackberry jam
Vegetable oil for frying
Powdered sugar to taste

In a mixing bowl, add the all purpose flour, pumpkin pie spice, baking powder, baking soda, salt, pecans and currants. Stir until combined. In a small bowl, add the buttermilk, brown sugar, egg, butter and vanilla extract. Whisk until combined and add to the dry ingredients. Whisk until the batter is moistened and combined.

Lightly flour your work surface. Place the dough on your surface. Knead the dough 10 times. Divide the dough in half. Wrap each piece of dough in plastic wrap. Chill the dough for 30 minutes.

In a sauce pan over low heat, add the butterscotch chips, caramels and evaporated milk. Stir constantly and cook until the butterscotch chips and caramels melt. Remove the pan from the heat. In a blender, add the blackberries and blackberry jam. Process until smooth and combined.

Lightly flour your work surface. Work with one piece of dough at a time. Roll each piece of dough to a 9" square. Cut each square into 16 squares.

Jam Cake Beignets With Blackberry Dipping Sauce cont'd

In a deep fryer or deep sauce pan, add vegetable oil to a depth of 2". The temperature of the oil needs to be 375°. You will need to fry the beignets in batches. If you add too many beignets at one time to the oil, the temperature of the oil will drop and the beignets will be greasy.

Add the beignets to the hot oil. Fry for 1 minute on each side or until the beignets are puffed and golden brown. Remove the beignets from the hot oil and drain on paper towels. Sprinkle powdered sugar to taste over the beignets.

Serve the beignets with the butterscotch caramel sauce and the blackberry puree.

Cinnamon Breakfast Fritters

Makes about 2 1/2 dozen

1 1/3 cups all purpose flour
1 cup Rice Krispies cereal, crushed
1/2 cup plus 2 tbs. granulated sugar
3 tsp. baking powder
1/2 tsp. salt
1/4 cup butter flavored shortening
1/2 cup whole milk
1 tsp. ground cinnamon
1/4 cup melted unsalted butter

In a mixing bowl, add the all purpose flour, Rice Krispies cereal, 2 tablespoons granulated sugar, baking powder and salt. Whisk until combined. Add the butter flavored shortening to the bowl. Using a fork, cut the shortening into the dry ingredients until you have small crumbs. Add the milk and stir until the batter is moistened and combined.

Form the dough into 1" balls. Preheat the oven to 425°. In a small bowl, add 1/2 cup granulated sugar and cinnamon. Stir until combined. Add the butter to a small bowl. Dip each ball in the butter and roll in the cinnamon sugar.

Spray an 8" round cake pan with non stick cooking spray. Place the balls, in a single layer, in the pan. Bake for 15 minutes or until a toothpick inserted in the fritters comes out clean. Remove the pan from the oven and serve.

Doughnut Fritters

Makes 2 dozen

1 1/2 cups all purpose flour
1/3 cup granulated sugar
1 tsp. baking powder
1/2 tsp. salt
1/4 tsp. ground cinnamon
1/2 cup whole milk
1 egg
1/3 cup creamy peanut butter
1 tsp. vanilla extract
Vegetable oil for frying
Powdered sugar to taste

In a mixing bowl, add the all purpose flour, granulated sugar, baking powder, salt and cinnamon. Whisk until combined. In a separate bowl, add the milk, egg, peanut butter and vanilla extract. Whisk until combined and add to the dry ingredients. Mix until the batter is moistened and combined.

In a deep fryer or deep sauce pan, add vegetable oil to a depth of 2". The temperature of the oil needs to be 375°. You will need to fry the fritters in batches. If you add too many fritters at one time to the oil, the temperature of the oil will drop and the fritters will be greasy.

Drop the fritters, by teaspoonfuls, into the hot oil. Fry for 1 minute on each side or until the fritters are golden brown. Remove the fritters from the hot oil and drain on paper towels. You can roll the hot fritters in powdered sugar if desired or glaze with one of the recipes below.

White Chocolate Strawberry Glaze: In a small bowl, add 1 cup powdered sugar, 2 teaspoons strawberry jam and 2 teaspoons milk. Whisk until combined and dip each fritter in the glaze. Drizzle 1/2 cup melted white chocolate over the top and serve.

Chocolate Peanut Butter Glaze: Drizzle cooked fritters with 1 cup melted peanut butter and 1 cup melted milk chocolate chips. You can combine the melted peanut butter and melted milk chocolate chips in a bowl if desired. Dip the fritters in the glaze and serve.

Apple Butter Doughnuts With Brown Butter Icing

Makes 3 dozen

2 eggs
1 cup granulated sugar
1/4 cup plus 2 tbs. unsalted butter, softened
1/2 cup apple butter
5 cups all purpose flour
2 tsp. baking powder
1 tsp. baking soda
1/2 tsp. salt
1/2 tsp. ground cinnamon
1/2 tsp. ground nutmeg
1 tbs. lemon juice
1 cup evaporated milk
Vegetable oil for frying
2 1/2 cups powdered sugar

In a mixing bowl, add the eggs, granulated sugar and 2 tablespoons butter. Using a mixer on medium speed, beat for 3 minutes. Add the apple butter and mix until combined.

In a separate bowl, add the all purpose flour, baking powder, baking soda, salt, cinnamon and nutmeg. Whisk until combined. In a small bowl, add the lemon juice and 3/4 cup evaporated milk. Whisk until combined and add to the mixing bowl with the eggs. Add the dry ingredients to the bowl and mix only until the batter is moistened and combined. Cover the bowl and refrigerate the dough for 2 hours.

Flour your work surface. Place the dough on your surface and knead the dough 6 times. Knead flour into the dough as needed to make a smooth dough. Roll the dough to 1/4" thickness. Using a floured doughnut cutter, cut out the doughnuts. Cut the doughnuts as close together as possible on the first rolling. Roll the dough scraps out and cut out the remaining doughnuts.

In a deep fryer or deep sauce pan, add vegetable oil to a depth of 3". The temperature of the oil needs to be 375°. You will need to fry the doughnuts in batches. If you add too many doughnuts at one time to the oil, the temperature of the oil will drop and the doughnuts will be greasy. When the oil is hot, add the doughnuts. Fry for 1 minute on each side or until the doughnuts are golden brown. Remove the doughnuts from the hot oil and drain on paper towels.

In a skillet over low heat, add 1/4 cup butter. Cook until the butter melts and turns golden brown. Remove the skillet from the heat and add 1/4 cup evaporated milk and the powdered sugar. Whisk until smooth and combined. Dip the warm doughnuts in the glaze and serve.

Applesauce Doughnuts

Makes about 2 dozen

4 1/2 cups all purpose flour
1 cup granulated sugar
3 tsp. baking powder
1 tsp. baking soda
1 tsp. salt
1/2 tsp. ground nutmeg
1/2 tsp. ground cinnamon
2/3 cup buttermilk
1/2 cup applesauce
1/4 cup melted unsalted butter
1 tsp. vanilla extract
2 beaten eggs
Vegetable oil for frying
Powdered or granulated sugar for dusting

In a mixing bowl, add the all purpose flour, granulated sugar, baking powder, baking soda, salt, nutmeg and cinnamon. Whisk until combined. In a separate bowl, add the buttermilk, applesauce, butter, vanilla extract and eggs. Whisk until combined and add to the dry ingredients. Mix only until the batter is moistened and combined.

Cover the bowl and refrigerate the dough for 1 hour or until the dough is chilled. Lightly flour your work surface. Place the dough on the surface and knead until the dough is no longer sticky. Divide the dough into two equal portions.

Roll each piece of dough to a 3/8" thickness. Using a floured doughnut cutter, cut out the doughnuts. Cut the doughnuts as close together as possible on the first rolling. Roll the dough scraps out and cut out the remaining doughnuts.

In a deep fryer or deep sauce pan, add vegetable oil to a depth of 3". The temperature of the oil needs to be 375°. You will need to fry the doughnuts in batches. If you add too many doughnuts at one time to the oil, the temperature of the oil will drop and the doughnuts will be greasy.

When the oil is hot, add the doughnuts. Fry for 1-2 minutes on each side or until the doughnuts are golden brown. Remove the doughnuts from the hot oil and drain on paper towels. Roll the hot doughnuts in powdered or granulated sugar to taste.

Beaten French Doughnuts

Makes about 18 miniature doughnuts

1 cup water
1/2 tsp. salt
2 tbs. unsalted butter
1 cup all purpose flour
3 eggs
Vegetable oil for frying
Powdered sugar to taste

In a sauce pan over medium heat, add the water, salt and butter. Cook until the water is boiling and the butter melts. Add the all purpose flour and stir constantly until the dough is smooth. Remove the pan from the heat and spoon the dough into a mixing bowl. Cool the dough for 5 minutes.

Add the eggs, one at a time, to the dough. Beat each egg into the dough with a wooden spoon. Do not add the next egg to the dough until the previous egg is well beaten into the dough. Cover the dough and refrigerate for 2 hours.

Spoon the dough into a pastry bag with a large star tip. Sprinkle all purpose flour on a baking sheet. Using the pastry bag, pipe out small doughnuts. Let the doughnuts sit for 2 hours at room temperature.

In a deep fryer or deep sauce pan, add vegetable oil to a depth of 2". The temperature of the oil needs to be 375°. You will need to fry the doughnuts in batches. If you add too many doughnuts at one time to the oil, the temperature of the oil will drop and the doughnuts will be greasy.

When the oil is hot, add the doughnuts. Fry for 1 minute on each side or until the doughnuts are golden brown. Remove the doughnuts from the hot oil and drain on paper towels. Sprinkle powdered sugar to taste over the doughnuts.

Old Fashioned Cake Doughnuts

Makes 2 dozen

4 eggs
2/3 cup granulated sugar
1/3 cup whole milk
1/3 cup melted vegetable shortening
3 1/2 cups all purpose flour
3 tsp. baking powder
3/4 tsp. salt
2 tsp. ground cinnamon
1/2 tsp. ground nutmeg
Vegetable oil for frying
1/2 cup granulated sugar

In a mixing bowl, add the eggs and 2/3 cup granulated sugar. Using a mixer on medium speed, beat for 3 minutes. The eggs and sugar should be light and fluffy when ready. Add the milk and vegetable shortening to the bowl. Mix until well combined.

In a separate mixing bowl, add the all purpose flour, baking powder, salt, 1 teaspoon ground cinnamon and nutmeg. Whisk until well combined and add to the wet ingredients. Mix only until the batter is moistened and combined. Cover the dough and refrigerate for 2 hours or until the dough is well chilled.

Lightly flour your work surface. Place the dough on your surface and knead the dough 6 times. The dough should be smooth when ready. Roll the dough to 3/8" thickness. Using a floured doughnut cutter, cut out the doughnuts. Cut the doughnuts as close together as possible on the first rolling. Roll the dough scraps out and cut out the remaining doughnuts.

In a deep fryer or deep sauce pan, add vegetable oil to a depth of 3". The temperature of the oil needs to be 375°. You will need to fry the doughnuts in batches. If you add too many doughnuts at one time to the oil, the temperature of the oil will drop and the doughnuts will be greasy.

When the oil is hot, add the doughnuts. Fry for 1 minute on each side or until the doughnuts are golden brown. Remove the doughnuts from the hot oil and drain on paper towels.

In a small bowl, add 1/2 cup granulated sugar and 1 teaspoon cinnamon. Whisk until combined. Roll the warm doughnuts in the cinnamon sugar and serve.

Sweet Cream Doughnuts

Makes 2 dozen

2 tbs. granulated sugar
1 cup heavy cream
1 cup buttermilk
1/2 tsp. salt
1/4 tsp. baking soda
3 beaten eggs
2 tsp. baking powder
4 cups all purpose flour
Vegetable oil for frying

Add the granulated sugar, heavy cream, buttermilk, salt, baking soda, eggs, baking powder and all purpose flour to a large mixing bowl. Stir until well combined. Cover the bowl with plastic wrap and refrigerate the dough for 2 hours.

Flour your work surface. Place the dough on your surface and knead the dough 6 times. The dough should be smooth when ready. Roll the dough to 1/4" thickness. Using a floured doughnut cutter, cut out the doughnuts. Cut the doughnuts as close together as possible on the first rolling. Roll the dough scraps out and cut out the remaining doughnuts.

In a deep fryer or deep sauce pan, add vegetable oil to a depth of 3". The temperature of the oil needs to be 375°. You will need to fry the doughnuts in batches. If you add too many doughnuts at one time to the oil, the temperature of the oil will drop and the doughnuts will be greasy.

When the oil is hot, add the doughnuts. Fry for 1 minute on each side or until the doughnuts are golden brown. Remove the doughnuts from the hot oil and drain on paper towels.

Coconut Doughnuts

Makes 1 dozen

2 eggs
1/2 cup granulated sugar
1/4 cup whole milk
2 tbs. vegetable oil
2 1/3 cups all purpose flour
2 tsp. baking powder
1/2 tsp. salt
1/2 cup sweetened flaked coconut
Vegetable oil for frying

In a mixing bowl, add the eggs and granulated sugar. Using a mixer on medium speed, beat for 3 minutes. Add the milk and 2 tablespoons vegetable oil to the bowl. Mix until well combined.

Turn the mixer speed to low. Add the all purpose flour, baking powder and salt. Mix until well blended. Turn the mixer off and stir in the coconut. Cover the bowl and refrigerate the dough for 3 hours.

Flour your work surface. Place the dough on your surface and knead the dough 6 times. The dough should be smooth when ready. Roll the dough to 1/2" thickness. Using a floured doughnut cutter, cut out the doughnuts. Cut the doughnuts as close together as possible on the first rolling. Roll the dough scraps out and cut out the remaining doughnuts.

In a deep fryer or deep sauce pan, add vegetable oil to a depth of 3". The temperature of the oil needs to be 375°. You will need to fry the doughnuts in batches. If you add too many doughnuts at one time to the oil, the temperature of the oil will drop and the doughnuts will be greasy.

When the oil is hot, add the doughnuts. Fry for 1 minute on each side or until the doughnuts are golden brown. Remove the doughnuts from the hot oil and drain on paper towels.

Cornmeal Doughnuts

Makes 2 dozen

3/4 cup whole milk
1 1/2 cups plain white cornmeal
1/2 cup unsalted butter
3/4 cup granulated sugar
2 beaten eggs
1 1/2 cups all purpose flour
2 tsp. baking powder
1/4 tsp. ground cinnamon
1 tsp. salt
Vegetable oil for frying
Powdered sugar to taste

In a sauce pan over low heat, add the milk. When the milk is hot, stir in the cornmeal. Stir constantly and cook for 10 minutes. Remove the pan from the heat and add the butter and granulated sugar. Whisk until well combined. Add the eggs and mix until combined.

In a separate bowl, add the all purpose flour, baking powder, cinnamon and salt. Whisk until combined and add to the wet ingredients. Mix only until the batter is combined and a soft dough forms.

Flour your work surface. Place the dough on your surface and knead the dough 6 times. The dough should be smooth when ready. Roll the dough to 1/4" thickness. Using a floured doughnut cutter, cut out the doughnuts. Cut the doughnuts as close together as possible on the first rolling. Roll the dough scraps out and cut out the remaining doughnuts.

In a deep fryer or deep sauce pan, add vegetable oil to a depth of 3". The temperature of the oil needs to be 375°. You will need to fry the doughnuts in batches. If you add too many doughnuts at one time to the oil, the temperature of the oil will drop and the doughnuts will be greasy.

When the oil is hot, add the doughnuts. Fry for 1 minute on each side or until the doughnuts are golden brown. Remove the doughnuts from the hot oil and drain on paper towels. Sprinkle powdered sugar to taste over the doughnuts and serve.

Taffy Apple Doughnuts

Makes 3 1/2 dozen

2 1/4 cups all purpose flour
2 tsp. baking powder
1 tsp. salt
1/4 tsp. ground nutmeg
1/4 cup vegetable shortening
1/2 cup granulated sugar
2 beaten eggs
1/2 cup whole milk
1 tsp. vanilla extract
3/4 cup honey
3/4 cup brown sugar
3 cups chopped peanuts

In a mixing bowl, add the all purpose flour, baking powder, salt and nutmeg. Whisk until combined. In a separate mixing bowl, add the vegetable shortening and granulated sugar. Beat with a heavy spoon until soft and fluffy. Add the eggs and mix until well combined. Add the milk and vanilla extract. Whisk until combined and add to the dry ingredients. Mix until the batter is moistened and combined.

In a deep fryer or deep sauce pan, add vegetable oil to a depth of 3". The temperature of the oil needs to be 375°. You will need to fry the doughnuts in batches. If you add too many doughnuts at one time to the oil, the temperature of the oil will drop and the doughnuts will be greasy.

Drop the doughnuts, by tablespoonfuls, into the hot oil. Fry for 1-2 minutes on each side or until the doughnuts are golden brown. Remove the doughnuts from the hot oil and drain on paper towels.

In a small bowl, add the honey and brown sugar. Whisk until combined. Add the peanuts to a separate bowl. Dip the warm doughnuts in the honey mixture allowing the excess to drip off back into the bowl. Roll the doughnuts in the peanuts and serve.

Texas Golden Puffs

Makes 2 1/2 dozen

2 cups all purpose flour
1/4 cup granulated sugar
3 tsp. baking powder
1 tsp. salt
1 tsp. ground nutmeg
1/4 cup corn oil
3/4 cup whole milk
1 egg
Vegetable oil for frying
1 cup cinnamon sugar

In a mixing bowl, add the all purpose flour, granulated sugar, baking powder, salt and nutmeg. Whisk until combined. Add the corn oil, milk and egg. Whisk until the batter is moistened and combined.

In a deep fryer or deep sauce pan, add vegetable oil to a depth of 3". The temperature of the oil needs to be 350°. You will need to fry the doughnuts in batches. If you add too many doughnuts at one time to the oil, the temperature of the oil will drop and the doughnuts will be greasy.

Drop the doughnuts, by teaspoonfuls, into the hot oil. Fry for 2 minutes on each side or until the doughnuts are golden brown. Remove the doughnuts from the hot oil and drain on paper towels. Roll the warm doughnuts in the cinnamon sugar.

Potato Doughnuts

Makes 3 dozen

4 cups all purpose flour
3 tsp. baking powder
2 tsp. salt
2 1/2 tsp. ground nutmeg
1/4 tsp. baking soda
2 beaten eggs
1 3/4 cups granulated sugar
1/4 cup melted vegetable shortening
1 cup cooled mashed potatoes
1 tbs. grated lemon zest
1/3 cup buttermilk
Vegetable oil for frying
1 1/2 tsp. ground cinnamon

In a mixing bowl, add the all purpose flour, baking powder, salt, nutmeg and baking soda. Whisk until combined. In a separate bowl, add the eggs, 1 1/4 cups granulated sugar and vegetable shortening. Using a mixer on medium speed, beat until smooth and creamy. Add the potatoes and lemon zest to the bowl. Mix until combined. Add the dry ingredients along with the buttermilk. Mix only until the batter is combined and a soft dough forms.

Flour your work surface. Place the dough on your surface and knead the dough 6 times. The dough should be smooth when ready. Roll the dough to 1/4" thickness. Using a floured doughnut cutter, cut out the doughnuts. Cut the doughnuts as close together as possible on the first rolling. Roll the dough scraps out and cut out the remaining doughnuts.

In a deep fryer or deep sauce pan, add vegetable oil to a depth of 3". The temperature of the oil needs to be 375°. You will need to fry the doughnuts in batches. If you add too many doughnuts at one time to the oil, the temperature of the oil will drop and the doughnuts will be greasy.

When the oil is hot, add the doughnuts. Fry for 1 minute on each side or until the doughnuts are golden brown. Remove the doughnuts from the hot oil and drain on paper towels. In a small bowl, add 1/2 cup granulated sugar and cinnamon. Whisk until combined. Roll the warm doughnuts in the cinnamon sugar and serve.

Orange Pecan Drop Doughnuts

Makes 2 dozen

2 cups all purpose flour
1/2 tsp. baking soda
1/4 tsp. salt
2 beaten egg yolks
1/2 cup granulated sugar
1/2 cup buttermilk
2 tbs. orange juice
1/2 cup chopped pecans
1/4 cup chopped raisins
1/4 cup chopped dates
1 tsp. grated orange zest
Vegetable oil for frying

In a mixing bowl, add the all purpose flour, baking soda and salt. Whisk until combined. In a separate bowl, add the egg yolks, granulated sugar, buttermilk and orange juice. Whisk until combined and add to the dry ingredients. Mix until the batter is moistened and combined. Add the pecans, raisins, dates and orange zest. Whisk until combined.

In a deep fryer or deep sauce pan, add vegetable oil to a depth of 3". The temperature of the oil needs to be 350°. You will need to fry the doughnuts in batches. If you add too many doughnuts at one time to the oil, the temperature of the oil will drop and the doughnuts will be greasy.

Drop the doughnuts, by teaspoonfuls, into the hot oil. Fry for 2 minutes on each side or until the doughnuts are golden brown. Remove the doughnuts from the hot oil and drain on paper towels.

Pumpkin Drop Doughnuts

Makes about 2 1/2 dozen

1 1/2 cups all purpose flour
1/3 cup granulated sugar
2 tsp. baking powder
1/2 tsp. salt
1 1/4 tsp. ground cinnamon
1/4 tsp. ground ginger
1/4 tsp. ground nutmeg
1/2 cup canned pumpkin
1/4 cup whole milk
2 tbs. vegetable oil
1/2 tsp. vanilla extract
1 egg
Vegetable oil for frying
1/2 cup granulated sugar

In a mixing bowl, add the all purpose flour, 1/3 cup granulated sugar, baking powder, salt, 1/4 teaspoon cinnamon, ginger and nutmeg. Whisk until combined. In a separate bowl, add the pumpkin, milk, 2 tablespoons vegetable oil, vanilla extract and egg. Whisk until combined and add to the dry ingredients. Mix until the batter is smooth and combined.

In a deep fryer or deep sauce pan, add vegetable oil to a depth of 3". The temperature of the oil needs to be 350°. You will need to fry the doughnuts in batches. If you add too many doughnuts at one time to the oil, the temperature of the oil will drop and the doughnuts will be greasy.

Drop the doughnuts, by teaspoonfuls, into the hot oil. Fry for 2 minutes on each side or until the doughnuts are golden brown. Remove the doughnuts from the hot oil and drain on paper towels.

In a small bowl, add 1/2 cup granulated sugar and 1 teaspoon cinnamon. Whisk until combined. Roll the hot doughnuts in the cinnamon sugar and serve.

7 SAVORY BUTTERS

Savory butters are great on savory breads, meats and vegetables. The butters are easy to make and add immense flavor to dishes.

Cajun Butter

Makes 1/2 cup

1/2 cup salted butter, softened
1 tsp. light brown sugar
1 tsp. chili powder
1/2 tsp. dried thyme
1/2 tsp. cayenne pepper
1/4 tsp. garlic powder
1/4 tsp. black pepper

Add all the ingredients to a mixing bowl. Stir until well combined. This is so good on corn on the cob but also delicious on vegetables and meats.

Avocado Butter

Makes 1 1/4 cups

2 ripe avocados
1 tbs. fresh lime juice
1/4 tsp. salt
1/8 tsp. garlic powder
1/8 tsp. black pepper
1/8 tsp. cayenne pepper
1/4 cup olive oil

Slice the avocados in half and remove the pit. Scoop out the avocado and place in a blender. Add the lime juice, salt, garlic powder, black pepper and cayenne pepper. Process until smooth and combined. With the blender running, slowly pour in the olive oil. Process until smooth.

Spoon the avocado butter into a small bowl. Cover the bowl and refrigerate for 1 hour before serving.

Citrus Chile Butter

Makes 1 cup

1 cup unsalted butter, softened
2 tbs. grated lime zest
2 tbs. grated lemon zest
3 garlic cloves, minced
1 tbs. fresh jalapeno pepper, minced
1 tsp. chopped fresh thyme
Salt and black pepper to taste

Add the butter, lime zest, lemon zest, garlic, jalapeno pepper and thyme to a bowl. Stir until combined. You can use salted butter and completely omit the salt if desired. I use about 1/8 teaspoon salt and 1/8 teaspoon black pepper. Omit the salt and black pepper if desired.

Use on meats, corn on the cob or vegetables. Very good on steaks or chicken.

Mustard Poppy Seed Butter

Makes 1/2 cup

1/2 cup unsalted butter, softened
1 tbs. minced green onion
1 tbs. Dijon mustard
1 tsp. poppy seeds

Add all the ingredients to a mixing bowl. Stir until well combined. This is so good on corn on the cob, biscuits, vegetables and meats.

Basil Butter

Makes 1 cup

1 1/2 cups fresh basil leaves
1 cup unsalted butter, softened
1 tsp. lemon juice
1 tsp. seasoned pepper
1/2 tsp. garlic salt

In a food processor, add the basil leaves. Process until the basil is chopped. Add the butter, lemon juice, seasoned pepper and garlic salt. Process until smooth and combined. Use on most any pasta, vegetable, fish or chicken.

Blue Cheese Butter

Makes 1 cup

5 oz. blue cheese, crumbled
1/2 cup unsalted butter, softened
1 green onion, minced
2 tbs. chopped fresh parsley
1 tsp. Dijon mustard
1/4 tsp. black pepper

Add all the ingredients to a mixing bowl. Stir until well combined. Use on breads, vegetables, corn or meats.

Buffalo Butter Spread

Makes about 1 cup

2 tbs. unsalted butter, softened
2 tbs. light brown sugar
3/4 cup mayonnaise
1/4 cup Tabasco sauce

In a mixing bowl, add the butter and brown sugar. Whisk until smooth and combined. Add the mayonnaise and Tabasco sauce. Whisk until combined. This is so good on burgers, pork or chicken.

Smoky Chipotle Lime Butter

Makes 1/2 cup

1/2 cup softened unsalted butter
1 1/2 tsp. chipotle hot sauce
2 tsp. fresh lime juice

Add all the ingredients and mix until combined. Use on meats, corn, rolls and vegetables.

Roasted Garlic Red Pepper Butter

Makes 3/4 cup

1 garlic bulb
1/2 cup softened unsalted butter
2 tbs. jarred finely chopped roasted red bell peppers
1 tbs. chopped fresh basil
2/3 cup grated Parmesan cheese

Preheat the oven to 400°. Cut the top off the garlic bulb. Place the garlic on a square of aluminum foil. Wrap the aluminum foil around the garlic. Place the garlic on a baking sheet. Bake for 1 hour. Remove the garlic from the oven and cool completely before using.

Remove the garlic cloves from the bulb. You need 1 1/2 tsp. garlic for this recipe. Use the remaining garlic for another recipe. In a small bowl, add the garlic, butter, roasted red bell peppers, basil and Parmesan cheese. Stir until combined.

Serve on breads, crackers, meats or vegetables.

Barbecue Butter

This is delicious on potatoes, bread, corn and most any vegetable or meat.

Makes 1/2 cup

1/2 cup unsalted butter, softened
2 tsp. dry barbecue seasoning
1 tsp. salt

Add all the ingredients to a mixing bowl. Stir until well combined.

Tequila Lime Butter

Makes 1/2 cup

1/2 cup unsalted butter, softened
1 tsp. minced jalapeno pepper
1 tsp. lime zest
1 1/2 tsp. fresh lime juice
1 tsp. tequila
1/2 tsp. salt

Add all the ingredients to a small bowl. Stir until combined. Refrigerate the butter for 1 hour before using. Delicious on savory breads, corn, chicken and fish.

Garlic Lemon Butter

Makes 1/2 cup

1/2 cup unsalted butter, softened
1 garlic clove, minced
2 tsp. grated lemon zest
1 tsp. minced fresh parsley
1/4 tsp. salt
1/4 tsp. black pepper

In a sauce pan over low heat, add all the ingredients. Stir constantly until the butter melts and you smell the garlic. Remove the pan from the heat. Spoon the butter into a small bowl. Refrigerate the butter until firm. Serve on breads, meats, seafood, pasta and vegetables.

Herb Butter

Makes 1 cup

1 cup unsalted butter, softened
2 tsp. chopped fresh thyme
2 tsp. chopped fresh sage
2 tsp. chopped fresh parsley

Add all the ingredients to a small bowl. Stir until combined. Refrigerate the butter for 1 hour before using. Delicious on corn, vegetables, bread, pork, chicken and fish.

Honey Ginger Butter

Makes 1/2 cup

1/2 cup unsalted butter, softened
3 tbs. chopped fresh chives
1 tbs. honey
2 tsp. crystallized ginger, minced

Add all the ingredients to a small bowl. Stir until combined. This is so good on breads, burgers, pork or chicken.

Brown Sugar Pecan Mustard Butter

Makes 1/2 cup

1/2 cup unsalted butter, softened
1/2 cup toasted pecans, finely chopped
1 tbs. light brown sugar
3 tbs. Dijon mustard

Add all the ingredients to a small bowl. Stir until combined. Use on biscuits, rolls and beef.

Orange Mango Butter

Makes 1/2 cup

1/2 cup unsalted butter, softened
2 tbs. mango chutney
1 tbs. orange zest
1/4 tsp. black pepper

Add all the ingredients to a small bowl. Stir until combined. This is so good on biscuits, cornbread, burgers, pork or chicken.

8 SWEET BUTTERS

Sweet butters are easy to make and add an extra depth of flavor to your quick breads, pancakes, coffee cakes, rolls and waffles.

Cinnamon Espresso Butter

Makes about 1/2 cup

2 tsp. instant coffee granules
2 tsp. water
1/2 tsp. vanilla extract
1/2 cup unsalted butter, softened
1 tbs. powdered sugar
1 tsp. ground cinnamon

In a small bowl, add the coffee granules, water and vanilla extract. Stir until the coffee dissolves. In a mixing bowl, add the butter, powdered sugar and cinnamon. Using a mixer on medium speed, beat until smooth and creamy. Add the coffee and mix until well combined.

Serve on waffles, pancakes, toast or over warm slices of pound or angel food cake.

Bourbon Pecan Butter

Makes 1/2 cup

1/2 cup unsalted butter, softened
1/3 cup toasted chopped pecans
1 tbs. bourbon
2 tbs. cane syrup

Add all the ingredients to a small bowl. Stir until combined. Delicious on biscuits, waffles, toast and pancakes.

Chocolate Cherry Butter

Makes 1/2 cup

1/2 cup unsalted butter, softened
1/4 cup grated semisweet chocolate
1 tbs. cherry jam
1/4 tsp. almond extract

Add all the ingredients to a small bowl. Stir until combined. Delicious on biscuits, waffles, toast and pancakes.

Cranberry Walnut Butter

Makes 1 1/3 cups

3/4 cup unsalted butter, softened
2 tbs. light brown sugar
2 tbs. honey
1 cup chopped fresh cranberries
2 tbs. toasted walnuts, chopped

In a mixing bowl, add the butter, brown sugar and honey. Using a mixer on medium speed, beat for 5 minutes. Add the cranberries and walnuts. Beat for 4 minutes or until the butter turns pink.

Place a piece of plastic wrap on your work surface. Spoon the butter into the center of the plastic wrap. Roll the butter into a log. Refrigerate until the butter is firm and chilled.

Orange Ginger Butter

Makes about 3/4 cup

1/2 cup unsalted butter, softened
1/2 cup orange marmalade
1 tbs. minced crystallized ginger
1 tbs. balsamic vinegar
2 tbs. grated orange zest

Add all the ingredients to a mixing bowl. Stir until well combined. Delicious on breads, asparagus, green vegetables, chicken and turkey.

Lemon Honey Pecan Butter

Makes 1/2 cup

1/2 cup unsalted butter, softened
2 tbs. honey
1 tsp. grated lemon zest
1/2 cup chopped toasted pecans

Add all the ingredients to a small bowl. Stir until combined. Spread on rolls and breads.

Mint Butter

Delicious on scones or just about any type of bread.

Makes 1 cup

1 cup unsalted butter
3 tbs. powdered sugar
2 tbs. chopped fresh mint
1 tbs. grated lemon zest
1 tbs. lemon juice

Add all the ingredients to a small bowl. Whisk until well combined. Cover the bowl and refrigerate for 2 hours before serving.

Sweet Cream Cheese Butter

Makes 4 cups

Perfect on pancakes, waffles and muffins!

8 oz. cream cheese, softened
1 cup unsalted butter, softened
3 cups powdered sugar
1 tsp. vanilla extract

Add the cream cheese and butter to a mixing bowl. Using a mixer on medium speed, beat until light and fluffy. Add 3 cups powdered sugar and the vanilla extract. Mix until smooth and combined.

Sorghum Butter

Makes 1 cup

1 cup unsalted butter
1/2 cup sorghum molasses

Add all the ingredients to a small bowl. Stir until combined. Delicious on corn, biscuits, toast and cornbread. Excellent butter to glaze chicken or turkey.

Pineapple Butter

Makes 1/2 cup

1/2 cup unsalted butter, softened
8 oz. can crushed pineapple, drained

Add the butter and pineapple to a small bowl. Stir until well combined. Delicious on muffins, toast, waffles, pancakes and quick breads.

Honey Spice Butter

Makes 1/2 cup

Seasoning blend

2 tbs. light brown sugar
2 tbs. ground cinnamon
4 tsp. ground ginger
1 tsp. ground nutmeg
1/2 tsp. ground cloves
1/2 tsp. ground cardamom

Butter

1/2 cup softened unsalted butter
2 tbs. honey
3/4 tsp. seasoning blend

To make the seasoning blend, add all the ingredients to a small bowl. Stir until combined. Store the blend in an airtight container in a cool dry place.

To make the butter, add all the ingredients. Mix until combined. Great on biscuits, waffles, pancakes and oatmeal.

Maple Butter

Makes 1/2 cup

1/2 cup unsalted butter, softened
2 tbs. maple syrup
1/2 tsp. ground cinnamon

Add all the ingredients to a small bowl. Stir until well combined. Delicious on muffins, toast, waffles, pancakes and quick breads.

CHAPTER INDEX

Savory Breads

Savory Muffins

Cheddar Pepper Muffins, 36
Bacon Cheddar Cornbread Muffins, 37
Bacon Cornbread Muffins, 38
Bacon Cheddar Muffins, 39
Onion Cheddar Muffins, 40
Garlic Cheddar Muffins, 41
Caraway Cheddar Muffins, 42
Rye & Wheat Muffins, 43
Ham & Swiss Corn Muffins, 44
Southwestern Chile Cheese Corn Muffins, 44
Curry Cornbread Muffins, 45
Cheese Cornmeal Muffins, 46
Maple Cornbread Muffins, 47
Mayonnaise Cornmeal Muffins, 48
Italian Parmesan Muffins, 49
Parmesan Cheese Muffins, 50
Rosemary Lemon Muffins, 51
Cheese Grits & Chive Muffins, 52
Ham & Cheddar Muffins, 53
Green Tomato Corn Muffins, 54
Mayonnaise Sesame Muffins, 55
Beer Pimento Cheese Muffins, 55
Sausage Cheddar Muffins, 56
Smoked Salmon Muffins, 57
Corn Dog Muffins, 58
Bell Pepper Biscuit Muffins, 59
Buttermilk Rosemary Muffins, 60
Sausage Pizza Muffins, 61
Pizza Muffins, 62
Hushpuppy Muffins, 63
Mushroom Muffins, 64
Apple Cheddar Muffins, 65
Golden Apple Cheese Muffins, 66
Apple Cornmeal Muffins, 67
Herb Cornbread Muffins, 68
Parmesan Pepper Cornbread Biscotti, 69
Jalapeno Pepper Jack Cornbread Biscotti, 70
Bacon Cheddar & Chive Cornbread Biscotti, 71
Parmesan Garlic Cornbread Biscotti, 72
Savory Herb Shortbread, 73

Old South Spoon Bread, 74
Southern Spoonbread, 75
Tomato Spoon Bread, 76
Vegetable Spoonbread, 77

Sweet Breads

Chocolate Chai Loaves, 79
Sweet Potato Bread with Pineapple Butter, 80
Coconut Bread, 81
Orange Sally Lunn Quick Bread, 82
Peanut Butter Bread With Ginger Cream, 83
Peanut Butter Chocolate Chip Bread, 84
Cinnamon Coffee Cake Loaf, 85
Cinnamon Swirl Bread, 86
Spice Bread with Maple Butter, 87
Orange Nut Bread With Orange Cream Cheese, 88
Orange Peanut Bread, 89
Chocolate Peanut Butter Banana Bread, 90
Strawberry Banana Nut Bread, 91
Chocolate Chip Banana Nut Bread, 92
Pecan Cream Cheese Banana Bread, 93
Pineapple Carrot Bread, 94
Golden Lemon Bread, 95
Lemon Cake Mix Bread, 96
Lemon Tea Bread, 97
Sweet Tropical Bread, 98
Lemon Pecan Poppy Seed Loaves, 99
Orange Poppy Seed Bread, 100
Pineapple Zucchini Bread, 101
Zucchini Honey Bread, 102
Lemon Poppy Seed Zucchini Bread, 103
Cranberry Zucchini Bread, 104
Lemon Zucchini Bread, 105
Zucchini Chocolate Chip Bread, 106
Cocoa Bread With Stewed Peaches, 107
Spiced Peach Carrot Bread, 108
Strawberry Bread, 109
Pumpkin Pecan Bread, 110
Caramel Glazed Pumpkin Pecan Bread, 111
Pumpkin Honey Beer Bread, 112
Pumpkin Crunch Bread, 113
Sweet Potato Bread, 114
White Chocolate Iced Blueberry Loaf, 115
Blueberry Crunch Bread, 116
Orange Cranberry Raisin Bread, 117
Cranberry Gingerbread Loaf, 118
White Chocolate Cranberry Bread, 119

Sweet Breads cont'd

Sweet Muffins

Upside Down Peach Cornbread Muffins, 144
Buttermilk Oat Muffins, 145
Miniature Orange Tea Muffins, 146
French Breakfast Muffins, 147
Peanut Orange Breakfast Muffins, 148
Applesauce Breakfast Puffs, 149
Apple Cinnamon Muffins, 150
Sweet Potato Muffins, 151
Snickerdoodle Muffins, 152
Blueberry Muffins with Lemon Cream Cheese Glaze, 153
Blueberry Spice Whole Wheat Muffins, 154
Berry Cheesecake Muffins, 155
Blueberry Yogurt Muffins, 156
Almond Berry Muffins, 157
Strawberry Jam Muffins, 158
Glazed Strawberry Lemon Muffins, 159
Cranberry Lemon Muffins, 160
Strawberry Rhubarb Spring Muffins, 161
Strawberry Muffin Ice Cream Cones, 162
Pecan Rhubarb Muffins, 163
Spicy Plum Muffins, 164
Tropical Muffins, 165
Morning Glory Muffins, 166
Cappuccino Muffins With Espresso Cream Cheese, 167
Cappuccino Muffins, 168
White Chocolate Chunk Muffins, 169
Peanut Butter Chocolate Crumb Muffins, 170
Toffee Crunch Muffins, 171
Mint Chocolate Chip Muffins, 172
Pumpkin Cornbread Muffins, 173
Blackberry Cornbread Muffins, 174
Banana Cornbread Muffins, 175
Peach Pecan Muffins, 176
Fresh Nectarine Muffins, 177
Nectarine Pecan Breakfast Muffins, 178
Nectarine Bran Muffins, 179
Nectarine Oat Muffins, 180
Raspberry Filled Almond Muffins, 181
Pineapple Bran Muffins, 182
Pineapple Raisin Muffins, 183
Gingerbread Pear Muffins, 184

Sweet Muffins cont'd

Banana Carrot Muffins, 185
Carrot Cake Muffins, 186
Chocolate Chip Cookie Carrot Muffins, 187
Wild Rice & Carrot Muffins, 188
Garden Harvest Muffins, 189
Oreo Muffins, 190
Super Easy German Chocolate Cake Muffins, 191
Graham Muffins, 192
Honey Pecan Sticky Bun Muffins, 193
Pecan Pie Muffins, 194
Pumpkin Streusel Muffins, 195
Sticky Bun Pumpkin Muffins, 196
Pumpkin Chocolate Chip Muffins, 197
Maple Pumpkin Muffins, 198
Pumpkin Ginger Muffins, 199
Coffee Cake Muffins With Brown Butter Icing, 200
Spice Cake Muffins, 201
Cream Cheese Carrot Muffins, 202
Simple & Delicious Lemon Muffins, 203
Lemon Walnut Muffins, 204
Cherry Rosemary Muffins, 205
Poppy Seed Pound Cake Muffins, 206
Marmalade Muffins, 207
Chocolate Chip Muffins, 208
Chocolate Chip Oatmeal Muffins, 209
Orange Cream Cheese Muffins, 210
Cream Cheese Cranberry Muffins, 211
Granola Streusel Cranberry Muffins, 212
Cranberry Oat Bran Muffins, 213
Cranberry Raisin Muffins, 214
Crumbcake Muffins, 215
Apple Oat Bran Muffins, 216
Caramel Apple Muffins, 217
Golden Delicious Sour Cream Muffins, 218
Apple Butter Spice Muffins, 219
Apple Pecan Streusel Muffins, 220
Apricot Oatmeal Muffins, 221
Anjou Pear Cheese Muffins, 222
Jumbo Oatmeal Muffins, 223
Basic Muffins, 224

Sweet Muffins cont'd

Biscuits & Scones

Sweet & Savory Fritters & Doughnuts

Sweet & Savory Fritters & Doughnuts cont'd

Savory Butters

Sweet Butters

ABOUT THE AUTHOR

Lifelong southerner who lives in Bowling Green, KY. Priorities in life are God, family and pets. I love to cook, garden and feed most any stray animal that walks into my yard. I love old cookbooks and cookie jars. Huge NBA fan who loves to spend hours watching basketball games. Enjoy cooking for family and friends and hosting parties and reunions. Can't wait each year to build gingerbread houses for the kids.